W0035929

SAGE was founded in 1965 by Sara Miller McCune to support the dissemination of usable knowledge by publishing innovative and high-quality research and teaching content. Today, we publish over 900 journals, including those of more than 400 learned societies, more than 800 new books per year, and a growing range of library products including archives, data, case studies, reports, and video. SAGE remains majority-owned by our founder, and after Sara's lifetime will become owned by a charitable trust that secures our continued independence.

Los Angeles | London | New Delhi | Singapore | Washington DC | Melbourne

Thirty Years of
SAARC

Thank you for choosing a SAGE product!
If you have any comment, observation or feedback,
I would like to personally hear from you.
Please write to me at **contactceo@sagepub.in**

Vivek Mehra, Managing Director and CEO, SAGE India.

Bulk Sales

SAGE India offers special discounts
for purchase of books in bulk.
We also make available special imprints
and excerpts from our books on demand.

For orders and enquiries, write to us at

Marketing Department
SAGE Publications India Pvt Ltd
B1/I-1, Mohan Cooperative Industrial Area
Mathura Road, Post Bag 7
New Delhi 110044, India

E-mail us at **marketing@sagepub.in**

Get to know more about SAGE

Be invited to SAGE events, get on our mailing list.
Write today to **marketing@sagepub.in**

This book is also available as an e-book.

Thirty Years of
SAARC

Society, Culture and Development

Edited by

RAJIV KUMAR
OMITA GOYAL

India International Centre

Los Angeles | London | New Delhi
Singapore | Washington DC | Melbourne

First published in 2016 by

SAGE Publications India Pvt Ltd
B1/I-1 Mohan Cooperative Industrial Area
Mathura Road, New Delhi 110 044, India
www.sagepub.in

SAGE Publications Inc
2455 Teller Road
Thousand Oaks, California 91320, USA

SAGE Publications Ltd
1 Oliver's Yard, 55 City Road
London EC1Y 1SP, United Kingdom

SAGE Publications Asia-Pacific Pte Ltd
3 Church Street
#10-04 Samsung Hub
Singapore 049483

Published by Vivek Mehra for SAGE Publications India Pvt Ltd, typeset in 10.5/12.5 pt Berkeley by Zaza Eunice, Hosur, Tamil Nadu, India and printed at Chaman Enterprises, New Delhi.

Library of Congress Cataloging-in-Publication Data Available

ISBN: 978-93-515-0881-6 (PB)

The SAGE Team: Supriya Das, Isha Sachdeva and Ritu Chopra

CONTENTS

FOREWORD

The South Asian region has had deep cultural and civilisational ties down the ages, and its rich and diverse religious, cultural and linguistic groups have coexisted for centuries. Rich in resources and mineral wealth, it attracted the unwelcome attention of Western powers across the globe, leading to a long era of colonial domination and exploitation. The advent of the 20th century saw the emergence and strengthening of nationalism and freedom movements across the region, led by our own freedom movement under the leadership of Mahatma Gandhi. The need for regional cooperation and a closer association among neighbours for the entire region of South Asia led to the setting up of SAARC in 1985.

In fact, the idea of cooperation in South Asia was discussed as early as the Asian Relations Conference held in New Delhi in April 1947. The two conferences following this, the Colombo Conference (1954) and the Bandung Conference (1955), contributed towards regional cooperation in South Asia. Regional bodies like ASEAN were a welcome step towards regional cooperation. Deliberations over the years among the neighbouring countries in the South Asian region enabled the establishment of SAARC exactly 30 years ago with its headquarters in Nepal. Coming at a time when the trend towards regional and international organisations was found useful for mutual understanding and peace, especially the spectacular emergence of the European Union that overcame centuries of enmity, animosity and constant warfare between the nations of Europe, in particular Germany, France and the United Kingdom, SAARC gave hope for a similar progression in South Asia. Unfortunately, these hopes have been largely belied.

In this era of globalisation, the challenges that we face today are crucial to the integrated development of the South Asian region. These include the protection of the environment and development of natural resources, provisions for protecting human rights, preservation of the cultural heritage of the region enabling transit facilities, sporting events, and so on. SAARC was established basically for promoting the welfare and improving the quality of life of the people of the region. Meaningful progress can be sustained by political understanding, mutual trust and confidence between the member countries. However, interstate relations within the region have not remained free from tension, and India's relations with its neighbours are a grim reminder that bilateral relations have vital bearing on the progress of SAARC.

More people live in the SAARC region than in China. It does lag behind in terms of contributing to global gross product, but most of South Asia is in a phase of rapid economic growth. Further, democracy in multiple forms is a variety of government now common to all SAARC members. This is a vital region at the crossroads of Southeast and West Asia, Inner Asia and the Indian Ocean Littoral. Its stability and progress are essential in the context of ensuring a sane and harmonious world order. Issues in regional cooperation must be defined and addressed so that they lead to mutual and balanced gains. SAARC, over the last 30 years, has made some strides in socio-economic cooperation, but there is tremendous scope to work together in a spirit of friendship, trust and understanding. Food security, climate change and disaster management require close cooperation, and SAARC's effectiveness has been disappointing in these areas. Though cultural exchanges between SAARC countries has led to a better understanding of the cultural ethos of the entire region, there is need to further encourage cultural tourism in the area. This includes religious tourism— Hindu, Buddhist, Sikh and the Muslim sufi shrines.

The recently concluded 18th SAARC Summit in November 2014 adopted 'Deeper Integration for Peace and Prosperity' as its motto and emphasised regional cooperation in trade, investment, finance, energy, security, infrastructure, connectivity and culture, and the implementation of projects and programmes in a prioritised, result-oriented and time-bound manner. It is the collective responsibility of all member states to maintain stability, protect democracy, preserve national unity and encourage regional cooperation. Mutual cooperation and understanding between member states will help SAARC realise its objective of giving every individual the opportunity to live in dignity and realise their full potential. The people of South Asia have been heirs to a great past and can be builders of a great future. If they face the challenges of the future together and cooperate to make use of all the available opportunities, they can be the veritable architects of a peaceful, healthy, vibrant and affluent region.

Our double issue this year brings together an interesting spectrum of chapters from all the SAARC countries which analyse various aspects from their respective viewpoints brought together painstakingly by our Editors Rajiv Kumar and Omita Goyal. We hope that this will be of interest to the membership of the India International Centre, and also the wider interested public in India and the SAARC nations.

KARAN SINGH

◆

PREFACE

The integrated development of the South Asian region is one of the greatest challenges we face today. The 30th anniversary of the establishment of SAARC, we felt, was an appropriate opportunity to bring out this volume on *Thirty Years of SAARC: Society, Culture and Development*.

People and areas comprising the South Asian region have had deep linkages and coexisted for a long time. Religious, cultural and linguistic bonds have brought people and nations together in the past. The large and expanding number of centres for South Asian studies in universities around the world that study historical, sociological and cultural issues, in addition to the economic and political scenarios, is testimony to the significance of the region. Common sense—and serious analyses—suggest that economic cooperation between the countries that comprise this region is more important now than ever before.

According to its Charter, SAARC was set up to 'promote peace, freedom, social justice and economic prosperity by fostering mutual understanding, good neighbourly relations and meaningful cooperation', but the hope generated by this development has largely been belied. Nations in other parts of the world have faced and overcome challenges to cooperation to create workable and meaningful associations of nations. It should be possible to make this happen in South Asia too.

Chapters in this volume endeavour to trace SAARC's journey so far and provide pointers for the future. Several chapters discuss economic and political issues. Economic cooperation is the core on which prospects for regional cooperation depend. This is even more important in the light of globalisation and the increasing role other countries wish to play in the region. While there is a long way to go, there has been some progress through trade agreements, infrastructure projects, pooling of energy resources and other measures that have been put in place, such as efforts at achieving ecological collaboration.

Economic integration must go hand in hand with political will. Limited regional cooperation in South Asia is largely attributed to political instability, as the contributors demonstrate. Recent attempts at building bridges between South Asian governments is a welcome step and has given hope for a new phase in South Asian cooperation.

The contributions also include discussions on human rights, trafficking, gender empowerment, literature and civil society efforts at people-to-people integration.

Were it not for constraints of space, we would have liked to include sport, music, tourism and many other areas of existing and potential cooperation between nations. Readers will find some repetition across chapters, which is inevitable but also necessary for those who might want to read the chapters selectively. We have had the enthusiastic support of our contributors from all eight countries. Without them, this attempt to revisit SAARC would not have been possible.

OMITA GOYAL

◆

INTRODUCTION
TOWARDS NEW BEGINNINGS IN SOUTH ASIA

South Asia, the geographic entity that lies between Kabul and Yangon and includes the island economies of Sri Lanka and the Maldives, continues to thwart attempts at deepening regional cooperation.[1] This is surprising on many counts. A large body of erudite literature, both empirical and analytical, shows that the economic case for deeper regional cooperation is beyond argument. This is further reinforced by several contributions in this volume. As Shyam Saran points out in his essay, the significant environmental challenge facing South Asia cannot be addressed without meaningful regional cooperation. Poverty, with its attendant ills of human trafficking, inhuman exploitation of child labour and other social evils can be tackled far more effectively if cross-border cooperation was to expand. Energy security will also be far better assured if a pan-South Asian electricity grid could be established and drew its energy inputs from hydro resources of Nepal and Bhutan and hydrocarbon reserves in other South Asian countries, including those in Afghanistan and Myanmar. Yet, despite these clear and irrefutable economic advantages, regional cooperation in South Asia has not progressed at the desired pace.

Socially and culturally too, South Asian countries share common traditions, religious practices and cultures that cross over national boundaries in all directions. There is surely more in common between the two Punjabs, located across the Wagah–Atari border, than either of these provinces have in common with others in their own country. The same can be said about the people living in the Terai regions of Nepal and India and in the Gangetic–Brahmaputra delta in Bangladesh, and the Indian state of West Bengal where Nasrul Islam and Tagore are claimed by both sides. Karachi and Mumbai have common social practices that originated with the coastal trade from their shores to Aden and beyond. Tamil is spoken on both sides of the Palk straits, and Sri Lankan

Buddhists regularly make the pilgrimage to Bodh Gaya in the Indian province of Bihar. The Kabuliwala was a part of my growing up and immortalised in Bimal Roy's classic film of the same name. One can continue with detailing such commonalities across the South Asian space. The question surely must be asked as to why regional cooperation in South Asia is not making satisfactory progress.

One can argue that those who are dissatisfied are simply displaying their impatience and do not appreciate the progress already made despite huge complexities inherent in South Asian societies. The extensive diversity within each country makes it difficult for consensus to emerge on any issue, including cross-border cooperation. Memories of past events are still rather fresh and militate against real cooperation. Domestic problems and challenges, numerous and urgent as they are, do not allow political leaders to pay attention to cross-border issues. Regional cooperation does not improve the electoral prospects of any political leader or party and so does not receive the attention it needs. Being relatively young nation states, SAARC member countries are hypersensitive to even the remotest challenge to sovereignty and thus not particularly enthused about collective endeavours, which are premised upon a partial surrender of sovereignty. In the case of South Asia, where India accounts for 80 per cent of the population and 83 per cent of the regional economic output, regional cooperation is perceived as reinforcing India's hegemonic position in South Asia. This is simply not acceptable to India's neighbours, especially Pakistan.

These are valid arguments. However, they are also obtained in other regions where regional cooperation has been far more successful. We want to argue that in South Asia's case, regional cooperation has not progressed satisfactorily for five reasons. First, those who argue in support of regional cooperation have so far, rather surprisingly, neglected to point out the role of regional cooperation in addressing the real challenge facing all South Asian countries. This is the challenge of finding productive employment for the young population and thereby earning the demographic dividend. Second, regional cooperation has suffered because the process has remained rather centralised in the national capitals and has not involved provincial governments in all South Asian countries. Third, despite being democracies, there has been little effort at popularising the case for regional cooperation in the public domain, with the result that political leaderships do not face any pressure from their constituents for pushing forward with the regional cooperation agenda. Fourth, the lack of trust and open hostility on several occasions between the two largest member countries (Indian and Pakistan) has unfortunately vitiated the atmosphere against cooperation and set a negative example for other SAARC members. This continues to be an exogenous and uncertain factor in an unpredictable future. Fifth and finally, given India's predominance in the South Asian region, successful regional cooperation depended critically on India's sustained espousal and promotion of the cause. This has occurred only recently with India finally changing its stance towards SAARC in 2007, at the time of the 14th SAARC Summit in Delhi. Thus, while SAARC itself has been around for three decades, the push for successful regional cooperation in South Asia is of a far shorter vintage.

The most critical challenge facing South Asian societies today is of rising aspirations of an exceptionally young population and the growing chasm between these aspirations and achievements. This chasm, if not overcome urgently, has sufficient destructive potential to drive South Asian countries over the edge into an economic and social precipice, which could engulf the entire region irrespective of where it originates. So far, however, the substantial literature on the benefits of regional cooperation has not focused on the issue of growing youth unemployment in South Asia and the possible role of regional cooperation in generating more jobs needed to absorb the new entrants to the South Asian workforce. These are estimated to be nearly 20 million each year, with 12–15 million new entrants to the workforce in India alone. It is, therefore, time to single-mindedly focus the arguments and efforts for South Asian regional cooperation on meeting this formidable challenge of large-scale employment generation in South Asia. Successfully communicating this urgency to political leaderships in all South Asian countries will hopefully generate the political will for taking forward the regional cooperation agenda.

It is rather evident that the threat of social and political disruption arising from large-scale unemployment is faced more directly by sub-national authorities (provincial governments, district administrations, etc.) rather than national governments located in far away national capitals. Thus, for example, the threat from rising

Maoist activity along the Indo–Nepal border is a bigger threat for the Bihar government than either for New Delhi or Kathmandu. Similarly, widespread drug abuse in the Indian Punjab and rising militancy in Pakistan Punjab is in large part due to the lack of productive employment opportunities for the youth in these two provinces. This constitutes a major challenge for the two provincial governments which have also demonstrated a greater urgency for cross-border cooperation. This is presumably done in the hope that it will promote fresh trade and investment activity in border regions and result in greater employment opportunities, and help wean the youth away from illegal activities. For sub-national governments, therefore, regional or cross-border cooperation offers direct and tangible benefits in tackling the challenges facing them. It is time, therefore, to expand the discussion and efforts at regional cooperation beyond national capitals to provinces in all countries of South Asia.

The failure so far to involve provincial governments and civil society in the discussion on, and efforts for, regional cooperation can be seen as a missed opportunity. One of the reasons for keeping state governments out of the discussion and efforts towards regional cooperation is that federal governments in South Asia demonstrate a degree of insecurity in involving state governments to participate in cross-border initiatives for fear that this could encourage latent separatist urges.[2] This has meant that on occasions, an agreement reached between two central (federal) governments has not been implemented due to active opposition from the concerned state government.[3] In contrast, the Chinese government has, with good effect, actively involved its border provinces like Yunan in the programmes for the Greater Mekong Sub-regional Cooperation, and Xingiang for cooperation with Central Asian Republics. It is to be hoped that with the maturing of federal institutions in South Asian countries, federal governments will reverse their stance towards involving state governments and regional political parties in cross-border initiatives in the coming period. That should provide a strong fillip to these efforts.

Third, as the veteran observer of South Asian regional cooperation Sumanta Bannerjee had warned with uncanny prescience at the time of the first SAARC Summit in Dhaka, the entire exercise has remained confined to the political and bureaucratic elite.[4] While the region's business class has been brought into the regional cooperation process with the setting up of the SAARC Chambers of Commerce in 1985, the common people are surely still not aware of the process itself or the benefits from it. There is hardly any sustained effort to spread awareness about SAARC and its benefits among the middle classes, especially in the largest member country, India. This is reflected in a near complete absence of any discussion on SAARC-related issues, both in the federal parliament and in provincial legislatures. The Indian political class, as also to a large extent its counterparts in neighbouring countries, do not see SAARC or regional cooperation in South Asia as an issue relevant to their constituencies. In Pakistan, for example, it will be a rare occasion when the Urdu media takes up the issue of regional cooperation even when SAARC summits are being held. There have been some abortive suggestions to bring SAARC and regional cooperation into the consciousness of the region's growing middle classes. For example, the ideas of having separate SAARC immigration counters, as is done in ASEAN member countries, or starting a chain of SAARC primary health centres have been put forward, but so far to no avail. This must change if SAARC has to make more progress in the future.

Fourth, Indo–Pak relations cast an ominous shadow over SAARC. The open hostility between the two largest member countries results in most SAARC initiatives being marred by bureaucratic red tape and inertia, often consciously encouraged to thwart progress. This is eminently understandable in the light of both governments perceiving any real progress in regional integration as providing greater opportunities to forces and agencies inimical to their national security. Highly restrictive bilateral visa regimes, restrictions of trade and investment flows and a degree of mutual mistrust continue to characterise the bilateral relations between these two countries. This often spills over into third countries as well when that is seen to offer preferential treatment to either Delhi or Islamabad, or sanctuary to forces working against the interest of either of the two countries. Attempts at isolating regional cooperation efforts from this bilateral rivalry, for example in the case of ADB's SASEC initiative, have yielded only modest results. It is difficult to imagine successful South Asian regional cooperation without the resolution of the bilateral Indo–Pakistan rivalry. The key perhaps lies in a change in the attitude of the Pakistan Establishment which, at present, does not see a greater integration of Pakistan's economy in South Asia to be in its national interest. It will allow Pakistan to earn rising revenues from transit trade between Central Asia and South Asia, and also improve its export prospects in the large Indian, and other South Asian, markets. Friends of Pakistan and other SAARC member countries would do well to convince the Pakistan Establishment of the benefits of a successful SAARC.

Given that India has a hugely dominant position in South Asia (the region was historically referred to as the Indian subcontinent), it has cultural and ethnic ties with all the countries in the region as a result of large domestic populations of people from neighbouring countries. It is the only country with borders with all other SAARC member states, except with Afghanistan. Given this geostrategic and economic domination of the South Asian space, India's initial and prolonged lukewarm and often hostile stance towards SAARC destined it to slow and halting progress. This stance thankfully began to change with the first NDA government (1998–2004) and was jettisoned in 2007 when India hosted the SAARC summit.

The rise of China, and its declared objective of playing a more active role in South Asia and capturing a larger share of South Asian markets, was perhaps one of the important triggers for this changed Indian stance towards SAARC. The Indian government has also recognised that its national interests in fields like energy security, environment conservation, anti-militancy operations, etc., were better served through deeper integration of South Asian economies. As a result, India has ostensibly taken on asymmetric responsibilities for promoting South Asian regional cooperation. This is demonstrated in several recent measures taken by India which, inter alia, include financial support for the SAARC Development Fund; tariff and quota-free access to exports from least developed South Asian countries to Indian markets; hosting of the first South Asia Forum in Delhi in 2012; agreement on a larger number of SAARC visa stickers that facilitate travel of business people within SAARC countries; and support for the South Asian University, which has been established in Delhi.

India's positive stance is a welcome development. This is likely to be sustained irrespective of the nature of Indo–Pakistan bilateral ties. India will, hopefully, also find the confidence to take some unilateral steps for improving its ties with Pakistan. This will have an immediate positive impact on regional cooperation prospects. A key measure that India can take is to open its geographic space to all its neighbours for facilitating passengers and freight transit across South Asia. This will allow SAARC members to take full advantage of proximity, which is one of the region's major advantages. Delhi is now more comfortable with provincial governments playing a more active role in cross-border initiatives. This tendency should be further reinforced and institutionalised. The Government of India could also encourage multilateral agencies like the World Bank and the ADB to play a more active role as neutral and pro-active intermediaries, to give greater assurance to the smaller SAARC members with regard to the sharing of potential benefits from regional projects. This will also help in minimising their fears about threats to their sovereignty.

India's role in promoting regional cooperation can hardly be overstated. Perhaps its more important role in South Asia is to ensure a high and sustained rate of growth of its domestic economy. This will generate a demand for exports from its neighbouring countries, giving their economies a much-needed external impetus; give India greater confidence to continue with its asymmetrical approach towards its neighbours and not look for reciprocity and allow India to contribute more financial resources for regional projects.

Some of these five steps have been elaborated in the contributions to this volume. If implemented, it will mark a new beginning for South Asia. There is reason to believe that once a new positive beginning is made, strong structural features present in South Asia will propel the region forward, initially towards deeper regional cooperation and, subsequently, towards greater regional integration. That will see the emergence of a vibrant, multifaceted South Asian regional identity, which is an integral, though at present a somewhat dormant, part of individual identities in South Asia. That is a future well worth working towards, and India will have a very important role in that endeavour.

RAJIV KUMAR

◆

NOTES

1. This is reflected in the statement by Prime Minister Modi at the 18th SAARC Summit that '… as SAARC, we have failed to move with the speed that our people expect and want'.

2. It is conceivable that the Sri Lankan government would be wary of permitting greater cross-border interaction between its Northern Province (Jaffna) and Tamil Nadu for fear that Tamil nationalism would be reinforced. Similarly, the Madhesis in Nepal could be seen as joining up with their ethnic counterparts across the border in the Indian states of Bihar and UP to the detriment of overall control from Kathmandu. These fears arise because of ethnic communities spread across national borders and in some cases have been only been recently separated when new nation states came into existence after independence from colonial rule.

3. The examples of the Indo-Bangladesh river water and border enclave agreements readily come to mind. While Delhi and Dhaka had apparently come to an understanding on these issues prior to the visit of Dr Manmohan Singh to Dhaka in 2013, the opposition from Mamta Bannerjee, the West Bengal Chief Minister, scuttled the agreements and the deal could not be clinched.

4. He had made this comment while covering the first SAARC Summit for *Mainstream Weekly.*

1
REVIEWING REGIONAL COOPERATION IN SOUTH ASIA

ERIC
GONSALVES[#]

Regional organisation, and the benefits flowing from it, came to be better appreciated after World War II. Chanakya and Machiavelli, and other teachers of statecraft, had laid down a precept that no sovereign should trust his neighbours. Acquisitions of territory, colonies, revenues and people were all legitimate, depending on the power a state exercised. Colonialism and Empire were, eventually, gradually discarded by the latter half of the 20th century, although colonial powers were reluctant and their subjects often had to force the pace. For a while, alliances and spheres of influence, allegedly based on ideology, remained in vogue under the rubric of the cold war. This, too, collapsed as first one and later the other protagonist found they did not have the resources to manage the international system. However, the desire to dominate brought out a new doctrine of exceptionalism that sought to place the 'international community' in the driver's seat of managing world problems and crises.

Throughout the 19th century, ever since the Congress of Vienna, a cabal of major powers had tried to manage their own confrontations, as well as maintain a modicum of order elsewhere. The basic dilemma in establishing a world system was, and is, the need to accommodate sovereign nation states which are averse to accepting rule-based arrangements. Nevertheless, these are essential, given the exponential growth in technology that has ensured increasing interdependence of the ever larger and more complex economies, as well as weapons that can destroy the entire planet. Further, governments have to cope with a better-educated public with a surplus of information at their disposal as well as the media, whose greed for revenues milks every sensation. Simultaneously, non-state actors have been able to grab substantive roles. Ironically, as they gain traction, they often abandon and even turn on their original sponsors and become fanatic proponents of the ideology, usually religious, that was used to create them. (For instance, the US and Pakistan may portray themselves as principal victims of Al Queda and the Taliban, but they initially created the monsters.) The UN, in giving the P5 a veto in the Security Council, destroyed its capacity to enforce rules. Settlement of major conflicts has had to be done outside the UN. Major powers, intent on using force, usually invoke absurd grounds of self-defence under the UN Charter to cover their actions. A durable system is still to be found.

At the same time, other statesmen sought closer associations among neighbours to curb the conflicts that had been the earlier norm. That considerable economic and other benefits resulted from such cooperation was a welcome discovery. The European Union (EU), once able to flaunt the benefits of regional cooperation, soon sought to confer them on other regions. The Association of Southeast Asian Nations (ASEAN) also reinforced this trend. Parallel to this was the movement towards globalisation, a concept fostered by the US, its allies and their transnational corporations. The G7 was their clearing house, and the dominating role of the US economy and the US dollar made it work along with the exceptional role also accorded to the US. The post-cold war unipolar system proved unsustainable, and the world is now moving towards a multipolar system. This could be a more representative version of the Congress of Vienna model, which would accommodate the views of the new nations that have emerged since 1945 and the regionalism that has spread in the post-imperial period. The new nations in the Asia Pacific Indian Ocean region will provide many of the new major players—some like China and India—seeking a place in the sun alongside the US. The G20, suitably modified, could become the new clearing house and management centre for this emerging system.

SAARC EVOLUTION

South Asia was very late in seeking the advantages of regional cooperation. Its state structure emerged from the bloody partition of Britain's Indian Empire into the hostile successor states of India and Pakistan. After the breakup of Pakistan, and the creation of

Bangladesh, it began to dawn on some of the smaller states in the region that much of their backwardness and lack of development resulted from regional tensions and barriers to most cross-border exchanges. Utilising resentment against their giant neighbour, India, to foster coherence and nationalism in the early years of independence, may have had some merit, but as they gained confidence the advantages of cooperation and a common forum in dealing with India, and each other, became more obvious. Bangladesh took the initiative in sending a proposal to all South Asian governments in 1980. India and in particular Prime Minister Indira Gandhi were opposed, as they feared it would encourage all its neighbours to gang up against India. Pakistan, too, was lukewarm as it feared that regional cooperation would enable India, with its larger and more sophisticated economy, to dominate the region just when Pakistan had successfully utilised great power rivalries to gain rich and powerful patrons in America, China and the Gulf States for its bid to establish equality with India. In retrospect, peaceful cooperation and competition might have served it better than by pursuing armed conflict and terrorist attacks against India over tenuous claims to territory in Kashmir, based on an ideology that nationalism should be based on religion. This had been set aside at Westphalia, and was to be roundly repudiated by the establishment of Bangladesh. The most recent elections in Jammu & Kashmir have thrown up a coalition government of a Hindu majority party in Jammu, with a Muslim majority party in Kashmir, which should provide a quietus to Pakistani illusions.

Gradually, discussions over some years enabled the formal establishment of the South Asian Association for Regional Cooperation (SAARC) in 1985. The reservations from India, and also from others, were duly incorporated in the Charter. All bilateral and contentious issues were excluded. No secretariat was provided till some years later. Links with other institutions were discouraged. By and large, it was to be a talking shop where some common programmes on non-controversial subjects might be instituted. This has been modified over the years as collaboration came to be found acceptable, and even desirable, on some subjects. Discussion and collaboration between professional groups such as the legal, medical, financial, accounting and other professions, as well as Chambers of Commerce and similar bodies, has taken root and gives ground for hope that someday civil society and business circles will amplify their role in seeking greater exchanges and better relations, and thereby give governments welcome leads.

SAARC EVALUATION

The Declaration issued after the 18th Summit in Kathmandu in November 2014 and the discussions there provide a vantage point from which to survey the state of play in SAARC after 30 years. There is a lot of activity: framing agendas, preparing papers and arranging discussions, but the progress towards greater cooperation remains limited. Issues such as imparting skills to youth, caring for women and children, social protection for the aged, problems of migrants in third world countries can provide for useful cooperation as there can be no political agenda. Food security and disaster management are slated for more cooperative action. However, major issues, such as climate change and environment, where we share the same disadvantaged position of developing countries, have not attracted common action.

Cultural exchanges are encouraged, but not on a meaningful scale. There are the usual bureaucratic exercises, such as declaring 2016 as the Year of Cultural Heritage, with each country zealously claiming its uniqueness in most things. Ironically, one major heritage of the Indic civilisation is its syncretic and plural nature. Most major official projections are directed at the developed world and not to our neighbours. Ideally, it would be best to allow the artistes and performers to bond together and provide them with generous resources, as they have admirers and audiences, which can be exploited to build goodwill. Rather, frustration is often generated by negative attitudes on granting visas or providing facilities, etc. Bollywood and the Indian film industry are popular and have a multitude of enthusiasts. There is, however, not much collaboration in this field, except that promising actors from neighbouring countries do get hired easily in Bollywood, with its overwhelming financial capacity, something that happens even within India itself. With a little more self-confidence, cultural activities could become a major field for cooperation, giving cohesion and momentum to SAARC.

Education is a common concern, where all members face the enormous task of removing the deficit and give the new generation the skills and jobs that would make a fundamental contribution to development and growth in the entire region. The suspicions of security agencies, allied to the unwillingness of local elites to surrender seats now available to their own constituencies, particularly in sought after professional colleges, do hinder a valuable avenue of cooperation and diminish the prospects of establishing a group of permanent well-wishers. We have only ourselves to blame if we do not gain the advantages of working together.

Collaboration on health and combating epidemics that recognise no borders could provide another welcome source of cooperation. However, we have to do this better at home first.

A South Asian University is now functioning in Delhi, with faculty and students from all eight countries. Let us hope it will be allowed to grow and thrive mainly under academic guidance. The more fortunate countries need to open up their professional and popular courses with generous scholarships. Funding for exchanges and training should be equally generous. Some of us will never forget the goodwill generated by even a year or two spent in a foreign institution. The very limited youth exchanges, between schools and colleges and the summer schools in specialised institutions, do encourage better knowledge and understanding. These need to be increased greatly to lay the seeds for greater people-to-people exchanges.

Needless to say, sports should be a major field for common endeavours. South Asia has jointly hosted a Cricket World Cup successfully. However, Pakistan is somewhat left out because of the overzealous hostility easily aroused towards foreign competitors. Circles that harbour similar sentiments also exist in India. It is time all the concerned authorities joined together to hammer out a regime for sporting fixtures that eliminates such demonstrations. And that should be extended to all chauvinistic actions against artistic and cultural activities on spurious grounds.

Encouraging tourism is an excellent component in expanding people-to-people exchanges as well as earning revenue. Here, again, we run into the ever-present question of visas. Granting them is usually made difficult and is often irrational. We have no visa system with Nepal and Bhutan and yet have managed, with some limited problems. Sri Lanka and the Maldives have made entry easy for tourists, with consequent benefit. One cannot expect to go immediately to a Schengen system, but we can harness intelligence and technology—as we have done for visas online, or on arrival for other tourists—and guarantee visas on a much faster basis. The present reporting requirements are often only used to harass particular groups. Gradually, country by country, we should seek to put all SAARC visitors on a visa-on-arrival basis.

The motivation for the creation of the EU and ASEAN was political. However, the processes utilised were economic. After centuries of conflict in Europe, its leaders sought to end that by putting weapons material production under common control. This was further reinforced by insistence that membership was only available to democratically governed countries. The first steps to the EU began with the setting up of the European Steel and Coal Community (ESCC) and the European Atomic Energy Community (EURATOM or EAEC). The ASEAN too began by concentrating on economic and people-to-people exchanges, while freezing territorial disputes. Drawing lessons from these efforts, SAARC has accepted in principle the objective of establishing an Economic and Monetary Union after uniting in a Free Trade Area (FTA), then a Customs Union and a Common Market. Not only do the goals remain elusive, but even the methodology is more negative than positive, with the FTA lists being used more to deny than to encourage trade and remove barriers. Pakistan has refused to grant India Most Favoured Nation (MFN) facilities, which it is obligated to do under international agreements. The transit movement of goods across Pakistan from India to third countries is barred. Bangladesh has long resisted seamless transit across her territory, even to and from one part of India to another. Before the Kathmandu Summit, a proposal had been accepted in principle by all participating governments that a transit agreement for road and rail traffic be concluded on the lines of similar agreements, which have been in force for decades around the world. Pakistan blocked this on the specious grounds that internal formalities had to be completed. It might be recalled that before 1971, trucks from Eastern Europe used to take cargoes from India all the way to Europe after crossing Pakistan. That one member, or a few, should be permitted to block the implementation of decisions of a large majority has been a problem which has plagued all international organisations. It has been solved in various ways and many can be used in SAARC, such as selective agreements operating on a subregional basis. However, it must be recognised that a mindset that places bilateral hostility above regional cooperation, even when that cooperation is clearly in the national interest, really sets regional arrangements largely at naught.

To grasp the lack of understanding on the importance of facilitating economic exchanges, the consideration of the Report of the Group of Eminent Persons (GEP), set up to provide a vision and road map for achieving an economic community in 1997, provides useful insights. After much labour, they produced a report suggesting a fairly modest, but viable programme, which would lead to a Common Market and Economic Union by 2020. In typical SAARC fashion, the report was accepted by the next summit, watered down in the next two summits and forgotten thereafter. Why does SAARC refuse to take the path to effective cooperation? My own view is that the political elites in all our countries do not realise that political will is required to make regional cooperation successful, nor have they educated the public on its benefits. They then allow smaller domestic vested interests, or their own personal and party predilections, to overrule the larger process without caring about the long-term negative consequences, both to their national interest and that of the region. The long-term approach to this problem may be to work around Pakistan by concluding subregional or bilateral agreements and making even Indo–Pak agreements more palatable. It may also be useful to consider a wider basis for purely economic arrangements, for instance, by the Economic and Social Commission for Asia and the Pacific (ESCAP).

Transit arrangements have become a fundamental part of connectivity, which is rightly identified as central to the expansion of economic and even other exchanges. Connectivity should not be restricted to developing transport infrastructure alone. It should encompass all cross-border arrangements such as government formalities, communications, banking and financial arrangements and tariffs, insurance and transit documentation. The efficacy of such facilitation can be measured in the time taken and additional costs paid to deliver passengers, goods and services. Currently, both in terms of time and money, moving goods and services across South Asia is both costly and slow. Since other regions have found solutions, we can adapt suitably from their experience. However, the first lesson would be to do the job in a fixed time frame and not let it get sidelined in a maze of committees and bureaucracy.

Even at the bilateral level, this element of grandstanding is difficult to avoid or restrain. The subcontinent has always been very dependent on the efficient use of the limited water resources. Before independence, disputes between provincial administrations had to be mediated at times by outsiders. The Kaveri River Agreement is one well-known example. After independence, with the World Bank's help, the Indus Waters Agreement was reached between India and Pakistan and has been implemented faithfully despite much pressure from lobbies on both sides. A similar agreement to share the Ganga–Brahmaputra waters between India and Bangladesh below the Farraka barrage was reached after a tortuous process, where an earlier agreement had to be abandoned. To the credit of both parties, it came about after recognition by both sides of the need for compromise, which was accepted at the technical and highest political levels, and also by the public, once the agitation had died down. Unfortunately, we have not so far been able to replicate this with Nepal as political parties and their leaders have been prone to switch positions from compromise to opposition as soon as they demit government. This would illustrate how necessary it is to avoid using sensitive cross-border issues for short-term, populist, political advantage. It is to be hoped that the agreement on Teesta River flows and the Land Boundary Agreement will soon be ratified and proved that short-term political gains can be trumped by long-term real gains. This would also be true if Tamil Nadu could change its negative attitude to cooperation with Sri Lanka to positive action, to improve the economic and political position of the Tamil areas in Sri Lanka. It may be noted that India and Bangladesh made an encouraging departure by settling the maritime boundary by going to arbitration. It provides hope that there may be no need for disputes to be allowed to simmer.

Energy is a subject where cooperation today will pay handsome dividends, as the entire region is suffering from shortages, with negative effects on the economy and on almost every aspect of everyday life. Fortunately, some cooperation appears to have succeeded beyond expectations. The fortunate example of the Bhutanese economy being boosted by the sale of hydroelectric power, produced with Indian assistance, to India is now encouraging the establishment of power grids connecting Bangladesh, Bhutan,

Nepal and India, with a possible extension to Myanmar. Technical questions required to add Sri Lanka to other grids have been studied. The advantages of similar connections with Pakistan are obvious. The crippling shortages experienced in Pakistan have caused voices to be raised there that favour power trading with India.

In the area of petroleum products, to be self-supporting was once the sole policy as security would otherwise be undermined. With the creation of better storage facilities, which incidentally help to stabilise prices, cooperation in all aspects now appears more rational. As with other transit facilities, grids, as well as oil and gas pipelines, are drivers for development and the economy. They also provide a more favourable concept of cooperation as a key contributor to stability not only for the economy, but also in political and security scenarios. The obvious lesson is to proceed from the bilateral to subregional cooperation. It could then extend to the whole region and, maybe, even beyond.

One encouraging innovation was the establishment of the SAARC Development Fund (SDF) where smaller projects were funded from resources provided by members. This got off the ground reasonably well, mainly with Indian funds, and contradicted the impression that SAARC was unwilling to do anything for itself, and that while all members are developing countries, some can help the Least Developed Countries (LDCs). This is more a matter for establishing a mindset that assistance does not always have to come from developed nations and that members can also contribute. The SDF should be expanded as members' economies grow, as mutual assistance should enhance the trust level and, consequently, cooperation.

Economic cooperation is extremely beneficial for all members of SAARC, and the policies of beggar-my-neighbour and autarchy are out of date. Economists, statesmen and the general public need to band together to moderate irrational restrictions supported by ultra-nationalists and often prompted by vested interests.

THE FUTURE OF INDIA, SAARC AND ASIA

Major changes are taking place in Asia and the world. As India seeks to position itself as a major player, this would be aided by a positive scenario for SAARC, given that India is a major constituent.

The presence of all SAARC leaders at the investiture of Narendra Modi as prime minister had signalled warmer attitudes, and was further improved by bilateral visits soon thereafter and the Sri Lankan presidential election. Pakistan's cross-border adventures and negative attitude to the transit agreements at the Kathmandu summit are a disappointment. Given that the military leadership is the major component in Pakistan's governance, establishing a regular dialogue with them is essential.

Projects on the ground providing visible benefits to the public are essential. Political will in favour of SAARC will then become established. India may have 75 per cent of the population and 80 per cent of the GDP of SAARC, but its proportion in intra-SAARC economic flows is still too low. Lessons can be drawn from how Germany's prosperity was built on exports to the EU, and America's on flows within the North American Free Trade Agreement (NAFTA). The effect of the FTA with Sri Lanka has been to create an autonomous movement for economic exchange, which needs to be replicated everywhere in the region.

Helping the continuing stabilisation of Afghanistan could also aid in providing another demonstration of the region's desire to help itself. To be seen to be a benevolent, but not ostentatious, leader in SAARC would boost India's position in Asia and the world.

The domestic scenario plays a fundamental role in the perception of a country's capacity. Political and military power is important. However, in the short term, it is the perception of economic capacity and its ability to assist partners in development and growth that matters. The economy is set to improve, and while the external economic exchanges that growth may be able to stimulate have to be aimed in many directions, more attention must be paid to the developing world and the immediate neighbourhood: first East, and then South, North and West. More targeted efforts to trim subsidies and rein in the corruption caused by unfair allocations of scarce public goods could help externally, as well as at home. External policies must be set with care and kept stable. Neither appeasement nor arrogance will pay dividends in the long term, and alternating between them is even worse. Our national strength lies in our managing our diversity and plurality into increasing our capacity and output within the democratic framework. Maintaining that and improving it, while gaining a larger international role, is the only way to go.

China has been active all over the world, and especially Asia, in the last few years. While its actions in the East and South China Seas have had negative repercussions, it has recently begun to display a more generous attitude towards its western and southern neighbours under the rubric of reviving the land and maritime Silk Routes. South Asian countries have reacted favourably as greater aid in the key areas of infrastructure and connectivity is being offered. In the case of Pakistan, this extends to political support and military aid. Hence, a bigger role for China in SAARC, even to the extent of making it a member, has been aired. We have to live in a real world. Our disapproval will mean little against hard cash. India will have to compete in providing similar development assistance. We can also get involved in the same projects and provide some resources, or utilise Chinese resources, or bring in Japanese or multilateral resources. Indeed, there is a case for harnessing Chinese resources and technology for investing in our development plans, subject to the same safeguards as the Chinese themselves use.

South Asia is a geographic unit with much in common in history and civilisation. As part of the British Empire, it inherited a common system of governance. However, in the pre-colonial era, most contiguous regions, including the Indian Ocean, were linked in many ways with India. The ASEAN and the institutions it has spawned, such as the Forum and the East Asia Summit, have shown that beneficial links can, and should, be established across the old colonial boundaries harking back to earlier times. Historians used to refer to the 'Other India', where Hinduism and Buddhism spread. Today, it would seem appropriate if we looked beyond SAARC in all directions as we seek to engage with all of Asia, and the Indian and Pacific Oceans. This would mean joining Asia–Pacific Economic Cooperation (APEC) and Shanghai Cooperation Organisation (SCO) as a full member. Newer economic groupings like the Trans Pacific Partnership (TPP) and the Free Trade Area of Asia–Pacific (FTAAP) have merit and should be examined further.

The world's future lies in achieving a multipolar system using the benign forces of regionalism to build layers of concentric cooperation in Asia. SAARC, with India as a major driver, can make a key contribution.

◆

#This chapter was first published in 2015 in the *IIC Quarterly,* Vol. 41, Nos 3 and 4.

2
AFGHANISTAN, SAARC AND THE ROAD AHEAD

HAROUN
MIR
HABIB
WARDAK#

Afghanistan, as the new entrant to the South Asian Association of Regional Cooperation (SAARC) since 2007, has great expectations from the Association, particularly because of its unique geographical role as a land bridge between South and Central Asia. Indeed, the survival of Afghanistan as a viable state relies on its ability to find itself a meaningful economic purpose in the region, a possibility only within the framework of regional cooperation.

However, South Asia has been one of the least economically integrated regions because, instead of exploring common opportunities, countries of the region have been dwelling on their differences. For instance, despite continuous efforts, such as the creation of SAARC, limited regional cooperation has been achieved. Nevertheless, the bulk of the trade of member countries takes place with countries outside the region, rather than within. Tariff and non-tariff barriers are serious obstacles to regional economic integration, which are direct consequences of unresolved regional issues.

Despite setbacks in the development of SAARC as a functioning framework for regional economic cooperation, the recent trend towards globalisation and the emergence of India as an important global player could help reinvigorate regional cooperation in South Asia. The biggest question for many of us in the region is the faith reposed in SAARC and its contribution towards member countries.

In the case of Afghanistan, the question is whether SAARC can open up an opportunity for the country to realise its inspiration as one that contributes to the peace and economic prosperity of the region. In order to answer this question, one has to first examine the opportunities that Afghanistan could offer to the region and, second, the political will among key regional players regarding regional cooperation.

A RENEWED HOPE

Ever since the communist coup in 1978, followed by the Soviet invasion of the country, Afghanistan has regressed; it has lost its traditional position in the region and has remained mired in conflicts. After the former Red Army's withdrawal in 1989, Afghanistan became a bloody field for geostrategic competition among key regional powers.

The collapse of the Taliban regime in 2001 and the start of the new democratic process, which began in 2001 in Bonn, known as the 'Bonn Process', led to new hope and an opportunity for Afghanistan to re-emerge from the ashes of civil war and reintegrate with the world community. The focus of the international community for the past 13 years has been on rebuilding state institutions, the economic infrastructure and a new political framework through the introduction of democracy.

There is an ongoing debate about the international community's achievements in Afghanistan, and particularly the North Atlantic Treaty Organization's (NATO) military mission, known as the International Security Assistance Force (ISAF), from 2001 to 2014. As Afghans, we look at the state of affairs in our country in relative terms and compare today's Afghanistan with the 1990s, when civil war raged and when the Taliban ruled over most parts of the country from 1996 to 2001.

We admit that, currently, the international community's mission is half done, but believe that complete achievement is still possible. We see better prospects for the future of our country, particularly after a democratic and peaceful transfer of political power for the first time in its history. We need another decade of international assistance in order to make the current gains and achievements sustainable and irreversible. We believe that the international communities' promises for Afghanistan for the decade to come, from 2014 to 2024, and its generous financial and military pledges during the Bonn Conference (2011), Tokyo

Conference (2012) and Chicago Summit (2012), will be enough to make us realise a true transformation of our country.

We trust our security forces, which are capable of meeting our challenges. If we continue receiving financial, technical and military support from the US government and our NATO partners, as was stated during the NATO Summit in Wales in 2014, we will be able to contain the insurgency and reduce it to a level which will allow us to consolidate government authority, and provide an incentive for the insurgents to accept our peace process.

We are witnessing the rise of a new generation of political leaders committed to political pluralism, good governance, democratic values and political integrity. In addition, a considerable number of our very young men and women have received higher education and have access to social media, which has had a positive impact on their views about the global political system. Once a critical mass is reached, the social and political changes in the country will become permanent.

We are also enthusiastic about our underground mineral resources, valued between USD 1 to 3 trillion, which could be of tremendous help.[1] We will not eternally remain a financial burden on the international community, and this much-needed capital could help us meet our economic development goals, as also lift us out of the infernal circle of conflict and poverty.

Therefore, the current National Unity Government's foremost agenda is to create an economic vision for Afghanistan, which was stated by President Mohammad Ashraf Ghani during his speech at the London Conference in December 2014:

> Afghanistan has the potential to be self-supporting, enhanced our paper on self-reliance but our self-reliance is not the old fashioned to close ourselves against the world. Our self-reliance is going to come and embrace the world in a competitive economy so creation of a legal economy that can drive the citizenship agenda and ensure that we can pay for our security is essential.[2]

Despite a worsening security situation and a grim economic outlook for the next couple of years, this economic vision must be realised in the backdrop of economic transition, where Afghanistan must reduce its financial reliance on the international community and boost its internal revenues.

WHAT CAN AFGHANISTAN OFFER TO SAARC MEMBERS?

Afghanistan, as a poor country, has suffered enormously in the past decade due to continuous civil strife. However, the country is resourceful and has the potential for rapid economic development.

Afghanistan's unique geographical position opens up tremendous opportunities for it to become a hub for trade and transit between South and Central Asia. Since the early 1990s, India and Pakistan have shown great interest in fossil fuel reserves in Central Asian Republics such as Uzbekistan, Turkmenistan and Kazakhstan.[3] After the US involvement in Afghanistan, the idea of making Afghanistan an energy bridge gained momentum and the trans-Afghanistan pipeline, widely known as the Turkmenistan–Afghanistan–Pakistan–India pipeline (TAPI), received the support of the United States and funding pledges from the Asian Development Bank (ADB).[4]

Furthermore, the most recent project agreed upon between Afghanistan, Tajikistan, Kyrgyzstan and Pakistan on the supply of electricity transiting via Afghanistan is an indication that Afghanistan could play a key role in helping an energy-starved South Asia meet its energy demands. In fact, the realisation of the Central Asia South Asia Electricity Transmission and Trade Project (Casa–1000)[5] is an important step in this direction because for the first time in recent history, Pakistan will become dependent on the transit routes of Afghanistan.

Similarly, Central Asian countries need an alternative exit gate to the outside world other than Russia. Therefore, the US military's effort to reduce its reliance on Pakistan's supply road has contributed to the opening of another transit corridor via Russia and the Caspian Sea to the Central Asian Republics and to Afghanistan, known as the Northern Distribution Network (NDN).[6] In fact, this new corridor opened up the 'Old Silk Road', which had been an important trade and transit route within the Eurasian landmass.

Meanwhile, the US administration adopted the concept of the 'New Silk Road', which was mainly developed by US national security and foreign policy experts and scholars, and through a paper by scholars from the Central Asia–Caucasus Institute Silk Road Studies Program in 2010.[7] Later, in 2011, this concept received the US government's support, as stated in US Department of State public remarks by the office of the Special Representative for Afghanistan and Pakistan.[8]

Lately, China, as an emerging world power and a de facto regional leader, has put forward its own initiative for regional cooperation, known as 'The New Silk Road', which consists of inter-regional economic integration, by reviving the old silk road in the Eurasian landmass.[9]

Indeed, there is a general consensus that trade and transit will become an important factor in the economic integration of Eurasia; thus, we are eager to finally see the benefit of Afghanistan's geographic position, which can offer an opportunity for landlocked countries such as ours to regain its old strategic importance by becoming a trade and transit hub between South and Central Asia, as well as China and the Middle East.

We are located close to two emerging world powers, China and India, which are in dire need of mineral resources to sustain their current economic development needs. Thus, Afghanistan, with its untouched and large reserves of mineral resources, will offer the best deals for both countries.

The riches of Afghanistan's mineral resources have attracted the attention of all major world players. According to an article in *The New York Times*:

> The United States has discovered nearly $1 trillion in untapped mineral deposits in Afghanistan, far beyond any previously known reserves and enough to fundamentally alter the Afghan economy and perhaps the Afghan war itself, according to senior American government officials.[10]

In fact, the only economic sector that could help Afghanistan through the period of economic transition is the mining sector. The country is in dire need of capital for investment in its economic infrastructure in order to overcome challenges related to poverty and dependency on foreign assistance. This vision of the new National Unity Government in Kabul is summarised in one sentence, delivered by President Ghani during his inauguration ceremony in Kabul:

> We believe the geographic location of Afghanistan can change this country to a transit route. The mines can change Afghanistan

to an industrial country; similarly, our land and water can change Afghanistan to a dynamic agricultural land.[11]

Indeed, Afghanistan offers a tremendous opportunity for regional countries to invest in its mining sector. So far, Chinese and Indian companies have shown interest in this sector and have already secured important contracts in the copper and iron mines, respectively. In order to extract these mines and transport the ore out of Afghanistan, both China and India are required to cooperate in stabilising the country and in modernising its transportation infrastructure. Therefore, the Afghan mining sector offers a unique opportunity for collaboration and cooperation among key regional powers.

Another opportunity that Afghanistan provides for regional economic cooperation is its sources of water. The country is largely part of the Hindu Kush Himalaya (HKH) region,[12] which is a rich source of water in South Asia. Moreover, rivers originating in Afghanistan flow into Iran and its three northern neighbours in Central Asia.

It is needless to mention the importance of water and how it has become a major source of conflict in today's world. There is ample literature on this subject; we, in Afghanistan, have been witnessing the belligerent intervention of our neighbours in this conflict because of their keen interest in controlling our water flows to their benefit. Therefore, there is a need for regional cooperation on water management because, sooner or later, water scarcity in this region could lead to serious conflicts.

AFGHANISTAN'S RESOURCES: A CURSE OR AN OPPORTUNITY?

So far, Afghanistan has not been able to use its resources to its own advantage. The continuation of conflict and outside intervention is certainly linked to its geographical position, mineral mines, its sources of water, among others. Afghanistan has been a resource-cursed country thus far.

However, because of new political and economic development since the collapse of the Taliban regime in 2001, some of the countries of the region, such as China, India, Pakistan and Iran, are keen to invest in Afghanistan. The extensions of both the Iranian and Uzbek railroads and their electric grids into Afghanistan are encouraging examples of cooperation. In addition, the TAPI project, which will enable Turkmenistan to export its natural gas to Pakistan and India via Afghanistan, is an important test for an effective multilateral agreement between Afghanistan, Pakistan and India.

Therefore, there is renewed hope in Afghanistan that the emergence of China and India as global powers will provide political stability to the region. Afghan leaders, particularly President Ghani, well understand the importance of an active regional diplomacy. He elaborated on his foreign policy and, particularly, regional diplomacy during his inaugural speech: 'For stability, security and economic development, we will try to reach to a regional cooperation pact with all our neighbours.'[13]

The biggest challenge for the Afghan government will be reaching out to regional stakeholders in order to transform the current resource curse into an opportunity. President Ghani, in his closing remarks at the London Conference, summarised Afghanistan's expectations from its neighbours and regional partners:

> We have a choice, we either become the lynch pin of Asian integration where only roads will come to our countries and go out of our countries to connect Central Asia, South Asia, West Asia and East Asia or we will become the cul-de-sac, the forgotten piece of history, because time will not wait. We master a sense of urgency. This is the moment where the third phase of globalization can lift us out of poverty in the region and [it] behooves us to seize that moment to cooperate fully so that we can curve [carve]a new future for our people.[14]

However, this endeavour will not be possible without the consent of major regional players in Afghanistan. Before we transform our natural resources into economic opportunities, we require strong regional diplomacy and leadership from emerging regional powers.

CAN SAARC HELP AFGHANISTAN MEET ITS REGIONAL ASPIRATIONS?
The rationale behind Afghanistan's membership of SAARC is mainly for economic reasons. Former President Karzai, in his speech during the 14th SAARC Summit in New Delhi, clearly stated: 'After decades of instability, there is a unique opportunity for Afghanistan to realize

its potential as a "land bridge" between Central Asia, South Asia and the Middle East region.'[15]

A perusal of the text of the SAARC Charter is indeed encouraging as we see that politicians at the highest level have understood the need for, and importance of, a common regional mechanism to foster economic cooperation and overcome geopolitical challenges that the region has inherited from the colonial era.

Alas, SAARC has never gained momentum because political and geostrategic rivalries have superseded regional cooperation. Indeed, the partition of the subcontinent and the Cold War deeply affected relations among countries of the region, which could not be righted in view of the enmity between the two major regional powers, India and Pakistan. Their adversarial relationship has severely affected the entire region and is considered the main cause for conflict and economic decline.

The signing of SAARC was not enough to transform the goodwill generated into political action. There have been several studies on conflicts and the lack of economic development in South Asia by explaining the origin of the conflict in the region. As in the Middle East, South Asian countries also suffer from arbitrary demarcations of borderlines after the independence of the subcontinent in 1947. In the particular case of Afghanistan, the continuation of conflicts is mainly due to the artificial creation of Pakistan and the ongoing rivalry between Pakistan and India.

There is a consensus among scholars, analysts and politicians in the region that without an honest territorial settlement and a resolution of the Kashmir conflict between India and Pakistan, a lasting peace might not be realised in the near future. Thus, without peace and the spirit of cooperation, any initiative for regional cooperation, be it SAARC or ECO, is bound to fail.

In a chapter from a book for the Carnegie Endowment for International Peace in 2010, I wrote:

> Nevertheless, despite the breadth of such opportunities, lack of political will, among many other factors, has complicated the prospect for effective regional cooperation. The countries have yet to look beyond historical differences and open a new chapter of cooperation and collaboration for the benefit of their peoples.[16]

Yet, continuous efforts by the United States and the European Union (EU) to help resolve contentious issues between Afghanistan and Pakistan did not bear fruit. In fact, because of NATO's military presence in Afghanistan, the US and other prominent European countries conducted a joint effort by naming a single special representative for both Afghanistan and Pakistan, thus treating the Afghan and Pakistani file as one.

However, despite tremendous efforts, Pakistan has remained indifferent to political pressures and even the US' financial incentive did not help change the country's belligerent policy in Afghanistan. For instance, despite the formal Trade and Transit Agreement (TTA)[17] between Afghanistan and Pakistan, which was signed in June 2011, Pakistan's territory is off limits to Afghan trucks.

The interest of the countries of NATO in Afghanistan and in the region is fading, and regional countries will thus regain their importance, as was the case in the pre-NATO intervention of the 1990s. In this new post-2015 context, Afghanistan's place within SAARC will depend on the whims of Pakistan. Therefore, our hopes for economic integration with South Asia, and any benefit from the Indian economic spillover, will depend on political developments within Pakistan.

In addition, most political and security developments in South Asia, as well as in the Middle East, have been significantly altered over the past decade owing to US interventions in Afghanistan and Iraq. The emergence of new, violent non-state actors, such as the Islamic state in Iraq and Syria, and its potential emergence in Pakistan and Afghanistan, will further change the security and political dynamics of the region. Furthermore, common challenges, such as climate change, the uncontrolled growth of population, the lack of water management and the energy crisis are some important factors which will deeply impact inter-regional relationships.

Meanwhile, in the backdrop of these tremendous challenges, the actual purpose of SAARC will be considered utopian and will never be able to achieve its ends and targets, unless and until the trust deficit, which has been created over the past several years, is not eliminated.

Like many other small countries, Afghanistan will also be deprived of enjoying the crucial benefits of SAARC unless India and Pakistan cooperate in the manner laid out in the SAARC mandate.

More than 35 per cent of the population of South Asia lives below the poverty line; yet both Pakistan and India spend huge amounts on building large armies and producing sophisticated military technology and hardware.

The lack of trust is another major obstacle in making SAARC a successful regional socio-economic and political bloc, with member nations accusing each other of abetting separatist and secessionist forces on their soil. Rather than dealing jointly with the problem, member nations are becoming increasingly isolated from one another. As a result, SAARC has failed to resolve the deadlock on several key issues and conflicts in South Asia.

Moreover, no major step with actual positive implications has been taken to promote peace and trust amongst member nations that are still in conflict. The promotion of trade and economy can only be possible if relations amongst member nations are stable. SAARC has failed to generate trust amongst its nations in a manner that could help achieve the objectives of the organisation. The best example is that of the differences between India and Pakistan over the Kashmir issue and the Pakistan–Afghanistan Durand–Line issue. Lives are lost every other day on the borders of these nations. Yet, SAARC has failed to take sensible steps to resolve these matters.

The current state of SAARC has been well highlighted by Prime Minister Modi at the SAARC meeting in Kathmandu on 26 November 2014:

> Today, less than 5 per cent of the region's global trade takes place between us. Even at this modest level, less than 10 per cent of the region's internal trade takes place under SAARC Free Trade Area. Indian companies are investing billions abroad, but less than 1 per cent flows into our region. It is still harder to travel within our region than to Bangkok or Singapore; and, more expensive to speak to each other.[18]

If SAARC is to become a successful model of regional cooperation and continue to be relevant in the future, one has to appraise the various accords and agreements signed by the member countries over the past many years. For example, the South Asian Free Trade Agreement (SAFTA) was signed in 2004; ten years later, intra-regional trade accounts for only 5 per cent. For Afghanistan, the TTA with Pakistan has not materialised as well due to the lack of Afghan access to Indian markets, mainly because of the increasing enmity between India and Pakistan. Therefore, the future of SAARC is directly co-related with the Indo–Pak relationship. Given this scenario, if the relationship between India and Pakistan is to improve, there is more likelihood that SAARC will move forward; if not, it will merely be a dead end. Resources will be wasted, with no positive implications for the member nations.

A NEW OPPORTUNITY

The balance of power in the region has been shifting during the past decade because of important events such as the US–India strategic alignment, Pakistan's deteriorating relationship with the US and China's emergence as a global power. In addition, new events such as the US–Iran detente and the new cold war between Russia and NATO could further alter the balance.

Further, Pakistan's political and military elite recognises that the biggest threat to the security of Pakistan is internal, and it emanates from radical and terrorist groups such as the Taliban.[19] The most recent ruthless Taliban attack on a Peshawar school that killed 145 people, most of them innocent children, has further galvanised anti-Taliban sentiment inside the country.

In addition, the new Afghan government has been trying to reach out to Pakistan and other powers in the region, such as Saudi Arabia and China, which have tremendous leverage over Pakistan. The aim of the Afghan government is to convince Pakistan to abandon its hostility towards Afghanistan.

Meanwhile, Pakistan has been suffering from an energy shortage and its economic growth is lagging behind the other regional countries; thus, economic recovery and development has become the priority of Nawaz Sharif's government.

We, in Afghanistan, believe that the time is ripe for improved regional economic cooperation, and we are expecting that the trade and transit agreement between Afghanistan and Pakistan will finally materialise; this will allow Afghan traders to access the rest of SAARC markets.

We expect that the new leadership in India and Afghanistan, as well as a shift in Pakistan's foreign policy vis-à-vis the two countries, might lead to a renewed hope for regional cooperation; SAARC could then establish its meaningful role in South Asia.

◆

#This chapter was first published in 2015 in the *IIC Quarterly*, Vol. 41, Nos 3 and 4.

NOTES

1. An estimate of the US survey.

2. Closing remarks delivered by Mohammad Ashraf Ghani, President of the Islamic Republic of Afghanistan, at the London Conference on Afghanistan, 2014.

3. 'When the Taliban was governing Afghanistan, two consortia vied for the right to take on the project, one led by Unocal (an American firm) and the other by Bridas (an Argentinean firm). The US government supported the Unocal consortium; it was negotiating with the Taliban regime from 1997 to August 2001, during both the Bill Clinton and George W. Bush administrations.' See Foster (2008).

4. Asian Development Bank, 13 November 2014: http://www.adb.org/news/turkmenistan-afghanistan-pakistan-and-india-establish-landmark-tapi-pipeline-company

5. http://www.worldbank.org/projects/P145054?lang=en

6. 'New Supply Front for Afghan War Runs Across Russia Georgia and the Stans', Bill Marmon, March, 2010: http://www.europeaninstitute.org/index.php/93-european-affairs/february—march-2010/959-new-supply-front-for-afghan-war-runs-across-russia-georgia-and-the-stans

7. 'The Key to Success in Afghanistan: A Modern Silk Road Strategy', S. Frederic Starr and Andrew C. Kuchins, http://csis.org/files/publication/100610_key_to_success_in_afghanistan.pdf

8. US Support of the New Silk Road: http://www.state.gov/p/sca/ci/af/newsilkroad/

9. 'China's Way: The New Silk Road', Camille Brugier, Europian Union Institute for Security Studies: http://www.iss.europa.eu/uploads/media/Brief_14_New_Silk_Road.pdf

10. http://www.nytimes.com/2010/06/14/world/asia/14minerals.html?_r=0

11. President Mohammad Ashraf Ghani's inauguration speech: http://president.gov.af/en/news/36954

12. 'Research Insights on Climate and Water in the Hindu Kush and Himalaya.' SWAMI, South Asia Water Initiative: https://www.southasiawaterinitiative.org/sites/sawi/files/documents/Research%20Insights%20on%20Climate%20and%20Water%20in%20the%20Hindu%20Kush%20Himalayas.pdf

13. President Ghani's inaugural speech in Kabul: http://president.gov.af/en/news/36954

14. Closing remarks delivered by Mohammad Ashraf Ghani, President of the Islamic Republic of Afghanistan, at the London Conference on Afghanistan, 2014.

15. Quote from Karzai's speech.

16. http://carnegieendowment.org/files/regional_approach.pdf
17. TTA agreement: http://moci.gov.af/en/page/8604
18. President Narendra Modi in Kathmandu, Nepal, 26 November 2014.
19. Pakistan's new Army Doctrine.

REFERENCE

Foster, John. 2008. *Foreign Policy Series*, Volume 3, No. 1, 19 June.

◆◆

3

CHANGING FACE
The Trials and Fortunes of Regional Cooperation under SAARC

SAMAN
KELEGAMA[#]

INTRODUCTION

The proliferation over the last few decades of various multilateral organisations to promote regional cooperation reflects a global society which is acutely aware of, and has come to embrace, its growing interconnectedness. The formal establishment of SAARC represents one instance of this. As set out in the charter, the primary objective of SAARC is to utilise cooperation amongst its eight member states as a springboard for achieving cohesive development in the economic, cultural and socio-political lives of its 1.6 billion citizens. Nevertheless, despite enormous potential for facilitating such development in a region populated by over 40 per cent of the world's poor, SAARC's effectiveness has been limited and its successes far too few. In acknowledgement of such failings, a Group of Eminent Persons (GEP) Report was commissioned by the organisation for consideration at its 1998 summit in Colombo. The Report points to SAARC's inadequate role in fostering regional cooperation, and then goes on to articulate a vision of change, detailing the steps that must be taken in order to transform the organisation into the fulcrum of a truly integrated and self-sustaining regional society. This chapter considers the obstacles which, up to the present moment, have hindered SAARC from achieving such a transformation. It then discusses a number of new opportunities which, if appropriately exploited, could provide a means for SAARC to close the gap between the GEP vision of an effective and productive organisation for regional cooperation, and its far less desirable reality.

THE CASE FOR REGIONAL INTEGRATION

Despite persistently high levels of poverty, the South Asian region has enjoyed steady economic growth in recent years, notably spurred by a robust Indian economy. A gradual movement away from primary product dependence to a concentration on manufacturing and services has enabled these states to reposition themselves favourably in the arena of international trade (Muni, 2010: 42). As an indicator, the share of agriculture in South Asian GDP fell from approximately 40 per cent in the 1970s to under 20 per cent in 2006 (RIS, 2008: 18). Nevertheless, the success of these economies in this regard has been somewhat constrained by such factors as a lack of infrastructure, insufficient investment in private enterprise and skill shortages in the labour force. Regional cooperation is, ideally, a means of overcoming such obstacles to growth. Accordingly, various intra-regional infrastructure development projects, the establishment of a Common Investment Area and the sharing of resources at many levels have all been proposed at SAARC summits and meetings over the years. In the context of trade, increased regionalism would allow these economies to improve their competitiveness, increase the export of services and add value to traditional exports. Particularly at the current juncture, in the aftermath of a global recession that has profoundly impacted many developed economies which are the customary recipients of a large proportion of South Asian exports, cooperation and trade within the region seems increasingly important. Given that South Asia is inhabited by approximately 24 per cent of the global population, the potential benefits to be reaped are extensive and thus, the burden of responsibility borne by SAARC is immense.

This is, in fact, the very conclusion arrived at by the Group of Eminent Persons in their seminal Report on SAARC. The Report, aptly titled *SAARC Vision Beyond the Year 2000*, 'attempts to define a long-range vision for SAARC...including a SAARC agenda for 2000 and beyond'.[1] In the context of trade, the Report calls for the implementation of a South Asian Free Trade Area (which SAARC achieved in 2006), the elimination of tariff barriers over an eight-year period and the removal of all non-tariff barriers (NTBs) to trade. Inspired by the successes of the European Union (EU), the GEP Report further recommends the creation of a similarly integrated South Asian Economic Union (SAEU) by 2020, preceded by the establishment of a Customs Union by 2015. The Report advises the adoption of the following measures as first steps towards the achievement of the SAEU: first, the creation of a Single Market for South Asia, involving an integration of transportation, energy, telecommunications and other services; and second, the espousal of a common competition policy for all states in the region. Nevertheless, given prevailing geopolitical tensions in the region, as well as the fact that the establishment of SAFTA was already well behind schedule, the achievement of these goals by the specified deadlines seems difficult. The ideas of a Common Investment Area, a South Asian Development Bank (SADB), a reshaping of SAARC's institutional structure and the signing of a Social Charter also feature in the Report, amongst other recommendations for regional cooperation in terms of infrastructure, trade in goods and services, investment and finance and macroeconomic policy.

The bulk of such recommendations have not, however, come to fruition. Indeed, despite its influence, the GEP Report in its entirety has not been fully endorsed by SAARC (Behera, 2009: 37). Many of the ideas contained in the Report have been the subject of discussions at subsequent SAARC summits (examples are the notion of a common currency for South Asia and a 'Schengen'-style visa for the region), and the SAARC Research Network was appointed to consider the viability of some of these options (such as the establishment of the SADB and creation of a common stock exchange), but the Network has hardly met after 1998–1999. In fact, SAARC's persistent inability to convert ideas into substantive action has long been a point of censure for critics of the organisation (Muni, 2010: 1–3). The reasons for such a failing are both geopolitical and structural in nature, and will be discussed later in this chapter. First, however, we consider the scope of its achievements to date.

SAARC SUCCESSES

It must be noted that while SAARC's practical successes have been few, several are worthy of acknowledgement. The commissioning of the GEP Report is certainly one of them. The formation of a Network of Researchers on Global Financial and Economic Issues to aid SAARC in dealing with macroeconomic concerns is another notable development. Arguably, the most significant of the organisation's achievements to date is, however, the establishment—following many delays—of the South Asian Free Trade Area (SAFTA) in 2006. The SAFTA agreement calls for trade liberalisation in the region through the reduction of tariff barriers. It envisions the removal of all regional tariffs at the end of 2015 by South Asia's least developed countries (Bangladesh, Bhutan, the Maldives and Nepal), and three years earlier by their more developed counterparts. Such an agreement is clearly an important step in the direction of fostering regional trade opportunities. The foregone benefits from regional trade in the absence of an agreement of this nature are considerable: in 2006, potential intra-regional trade was estimated to be approximately USD 40 billion, compared to an actual trade valuation of USD 10.5 billion (RIS, 2008: 63). As previously noted, such potential gains are of particular significance in the current global economic climate. Nevertheless, such regional trade agreements are desirable not only as a means of encouraging intra-regional trade flows but also in enabling states to reorganise their economies in a manner that derives the maximum possible advantage from specialisation and economies of scale, following the example of the EU (ibid.: 59–60).

However, a large proportion of this array of potential benefits remains to be enjoyed due to a number of factors which have inhibited SAFTA's efficacy. To begin with, the lengthy administrative delays involved in setting up the agreement mean that SAFTA is significantly behind schedule in its activities. The GEP Report advised that SAFTA be created in 2000, with all of its primary objectives to be completed by 2010. The current projected timeline lags substantially behind this. Second, member countries maintain lengthy negative lists for regional trade, a state of affairs the agreement fails to preclude. A 2006 study shows, for instance, that 42 per cent of Sri Lankan, and 58.5 per cent of Indian, exports to SAARC countries feature on negative lists, a fact which severely debilitates the practical workings of the agreement (Weerakoon and Thenakoon, 2006: 3922). In fact, the existence of parallel trade agreements which offer more favourable trade terms—such as the India–Sri Lanka Free Trade Agreement (ISFTA) and India's FTAs with both South East and East Asian nations—impacts negatively upon states' commitment to meeting SAFTA's targets and, indeed, calls into question its usefulness in the sphere of regional trade.[2] Another problem is the continued existence of non-tariff and para-tariff barriers to trade. The GEP Report calls for the removal of all such barriers by 2009 by LDCs and by 2007 by non-LDCs. Despite this, however, SAFTA makes no provision for such removal, and NTBs such as quotas, import licensing requirements and anti-dumping measures continue to limit trade opportunities in the region. Finally, the fact that SAFTA covers only trade in goods, and not in services, means that the agreement is lamentably parochial in nature. The inclusion of services under a separate agreement called SATIS (SAARC Trade in Services) in 2010—an issue which has been raised repeatedly at SAARC summits and within academic circles—represents an important step towards promoting the growth of services exports by these countries.

The SAARC Social Charter was initiated in 2003–2004. Like SAFTA, its implementation suffered from long delays, but might be considered another stride, however small, in the right direction for SAARC. The Charter was finally signed in 2004 at the 12th SAARC Summit in Islamabad and outlines a regional plan of action for the organisation, setting general targets in the areas of poverty alleviation, population stabilisation, the empowerment of women and protection of children, the promotion of health and nutrition and youth mobilisation. The Social Charter is frequently lauded for its inclusive nature: its development involved input not only from the governments of SAARC's member states, but also from civil society organisations, which were permitted to voice their own opinions concerning the important challenges that SAARC should aim to address in the future. Nevertheless, insufficient attention has been paid by SAARC to the monitoring of the Charter's targets, as Lama observes (2007: 26). This may be attributed partly to a lack of resources on the part of the SAARC Secretariat and a lack of commitment on the part of its individual member states. Furthermore, the targets outlined in the Charter are broad, and there remains a need for more specific, numerical targets to be agreed upon, adopted and worked towards if the Charter is to have any practical value.

Two other initiatives that SAARC can count among its partial successes in recent years are the establishment of the SAARC Energy Centre in Islamabad in 2006 and the South Asian University in New Delhi. The GEP Report emphasises, among other things, the importance to South Asia of energy cooperation. The uneven spread of energy resources throughout the region, with oil, coal and natural gas reserves in India, as well as natural gas reserves in Pakistan and Bangladesh, means that the region as a whole would benefit greatly from cooperative energy policies. The SAARC Energy Centre is charged with the tasks of developing existing energy resources, promoting conservation and energy efficiency, and working towards the development of alternative and renewable energy sources. Given the high costs invariably incurred by such endeavours, the pooling together of regional resources in order to fund energy development projects is important; it remains to be judged, however, whether the Energy Centre is able to achieve in practice the aims set out for it on paper.

The South Asian University is funded by the Indian government, and all SAARC members are expected to contribute towards its operational costs. The university has the potential to achieve some measure of the cross-border flows of skills that regional cooperation is envisaged to generate. Furthermore, in providing students with a regionally recognised qualification, the South Asian University goes some way towards achieving the equivalence of qualification that is a desirable characteristic of education in a truly integrated region.

Nevertheless, such limited successes remain overshadowed by a history of inaction and inefficacy, and some critics contend that the number of SAARC's achievements are markedly disproportionate to the length of the organisation's existence (Muni, 2010: 1–2). While the reasons for such a state of affairs are multiform, it may be considered that the cloud of geopolitical tension and mistrust that SAARC has laboured under—virtually since its inception—bears a significant proportion of the blame in this respect. The long-prevailing atmosphere of suspicion and animosity that characterises Indo–Pak relations is particularly important here.

THE BURDEN OF INTERSTATE HOSTILITIES

Disputes over Kashmir between India and Pakistan, resulting in a number of armed conflicts and highly strained relations between the two states, have existed since the collapse of British colonialism in the subcontinental region. Attempts to heal the political breach—such as the establishment of the Delhi–Lahore bus service in 1999 in the wake of nuclear tests carried out by both nations and the Indo–Pak ceasefire agreement of 2003—occurred at critical moments in the history of the conflict to cool hostilities. Nevertheless, such events as the attack on the Indian Parliament in 2001 and the 2008 terrorist attacks in Mumbai have led to a resurgence of political mistrust between the two nations. The prolonged existence of such a fraught relationship between SAARC's largest and most powerful member states has been a significant spoke in the wheel of progress for the organisation. The Kargil War of 1999, the last of the formal Indo–Pak wars and the only one to occur after the formation of SAARC, has particularly impeded efforts at regional integration.

One of the greatest resultant losses to SAARC has been Pakistan's refusal to grant India Most Favoured Nation (MFN) status, thereby preventing an accrual of benefits to the region from the largest potential segment of trade within South Asia. A 2006 ADB study estimates the value of potential Indo-Pak trade at up to USD 10 billion (ADB, 2006: 13). Although there were breakthroughs in regard to the MFN offer in recent years, there is more to be done by Pakistan for normalising trade relations with India. In addition, an atmosphere of mutual suspicion has also doggedly marked India's dealings with other SAARC member states since the organisation's establishment. In the absence of SAARC, South Asian states would need to engage bilaterally with the regional giant, India, in a manner that, given the clear economic asymmetries involved, would place the former parties in a highly disadvantageous bargaining position. Therefore, it is certainly in their interest to use SAARC as a means of levelling the diplomatic playing field. Similarly, such a balancing of power would ideally enable India to engage with its neighbours in a setting that posits it favourably, not as an evil overlord bent on achieving its own will, but as a fellow member state striving for regional benefits. Nevertheless, a distinct fissure exists between idealism and reality in this instance. Most member states have historically viewed India's participation in SAARC with mistrust, suspecting it of using the organisation as an indirect means of exerting control over its neighbours and increasing the scope of its regional dominance. Conversely, India has harboured reservations about SAARC in the past, believing it to be a tool of suppression for the other members in banding together against India. In fact, virtually all its members have displayed a wary attitude towards SAARC, particularly during its early years of existence.

This is, perhaps, an unfortunate repercussion of the region's relatively recent emergence from under the control of British imperialism. The independent nation state is, in South Asia, young and still evolving. Consequently, it guards its sovereignty jealously, and often views the actions of supranational entities as so many attempts to usurp that sovereignty. Therefore, most countries have hesitated to accept the powers of organisations such as SAARC and continue to regard them with suspicion.[3]

MEMBER COMMITMENT, HISTORY AND THE INFRASTRUCTURE GAP: MISSING LINKS

Partly as a result of this historical state of affairs, SAARC has suffered from a lack of commitment on the part of its members, a fact that has rendered problematic the formation of policy and the initiation of intra-regional projects. Consequently, many of the decisions passed by SAARC have been more for the sake of outward display than actual usefulness (Behera, 2009: 29). Furthermore, often, even when members have accepted certain SAARC protocols, practical implementation (left largely in the hands of individual states) has not necessarily followed. An example of this is states' failure thus far to substantially reduce their sensitive lists and remove non-tariff barriers under SAFTA, and SAARC's inability to impel any action in this respect. Although agreements may be reached at SAARC summits concerning the importance of addressing certain pressing issues such as poverty and food security in the present context, enthusiasm typically wanes in the aftermath of the summit, and SAARC has little institutional power or ability to sustain its momentum until the next summit. Other factors which impact unfavourably upon states' commitment to SAARC are the existence of alternative bilateral agreements between members (as previously discussed) as well as states' membership of parallel multilateral organisations such as the WTO. Unless SAARC is able to provide clear incentives for its members to prefer SAARC initiatives over any of these external options, it is unlikely to be able to inspire the degree of commitment that is required, at a national level, to make SAARC an effective actor in regional affairs.

Conversely, it may be argued that bilateral trade agreements of this nature could become an impetus for, rather than a hindrance to, regionalism and, as such, should not necessarily be discouraged

(Kelegama, 2001: 37). Yet this is only true if the bulk of such agreements exist between regional states. In reality, however, many of these FTAs are for the purpose of stimulating trade between a South Asian state and a non-regional partner. Examples are the FTA between China and Pakistan, the ASEAN–India Free Trade Area (AIFTA) and the EU–India FTA. The last is currently under negotiation. These clearly run counter to SAARC's aim of redirecting trade flows to regional destinations. Nevertheless, despite its importance as a first step towards regional integration, intra-regional trade has proved difficult to stimulate and, indeed, such difficulties have long occupied the attention of SAARC, though to little productive purpose. Key among the reasons for the persistence of such a state of affairs is a single factor, namely history.

As a consequence of their shared colonial past, the majority of South Asian states have historically directed their exports towards the markets of their former colonisers and the latter's neighbours. They also are accustomed to viewing each other as competitors in trade, rather than as potential trade partners, given their exportation of similar products. The weight of such a history, and the manner in which it has shaped the direction of South Asian trade policy, has certainly hindered SAARC, particularly during its earlier years. Nevertheless, a 2008 ADB–UNCTAD report suggests that the existence of competition between South Asian states is more a matter of perception than a true barrier to trade. The report points out that these countries can achieve complementarities through specialisation in different *stages* of production, or by working towards product differentiation (ADB/UNCTAD, 2008: 37). Further, it observes that, in the context of trade in services, various regional states have comparative advantages in different sectors, thereby opening potential pathways to regional trade (ibid.: 96). Examples of such comparative advantages are transport services for Pakistan and Sri Lanka, travel services for the Maldives and Nepal and financial services for Bangladesh.

Nevertheless, states' ability to take advantage of the benefits of trade in services has been limited to a certain extent by a lack of domestic infrastructure. The 2008 South Asia Development and Cooperation Report notes, for instance, the troubling fact of a growing disparity between infrastructure levels in developed and developing nations (ADB, 2006: 96). In recent years, the majority of South Asian states have experienced rapid economic growth, as well as inherent structural transformations within their economies as they expand from—initially—an almost exclusive concentration on agricultural products to include the development of services and knowledge production. The consequently widening infrastructure gap in these economies is, therefore, an issue that needs to be addressed.[4] Thus, projects to integrate transportation, energy and labour markets, as proposed in the GEP Report, would clearly benefit the region. Nevertheless, while SAARC bears a significant portion of the responsibility for improving regional infrastructure, the *lack* of such infrastructure equally hinders its effectiveness. SAARC suffers, therefore, from something of a vicious circle in this regard. Accordingly, the impetus for escaping this depends largely on the individual commitment of its member states which, as previously discussed, has been notably lacking in the past.

CIVIL SOCIETY: THE NEED FOR ALTERNATIVE SAARC CHANNELS

Another factor which might be viewed as limiting SAARC's effectiveness is an inadequate involvement of the regional business and academic communities in the organisation's decision-making processes. SAARC is, by nature of its construction, an organisation for cooperation among state actors. Thus, the voices heard at SAARC meetings, and the opinions, concerns and ideas expressed there, are largely those of government officials. Yet, in maintaining such insularity, the organisation becomes undesirably parochial in nature; it fails to benefit from a range of alternative sources of knowledge and expertise, as well as a more nuanced view of challenges and new ideas concerning the ways in which these challenges might be addressed. Indeed, given its purpose of achieving integration, it is somewhat ironic that one of SAARC's greatest problems has been its inability to achieve an integrated involvement of civil society with official government channels in its processes of policy-making and project implementation. One of the reasons that the SAARC Social Charter has been met with approval from critics is, in fact, its implicit acknowledgement that there are important contributions to be made to SAARC from non-governmental sources. Yet the involvement of civil society in the creation of the Social Charter is only a single step in a journey of many towards an integrated institutional structure for SAARC.

Behera (2009: 14–27) identifies three schools of thought concerning the manner in which civil society could be brought into engagement with official government channels in SAARC processes: by intervention from the top down, from the bottom up and through the creation of knowledge. For this purpose, we consider the existence of three parallel 'tracks' or channels of involvement in SAARC. Track I is the official channel of intergovernmental decision-making. Tracks II and III represent the involvement of civil society: Track II, the 'top-down' approach, consists of a form of 'shadow diplomacy' involving retired policy-makers, scholars and other individuals who have ready access to, and established relationships with, members of Track I. This group ideally serves to bridge the divide between the government and the domestic intelligentsia. Track III, the 'bottom-up' approach, involves 'NGOs, peoples' organisations, activist groups and networks that explicitly function apart from or beyond governments' (ibid.: 17). While the latter group likely has little or no direct access to government channels, its involvement is intended to broaden the scope of SAARC participation by stimulating public interest and thereby encouraging governments to take decisive actions within the SAARC framework.

Knowledge creation within these channels is also an important aspect of their contribution to Track I dialogues. Research bodies such as the South Asia Centre for Policy Studies (SACEPS), the South Asia Network of Economic Research Institutes (SANEI) and the Coalition for Action on South Asian Cooperation (CASAC) aim to infuse Track I processes with a more holistic and nuanced understanding of regional matters. Ideally, the formation of such a regional network outside the central sphere of policy-makers would facilitate the continuance of discussion and interest concerning SAARC affairs between official summits. Furthermore, the dissemination of information through regional journals, magazines and other publications ensures that the wider South Asian community remains cognizant of emerging challenges and opportunities for regional integration, as well as of SAARC's current initiatives in this respect.

Nonetheless, the full benefits of these alternative channels of SAARC participation remain to be enjoyed, largely due to lacunae of communication with Track I. Firstly, the lack of an inherent structural connection between governmental and non-governmental SAARC participants means that the information sets under which each operates are mutually exclusive, as Behera observes (ibid.: 34). This inevitably creates a cloud of suspicion and, sometimes, hostility that casts a shadow upon interactions between the two parties. Governments are, therefore, less likely to accept the views and policy advice that emerge from Tracks II and—particularly—III. Furthermore, due to the highly personalised nature of prevailing interactions with Track I, it is often the case that the body of information passed from Tracks II and III to Track I is not truly representative of the civil community in its entirety but, rather, is peculiar to certain factions that have preferential access to governments.

In fact, just as decision-making within official government channels is rendered problematic by the existence of conflicting views amongst domestic political parties, communication amongst Tracks I, II and III is somewhat garbled by the diverse, fractured and, sometimes, partisan nature of civil society. The prevalence of populist propaganda and infeasible suggestions among certain groups robs the entire channel of much of its credibility and requires a sifting of information from these sources on the part of Track I, which is time-consuming and expends resources wastefully. Thus, the lack of coordination and collaboration amongst these groups hinders the creation of useful and coherent policy advice by Tracks I and II, as well as Track I's ability to give credence to, and absorb, such information.

In fact, this issue of communication and coordination is one which equally characterises the institutional structure of SAARC itself. The highly bureaucratic chain of decision-making generates frequent delays in the creation of policy as well as in its implementation. In fact, the waning of members' enthusiasm between summits, which has posed such a problem for SAARC initiatives in the past, may partly be attributed to this. Another related concern is that the individual roles of entities within the broader SAARC structure are not clearly defined.[5] The inactivity of SAARC's regional centres may, for instance, be explained in this manner. Such a lack is highly detrimental to the organisation's effectiveness, as it inevitably dissolves any sense of accountability. In the absence of a clear-cut chain of accountability, any progress must be drawn with difficulty from a well of apathy and torpor.

CHANGING FACE : SAMAN KELEGAMA

CHANGING FACE

The portrait of SAARC's past is, therefore, a somewhat disconsolate image. Nevertheless, it does not follow that its future should be painted in a similar hue. Rather, changes in geopolitical attitudes and the emergence of important new opportunities within the region provide SAARC, at the current juncture, with the necessary tools for an institutional transformation. Critical among these changes is the fact that India's attitude towards SAARC has begun to adopt a more positive tone. In early 2008, for instance, it granted SAARC LDCs duty-free access to its domestic market, and recently contributed USD 100 million to the organisation for use by the SAARC Development Fund. India's emergence in the present context as a global power is undeniable. In terms of population and recent GDP growth (8.3 per cent in 2010), its statistics are impressive. Furthermore, it currently holds a two-year non-permanent seat in the UN Security Council, and is campaigning strongly to be given a permanent seat there. Thus, its positive involvement in SAARC is of tremendous importance to gain a permanent position in the Council.

Moreover, as previously discussed, the development of services is a crucial issue in South Asia, and one which SAARC has continually attempted to facilitate. India's fashioning of itself as a services hub, engaging in the fields of bio-information, drug testing, pharmaceutical research, engineering design and financial analysis, could have profound spillover effects for the region and, therefore, is a highly desirable development. Exports of IT services from India, for instance, soared from USD 4 billion in 2000 to USD 40.4 billion in 2008 (RIS, 2008: 39–41). In view of this, the importance of using India's lead as a springboard for establishing South Asia as a regional ICT hub has featured strongly in SAARC discussions of late (ibid.: 39).

Furthermore, several issues have emerged in recent years that are regional and often global in scope—difficult or even impossible to control at a national level. Consequently, the need for deeper regional integration in order to combat these challenges provides SAARC and its member states with a fresh impetus for collaborative action. Chief among these are an increasing awareness of the threat posed by climate change, concerns about food security in light of steadily rising global food prices and issues regarding regional migration and the steady influx of internally displaced persons in South Asia. Accordingly, SAARC has made a certain amount of progress towards an integrated response in this respect: for instance, a common SAARC position was adopted on regional climate issues such as coastal erosion and the melting of the Himalayan glaciers at the 2009 UN Climate Summit in Copenhagen. Member states have also agreed to form a SAARC Food Bank.

Nevertheless, far more effort is required by SAARC if it is to take full advantage of the fresh opportunities afforded to it at the present juncture. In particular, a progressive transformation of the organisation—in terms of its structure and the manner in which it approaches the task of achieving regional integration—is to be desired. This final section, therefore, considers the ways in which SAARC could attempt to overcome the obstacles that have impeded its progress in the past.

As previously discussed, an issue that has relentlessly beleaguered SAARC from the very outset is that of a geopolitical climate characterised by mutual tension, mistrust and jealously guarded state sovereignty. Within such a realm of neorealist politics, the effective functioning of any multilateral organisation is likely always to be obstructed. Therefore, an important step for SAARC is perhaps to acknowledge that such political realities are unlikely to change in the near future. Consequently, instead of viewing them as an obstacle to be fought against and thereby overcome, SAARC must find ways of working *with* them, ideally even using them to its advantage wherever possible. This would require, however, subtle and skilled diplomacy on SAARC's part, through the efforts of individuals who understand the nuances of South Asian politics.

For example, the area of infrastructure-building is one that merits SAARC's particular attention. This is because the costs of infrastructure development projects are often too great to be borne by a single government (particularly in a region comprised entirely of developing nations); therefore, cooperation in this regard is highly desirable. Nevertheless, region-wide infrastructure development projects have proven difficult to implement, largely as a result of political challenges to the process and difficulty of coordination. Consequently, the pursuance of smaller-scale bilateral deals could be an alternative and a more feasible means of working towards the same goal.[6] Furthermore, if peace talks resume between India and Pakistan, this would provide SAARC with ample opportunity to attempt a deeper involvement of these two nations in SAARC activity. In pursuance of the same goal of turning regional politics to its advantage, another desirable change is for SAARC to develop its relationships with other multilateral organisations, particularly regional ones such as ASEAN and the EU,[7] from which it can glean support, guidance and, most importantly in this instance, a better standing in the arena of regional power politics.

In addition to improving its skills at playing the game of neorealist politics, SAARC must also consider an overhaul of its organisational structure. The lack of clearly defined roles for individual SAARC entities, as well as the garbled and clogged lines of communication and authority, are (as previously observed) a severe impediment to SAARC activity. Although the establishment of the SAARC Social Charter has gone some way towards remedying this situation, much more work needs to be done by the organisation in this respect. Having acknowledged the importance of involving civil society in SAARC processes, one of its key tasks now is to improve the flow of interactions between Tracks I, II and III. SAARC could, for instance, greatly reduce the inherent segregation of official and non-official spheres of dialogue by encouraging Track I officials to participate in Track II and III dialogues and to pursue sabbatical work in these alternative tracks. Similarly, greater credence could be ascribed to Tracks II and III by frequently including representatives from these channels in selected Track I dialogues. The extensive participation of all tracks in events such as the SAARC Chamber of Commerce and Industry (SCCI) Business Conclave and the South Asia Economic Summit should also be promoted, as these represent arenas in which government officials can interact with members of the other tracks freely and on fairly even footing.

Within the organisation, moreover, the roles of regional centres and other SAARC entities need to be defined in more specific terms. Realistic deadlines must be set for these entities to achieve feasible goals, and a monitoring system needs to be implemented to ensure that they remain on track for meeting them. By setting targets and successfully completing a series of projects (regardless of their size or scope), SAARC can begin to change its reputation of inactivity and inefficacy, thereby improving its standing in the eyes of its member states. For this purpose of building confidence, it is perhaps advisable for SAARC to focus its attention on 'soft' projects, as well as those characterised by high visibility. The founding of the SAARC University is a good example of a success story in this respect. The creation of an airport channel for SAARC citizens and a green channel at Customs for SAFTA goods are other positive examples. SAARC could also work towards the promotion of greater regional air connectivity and the development of regional tourism. The latter, in addition to bearing relatively few political challenges, is important because of the notable spillover benefits that an improved tourism sector would afford economies, both domestically and regionally. In this way, by redirecting its energies into less controversial areas of integration, SAARC can begin to establish itself as a credible presence within the South Asian region.

Having consolidated its approach to achieving these central aims, SAARC could then seek to improve its efficacy by a range of other means. Given the centrality of trade to regional integration, measures should be taken to improve the functioning of SAFTA; significant among these are the shortening of states' sensitive lists, the removal of non-tariff barriers to regional trade and the deepening of SAFTA to expedite trade in services liberalisation under SATIS, as previously discussed. Furthermore, an allocation of resources for the purpose of hiring consultant experts for SAARC projects is also desirable, as this would prevent resources being wasted on initiatives that ultimately fail to be realised.[8]

CONCLUSION

Despite its past failings, therefore, SAARC retains the potential to radically impact the process of regional integration in South Asia. In order to fulfil that potential, however, it must successfully utilise such available tools as the GEP Report, the input of civil society, the advantages wrought by a changing politico-economic climate and its own historical experience to refashion its approach and begin to accumulate a portfolio of successes. Time will tell if, in this way, SAARC is able, in the coming years, to significantly contribute to the synthesised development of its regional community.

◆

#This chapter was first published in 2015 in the *IIC Quarterly*, Vol. 41, Nos 3 and 4.

NOTES

1. *SAARC Vision Beyond the Year 2000: Report of the SAARC Group of Eminent Persons Established by the Ninth SAARC Summit.* New Delhi: Shipra Publications, 1999, p. 23.

2. This issue is discussed in South Asia Centre for Policy Studies, *Assessing and Reformulating SAARC Road Map,* SACEPS Paper No. 18. Kathmandu: SACEPS, 2008, p. 8.

3. For a discussion of this, see Behera (2009: 30).

4. For a discussion of this, see RIS (2008: 22).

5. See SACEPS, *Assessing and Reformulating SAARC Road Map,* 2008, p. 46.

6. This is suggested in SACEPS, *Assessing and Reformulating SAARC Road Map,* 2008, p. 62, particularly with regard to improving the regional energy grid.

7. The importance of this is considered in ibid.: 50.

8. SAARC's shortcomings in this respect are briefly considered in: *Assessing and Reformulating SAARC Road Map*, 2008, p. 67.

REFERENCES

Asian Development Bank. 2006. *South Asia Economic Report.* October.

Asian Development Bank and UNCTAD. 2008. *Quantification of Benefits from Economic Cooperation in South Asia.*

Behera, Navnita Chadha. 2009. *SAARC & Beyond: Civil Society and Regional Integration in South Asia.* SACEPS Paper No. 19. Kathmandu: SACEPS.

Kelegama, Saman (ed.) 2001. *Impediments to Regional Economic Cooperation in South Asia.* No. 49. Colombo: FES Publications.

Lama, M. 2007. *Monitoring of SAARC Policies and Programmes.* SACEPS Paper No. 17. Kathmandu: SACEPS.

Muni, S.D. (ed.). 2010. *The Emerging Dimensions of SAARC.* New Delhi: Cambridge University Press.

RIS (Research and Information System for Developing Countries). 2008. *South Asia Development and Cooperation Report, 2008.* New Delhi: Oxford University Press.

Weerakoon, D. and J. Thennakoon. 2006. 'SAFTA: Myth of Free Trade', *Economic and Political Weekly.* 16 September.

◆◆

4
SAARC AND ECONOMIC COOPERATION

AMITA
BATRA[#]

The South Asian Association for Regional Cooperation was established in 1985 with the objective of accelerated economic growth and welfare of all people in the region. The regional association was to simultaneously promote cooperation with other developing countries, other regional organisations, and become a collective representation of South Asia at international forums. Provisions of SAARC included, inter alia, decisions based on the unanimity and exclusion of bilateral and contentious issues from the deliberations. Economic cooperation and integration became a part of the SAARC agenda seven years later when the council of ministers of the member countries signed an agreement to form the South Asian Preferential Trade Agreement (SAPTA). The agreement was prompted by the South Asian economies' desire to dismantle trade barriers, following the move towards unilateral liberalisation and global trade integration, initiated first by India, as part of its systemic economic reforms in 1991, and followed later by the other South Asian economies. The process of regional economic integration was also necessitated by the impending risk of isolation for South Asia, as the rest of the world was increasingly formulating regional preferential trade arrangements and a major proportion of global trade was being undertaken on a preferential basis. SAPTA was envisaged primarily as the first step towards the region's transition to a free trade area, leading subsequently towards a customs union, common market and economic union.

THE SOUTH ASIAN PREFERENTIAL TRADE AREA

Aimed at trade liberalisation through the exchange of tariff preferences and dismantling trade barriers among member nations, SAPTA included a Most Favoured Nation (MFN) clause so that any preference, extended within the framework of the agreement, was to be automatically extended to all members. SAPTA also provided for special and differential treatment of Least Developed Countries (LDCs) in the region. The rules of origin, to determine the source of imports for preferential treatment under the agreement, were finalised after a prolonged debate at 40 per cent local content requirement for non-LDC members and 30 per cent for LDC members, with a cumulative origin requirement of 50 per cent. Four rounds of negotiations towards preferential tariff reductions were initiated under the SAPTA agreement. Based on product-by-product and chapter-wise approaches, the negotiations were laborious and time-consuming.

The first round of SAPTA negotiations, which concluded in 1995, covered only 6 per cent of traded goods, i.e., about 226 products at the 6-digit level of the Harmonised System (HS–6) of tariff classification. The important issue of non-tariff barriers was not taken up in this round. The second round of SAPTA that concluded in 1997 was more ambitious in its scope, covering around 1,800 items at the HS–6 digit level and the easing of some non-tariff barriers. SAPTA's third round, signed in 1998, was the most ambitious, covering about 2,700 items. The three rounds of SAPTA negotiations thus brought about 4,700 tariff lines under preferential access.

However, tariff preferences granted in SAPTA negotiations implied only limited concessions given the initial high protectionist regimes of member countries. Additionally, the fear of enlarged trade deficits and competing structures of comparative advantage of member economies implied that preferences were granted to only a few sectors such as chemicals, textiles and clothing, machinery and appliances and some in the category of live animals and animal products. Major exporting sectors of South Asian economies were not brought under SAPTA preferences. Further, taking advantage of the more liberal enabling clause of the General Agreement on Tariffs and Trade (GATT), under which SAPTA had been notified, goods covered under preferential tariffs did not constitute a substantial proportion of the total goods traded among regional economies. The proportion of intra-regional imports covered by SAPTA preferences of individual member economies was, therefore, limited to a range of 12–39 per cent. The three rounds of SAPTA preferential trade, therefore, did not impact intra-regional trade in any significant manner and it remained at 4 per cent of the total trade of South Asian economies. The fourth round of negotiations, although initiated in 1998, had to be suspended owing to the military takeover in Pakistan in 1999 and nuclear tests by both India and Pakistan that led to an escalation of tensions between the two countries. SAPTA remained suspended thereafter till, in 2003, the India–Pakistan bilateral situation improved and heads of SAARC nations agreed to launch an agreement with the objective of creating a free trade area in the region.

SOUTH ASIAN FREE TRADE AREA

The agreement on South Asian Free Trade Area (SAFTA) was signed in January 2004 during the 12th SAARC Summit held in Islamabad. The SAFTA agreement, entering into force two years later in January 2006, was designed with the motivation of maximising the region's potential for trade and development through the elimination of barriers to the cross-border flow of goods. Towards this objective, SAFTA outlined a trade liberalisation programme, rules of origin, safeguard measures and provisions for a dispute settlement body. As initially designed, SAFTA was restricted to trade only in goods and aimed at creating a free trade area in South Asia in a period of 10 years through gradual tariff liberalisation, the removal of non-tariff barriers and introducing, strengthening and modernising trade-facilitating national infrastructure. The SAFTA agreement specified a negative list and a sensitive list which were to be subjected to periodic revision. Keeping in view the differential levels of development, the sensitive list specified for LDCs was more flexible in terms of time and coverage. India completed its Trade Liberalisation Programme (TLP) one year ahead of the schedule by reducing its tariff to zero per cent for LDCs under SAFTA, with effect from 1 January 2008. The other non-LDCs, i.e., Pakistan and Sri Lanka, also completed their TLP for LDCs by bringing their customs tariff down to the range of 0–5 per cent, as stipulated.

However, as originally designed, SAFTA had many flaws; it was a shallow agreement, with its liberalisation programme restricted to only trade in goods. The potentially more trade-creating, services sector liberalisation was excluded from the agreement. In a region in which the services sector contributes more than 50 per cent of the GDP of almost all economies, the 'only goods' agreement was inherently limited in scope. For the liberalisation of trade in goods, the more efficient negative-list approach was adopted for granting tariff preferences, but the size of these lists specified by member countries was large. Goods included in the negative lists comprised close to 50 per cent of the region's exportable commodities. Further, there was no target date for the complete elimination of these negative lists. Moreover, while the agreement included measures for trade facilitation and dispute settlement, these appeared more as a reflection of intent rather than an actionable agenda. Details for translating intent into action were missing in the provisions of the agreement. The intra-SAARC trade flows under SAFTA, therefore, continued to be low at around 5–6 per cent of the region's total trade, and well below potential. The inability of the agreement to accelerate the pace of economic integration in South Asia was in stark contradiction to the region's pace of integration with the global economy. The rate of global trade integration of South Asia was the fastest amongst all regions in the world between 2005 and 2007.

The implementation of SAFTA also coincided with the period when the Indian economy emerged as the second fastest growing economy in the world. Other countries in the region, with the exception of Nepal, also experienced an average annual rate of growth of over 5 per cent during these years. With a maximum share in regional trade, GDP and sharing borders with all the other regional economies, regional economic dynamism and India's centrality should have been the integrating force for the region. However, the fear of being overwhelmed by Indian imports and consequent enlarged deficits, not necessarily based on economic rationality, acted as a limiting factor in the operation of the regional preferential agreement. The economic dynamism of the region was not translated into a higher level of economic integration among the South Asian economies. South Asia, a region endowed with geographical, historical, cultural and linguistic proximity, all parameters that make the member economies potentially the most natural trading partners, is the least integrated region in the world.

Over the years, some of the design flaws in the SAFTA agreement have been rectified. The missing element of services sector liberalisation was provided for by the SAARC Trade in Services Agreement (SATIS), signed in 2010 at the 16th SAARC Summit held in Thimpu, Bhutan. SATIS, ratified by all member states, entered into force in November 2012. However, progress has been slow as operationalisation of the agreement has been held up by member states not having finalised their schedule of specific commitments. So far, 10 meetings of the expert group on SATIS have been held, and it has been agreed that all member states would table their final offer lists and schedules of specific commitments to be finalised and adopted at the next meeting. The 18th SAARC Summit in 2014 has also committed to the early operationalisation of SATIS by finalising the schedule for commitments. Sectors such as tourism, construction, power, education, health and telecommunication hold considerable potential for the enhancement of trade in services in South Asia.

The initial large negative lists under SAFTA have also been subsequently revised and implemented by all member states. Some progress is also evident with regard to trade facilitation wherein, through cooperation among member states, identification and classification of the non-tariff barrier is underway for the construction of a consolidated regional database. Cooperation on the acceptance of national standards is also being undertaken by SAARC.

While a shallow liberalisation programme and inadequate design were responsible for SAFTA's limited success in enhancing regional trade, it is also true that its implementation was adversely impacted by Pakistan's stance vis-à-vis its trade with India and that SAFTA stands undermined by more successful bilateral agreements that are operational among SAARC member nations, as also by unilateral policy announcements that may be more encompassing in terms of coverage and, hence, more advantageous for member countries.

INDIA–PAKISTAN BILATERAL RELATIONSHIP

It is recognised and accepted that the India–Pakistan bilateral relationship that has, unfortunately, not been led by economic rationality is the predominant factor in the regional landscape. This has been most evident recently at the 18th SAARC Summit when member countries anxiously waited till the last minute for India and Pakistan to sort out their differences and take forward the idea of regional cooperation in South Asia by signing three agreements: a South Asia power trade agreement, a motor vehicle agreement and a railway agreement to take forward the process of regional integration. However, only one of the proposed agreements—energy cooperation—could be signed before the conclusion of the Summit. Pakistan cited lack of preparedness with regard to the other two agreements.

The friction-laden relationship between India and Pakistan has also been a significant restrictive factor in the progress of preferential trade agreements in South Asia. Negotiations on SAPTA were suspended owing to escalating bilateral tensions between India and Pakistan following a military takeover in the latter country, and nuclear tests by both countries. The implementation of SAFTA was obstructed by Pakistan's stubborn stance of specifying a positive list for trade with India. This was in violation of the provision of the agreement whereby all SAARC nations, as signatories to SAFTA, agreed to specify a negative list indicating the items to be excluded from preferential treatment. Further, unlike India, Pakistan has not granted India MFN status, and it is now over three years since Pakistan announced its intention of granting India this status in September 2011. However, only a few positive measures have been taken by Pakistan in the direction of 'trade normalisation'. These include the replacement of the positive list by a short negative list and the conclusion of agreements on customs cooperation, mutual recognition of standards and redressal of trade grievances, along with announcements towards liberalisation of the visa regime and facilitation of business travel. These measures do not add up to MFN status, which has now been euphemistically termed by Pakistan as 'Non-Discriminatory Market Access' (NDMA). Conflict, both actual and anticipated, continues to define the bilateral relationship between India and Pakistan and bilateral trade remains below potential as a natural outcome of traders' risk-return calculations in an atmosphere of constant friction (Batra, 2013).

OVERLAPPING BILATERAL TRADE AGREEMENTS

Preferential terms of trade within the bilateral or through unilateral agreements, independent of SAFTA, cover almost all trade between India and its regional trade partners other than Pakistan. Sri Lanka signed the first formal bilateral free trade agreement with India in 1999. The India and Sri Lanka bilateral free trade agreement, implemented in 2000, is operating successfully with both sides desirous of its elevation to a comprehensive economic partnership. The India–Sri Lanka FTA is an example of a south-south trade agreement that has taken into account the asymmetric economic size and level of development of the two countries in its provisions and yet been successful in generating a positive outcome of increased trade for both economies. India's importance as an export market for Sri Lanka has grown since the implementation of the FTA. While India was ranked as the 14th largest market for Sri Lanka in 2000, it graduated to the 5th and 3rd rank in 2005 and 2012, respectively. The trade deficit between the two countries, viewed as the import–export ratio, improved from 10.3:1 in 2000 to 6.4:1 in 2012, indicating that the overall deficit improved in favour of Sri Lanka (Kelegama, 2014). India has also signed a preferential trade agreement with Afghanistan in 2005. India's bilateral trade treaties with Bhutan and Nepal that have been operational since the 1950s and revised several times thereafter are like de facto free trade agreements. The treaty of trade signed in 1991 and renewed in 1996 has been the milestone in India–Nepal trade relations as it provided for duty-free access to all Nepalese manufactured goods on the basis of merely a certificate of origin issued by Nepalese authorities. The elimination of the rules of origin requirement resulted in a phenomenal increase in India's imports from Nepal by 94 per cent in the following year (1997) as against the pre-treaty (1995) level. Rules of origin (RoOs), based on the twin criteria of 'Change in Tariff Heading' (CTH) at the 4–digit HS level and 30 per cent value addition for duty-free access to Indian markets, were introduced when the treaty was renewed in 2002. The 2009 renewal of the treaty saw some significant revisions, including relaxation of many rules for trade facilitation, such as granting recognition to Sanitary and Phytosanitary (SPS) certificates provided by competent national authorities and establishing Land Customs Stations (LCSs).

Bilateral trade between India and Nepal has greatly benefitted from the trade treaties.

From 2008 onwards, in addition to bilateral agreements, India has unilaterally extended duty-free, quota-free access to all LDCs. From August 2008 onwards, applied customs duties were to be removed over a period of five years with 20 per cent reduction each year on about 85 per cent of India's total tariff lines. In addition, preferential market access on some goods is also provided. In all, the scheme provides preferential market access on tariff lines that comprise 92.5 per cent of global exports of all LDCs.

Therefore, for SAFTA to be utilised and, in fact, redirect some of the trade that is being undertaken in the region outside SAFTA, it is necessary that within the ambit of SAFTA it makes its rules of origin and tariff preferences more attractive than those that prevail in the more successful bilateral agreements among member states. Recognising this, at the 18th SAARC Summit, members have emphasised the need for further tariff liberalisation and reduction in SAFTA sensitive lists. The Summit also emphasised the need for SAFTA to gather momentum and accelerate the pace of economic integration in South Asia as this is necessitated by evolving regional and global imperatives.

REGIONAL AND GLOBAL IMPERATIVES

In the South Asian neighbourhood, the 10-member Association for South-east Asian Nations (ASEAN) is expected to complete the process of formulating an economic community by 2015. The larger region of the ASEAN+3 (China, Japan, Korea) +3 (Australia, New Zealand, India) is negotiating a Regional Comprehensive Economic Partnership (RCEP) that is to be finalised by 2015. In addition, there are also other mega-regional agreements, such as the Trans Pacific Partnership (TPP) agreement, that are being negotiated and are, in fact, close to being concluded, thus making the regional trade scenario very competitive. In that context, therefore, South Asia needs to not just accelerate its efforts towards regional cooperation, but to move in the direction of deeper economic integration, failing which, it may have to bear the cost of trade being diverted away from the region.

This becomes even more critical as India is already looking east, having entered into a comprehensive agreement with the

ASEAN, Korea and Japan. India is also a member of the Regional Comprehensive Economic Partnership (RCEP) agreement. The RCEP will help India integrate into the larger regional production networks. This is a significant advantage for India as global trade patterns are changing in response to production fragmentation across borders. As ASEAN moves closer to achieving its vision of an economic community and becoming a globally integrated, highly competitive, single market and production base by 2015, India will gain through its membership of the mega-regional agreement. As RCEP is an ASEAN-centric configuration, the ASEAN–India FTA, implemented in 2010 will contribute further to India's economic integration in the larger Pan-Asian network. If South Asia is able to accelerate its regional integration process, member economies will have access through India, the South-east Asian and the larger Asian region. Conversely, the inability to integrate within will deprive the other South Asian economies of possible linkages with a dynamic region and networked production that is emerging as the core of global trade flows. Strengthening intra-regional economic linkages is also acquiring increasing importance in the post-global financial crisis period when many traditional Western markets are unable to generate sufficient growth and, hence, demand for exports of developing South Asian economies. Regionalism is a mode that is being actively pursued by the rest of the world. South Asia must, therefore, make the best of the available opportunities in this direction by strengthening SAFTA. In addition, SAFTA needs to be supplemented by a focus on the following aspects, which should form a part of the SAARC agenda, to further consolidate the process of economic cooperation and integration in the region.

FINANCIAL CONNECTIVITY

While transport connectivity has been a focus in the SAARC regional cooperation agenda for some time now, financial connectivity has received relatively less attention. It is, however, of critical importance for enhancing trade in the region. As banking channels are limited in many areas, financial support measures for trade capacity build-up could be of major assistance. Local currency swap arrangements, with assistance from central banks for settling payments in local currencies of cross-border charges and a fee for cross-border movement of goods, can be developed as a feasible option. By

May 2012, the Reserve Bank of India (RBI) had announced it would offer swap facilities aggregating USD 2 billion, both in foreign currency and the Indian rupee, to SAARC member countries for a three-year period. India and Bhutan have also signed a currency swap arrangement, whereby the Royal Monetary Authority of Bhutan (RMAB) is enabled to make withdrawals of USD, Euros or Indian rupees in multiple tranches up to a maximum of USD 100 million, or its equivalent. These swaps are denominated in USD and earmarked only as a line of reserve for partner countries during a balance-of-payment crisis, and not for enabling trade payment. These could, however, serve as the basis of evolving alternative arrangements for settling trade transactions in the near future.

Lack of financial connectivity is a particularly severe constraint for border trade in the region that, therefore, remains confined to a limited number of commodities and barter systems. Border regions and communities are amongst the poorest in South Asia. Setting up a regional fund, or a bilateral fund, for border trade could be taken up for consideration by SAARC. Trade finance could help border regions develop in such a manner that they become channels of absorbing and transmitting economic dynamism of neighbouring countries rather than being solely dependent on their own countries. This would help further the development of border communities, as also regional economic integration.

SUBREGIONALISM AS A PRECURSOR TO REGIONAL ECONOMIC INTEGRATION

Given that friction amongst some member states has been a constraining factor in the efforts towards regional economic integration, one alternative is for member countries to come together in smaller subregional groups with a focused agenda comprising both common challenges and aspirations that are cross-border in nature. Once they are successful in attaining the limited agenda, the aims and objectives can expand and so can the membership, as non-members would start to incur the cost of non-accession. In due course, subregionalism would serve as a preparatory ground for merging into larger groupings as it would be indicative of the members' willingness to act in a cooperative framework with their neighbours and a readiness to join larger groupings in the region that go beyond these members. The Bangladesh–Bhutan–India–Nepal growth quadrangle could be one such subregional grouping that could adopt a focused approach towards the regional issue of energy cooperation. Power trade and development are already on the agenda of cooperation amongst these countries. Similarly, other regional groupings could, with a focussed agenda on issues of regional significance such as transit, connectivity and economic corridors, become forerunners of the integration process in South Asia.

ROLE OF OBSERVER NATIONS IN SAARC

SAARC has nine observer nations, the contributions of which have so far been limited to training and capacity building. However, there must be a broader vision to utilise the expertise of these nations to build a more substantive association on a regional basis, given that some of these observer nations are our co-participants in emerging regional economic formulations, as also their expertise in achieving peaceful coexistence through economic integration in their respective regions. The EU, in particular, may have a useful role to play in this respect. Economic prosperity through cooperation, and its necessary placement over conflict, was the underlying principle for the success of the economic union. South Asia has much to learn from the experience.

In conclusion, the South Asian region requires a comprehensive effort that combines an upgraded SAFTA, with the necessary infrastructure and innovative approaches, to realise the objective of economic integration in the region.

◆

[#] This chapter was first published in 2015 in the *IIC Quarterly*, Vol. 41, Nos 3 and 4.

REFERENCES

Batra, Amita. 2013. *Regional Economic Integration in South Asia: Trapped in Conflict?* London: Routledge.

Kelegama, Saman. 2014. 'The India-Sri Lanka Free Trade Agreement and the Proposed Comprehensive Economic Partnership Agreement: A Closer Look', ADBI Working Paper. Series No. 458.

◆◆

5

SOUTH ASIA'S MOUNTING ECOLOGICAL CHALLENGE
Regional Cooperation is the Only Answer

SHYAM
SARAN[#]

The Fifth Assessment Report of the Intergovernmental Panel on Climate Change (IPCC) released recently has confirmed with scientific evidence what has been evident for several years: that global temperatures are on a secular upward trend; that this warming trend is causally related to the increasing accumulation of greenhouse gases, in particular carbon dioxide, in the earth's atmosphere; that this, in turn, is the result of the increasing use and burning of carbon-based fossil fuels such as coal, oil and gas, in the course of rapid industrialisation and that unless the increase in global temperature is limited to 2 degrees centigrade or less by mid-century or thereabouts, there is a serious risk of irreversible alteration in the life-sustaining and fragile ecological balance of our planet, with catastrophic consequences. Even if, by some miracle, global emissions of greenhouse gases fell to zero, the impact of climate change would be felt for an extended period of time, since these gases stay in the atmosphere for a 100 years or more. This implies that, even while the world makes determined efforts to reduce emissions, there needs to be an immediate and parallel focus on adaptation to the consequences of climate change. Thus, the challenge of climate change takes on a dual character: mitigation of emissions on the one hand and adaptation to climate change that is already taking place, on the other.

It is evident that climate change poses a more serious risk to developing countries than to developed countries. Most developed countries are now in the post-industrial phase where the component of services in their GDP is replacing manufacturing. Furthermore, with substantial financial and technological resources, they have a greater capacity and capability to adopt measures for increasing energy efficiency and for enhanced use of renewable and clean sources of energy than do developing countries. Possessing larger resources, they are also more capable of adapting to the consequences of climate change, such as increased frequency of extreme climatic events and climate-induced natural disasters, than are developing countries. This significant asymmetry is further exacerbated by the fact that in developing countries, the impacts of climate change tend to intensify all the stresses and strains that are inevitably generated in the course of rapid economic and social development. This includes unplanned urbanisation, water stress, deforestation, soil erosion and environmental degradation, in general. In developing countries, therefore, climate change action cannot be separated from the developmental process. Even if developing countries formulate sustainable development strategies, their efforts would be in vain, unless the world as a whole is able to make a strategic and accelerated shift away from an entrenched pattern of economic activity based on fossil fuels to one that is progressively based on renewables, such as solar and wind energy, and clean energy, such as safe nuclear energy. Global warming is a transnational, cross-cutting challenge which demands mitigation of emissions worldwide. The consequences of global warming, however, are usually manifest regionally and locally, depending upon geographical location, terrain features, demographic profile and the overall level of development. South Asia's ecological challenge must be examined against this backdrop.

◆◆◆

Despite its current political division into several independent and sovereign states, South Asia is a single geopolitical and economically complementary region, with a shared history and deep cultural affinities. But, more importantly, the region also occupies a distinct, clearly defined and densely interconnected ecological space. While there are good political and economic reasons for South Asian countries to expand regional cooperation, the ecological reasons for such cooperation are even more compelling. These countries are already experiencing an acute ecological crisis as a result of expanding populations, resource depletion and widespread environmental degradation. The stresses and strains generated by rapid economic development and social transformation are being made even more acute by the growing impact of climate change. Natural disasters, related to both environmental degradation and climate change, are increasing in frequency and intensity, making populations already suffering from poverty and deprivation even more vulnerable. What should be noted is that national boundaries cannot insulate any country in the region from these impacts, irrespective of where the events originate. If deforestation takes place in the upper reaches of the mountain ranges, the rivers which flow through several countries will be affected through higher siltation and increased run-off. The melting of the glaciers across the Himalayan range, which is shared by several South Asian countries, would affect the entire densely populated Indo-Gangetic plain, not just the countries adjacent to the mountains. Recent natural disasters, such as the severe cyclonic weather affecting the Eastern coast of India, or the unprecedented floods which ravaged Jammu and Kashmir, have been ascribed to climate change. They have impacts which respect no national boundaries. Quite often, such natural disasters, such as flooding or extended warm and moist weather, are followed by the spread of water or airborne diseases, which could easily and rapidly spread across political boundaries. This underlines the urgent need for a South Asian perspective on the region's ecological crisis, which is the cumulative result of both environmental degradation and the impact of climate change, and to find solutions to these shared challenges. It is only through an awareness of their interconnected destinies that they would be able to generate collaborative and transnational responses.

Success in this endeavour would not only serve the vital interest of 1.5 billion people who call South Asia their common home; it would also be an example to the world, which has so far been unable to set aside a competitive mindset in addressing what is clearly an elemental threat to human survival itself.

Through the mechanism of SAARC, South Asian countries have recognised the ecological challenge the region confronts, including the challenge of global climate change. Thus, in the Common SAARC Position, presented to the 16th Conference of

Parties to the UN Framework Convention on Climate Change (UNFCCC), they stated:

> The low-lying areas, long coastlines, island regions, flood plains, deserts, wetlands, mountain ranges, etc., of South Asia face serious threats from climatic variations, including sea level rise. Likewise, the Hindu Kush, Karakoram and Himalayan regions face catastrophic consequences of accelerated glacier melt, including Glacial Lake Outburst Floods (GLOF). Similarly, the region is threatened by other climate change-related phenomena, such as increased variability of monsoons and extreme weather events, e.g., floods, droughts, cyclones and heat/cold waves. In the long run, this would also negatively impact water security for the region.

The SAARC countries also adopted a SAARC Action Plan on Climate Change at the Thimphu Summit, held in April 2010, which lists a number of measures to be taken to deal with the challenge of climate change. These have yet to be translated into collaborative action on the ground.

What would be the main elements of a regional strategy, and which are the critical areas of the regions' shared ecology where urgent and effective collaborative regional initiatives should be deployed? There are four key pillars of regional strategy:

(i)   Mapping the Monsoons
(ii) Safeguarding the Fragile Ecology of the Himalayas
(iii) The Realm of the Seas and the Coastal Plains
(iv) Preserving the Region's Biodiversity

MAPPING THE MONSOONS

The monsoons have sustained the lives of the peoples of South Asia for millennia. They bring rain to the fields on which farmers grow food. They fill the rivers, lakes and ponds with water on which all life depends. They have been, through countless centuries and even now, indispensable to the livelihood of hundreds of millions. Without the monsoons, there would be no water or food security for South Asia's peoples. It is for this reason that much of the subcontinent's shared culture, its art and literature, remains permeated with the romance of the monsoons. Whatever other differences there may be among the countries of South Asia, there is none which would remain unaffected by any significant and extended variation in monsoon rainfall patterns.

There is now sufficient evidence to show that the monsoons are being affected by climate change. There is a greater frequency of extreme climatic events, such as prolonged drought in some areas and high intensity rainfall in others. The degree of unpredictability has increased and weather forecasting has become more difficult and complex. There appears to be an emerging pattern, not yet confirmed through rigorous research, that precipitation on an average has not changed much in recent years but that there is more intense rainfall over shorter time periods. This is leading to more frequent flash floods and storm surges. In the fragile mountain regions to the north, this is causing more frequent landslides and avalanches. There appears to be a gradual shift in the distribution of rainfall across the region. Formerly dry areas have begun to receive greater precipitation in recent years, leading to disruptions in age-old patterns of living and farming. These alterations in the patterns of monsoon winds are not well understood. Each country has a small piece of the total picture but the overall pattern is not clear. A fuller understanding may only be possible through a joint research project, spread over several years, studying the monsoons over the entire region, collecting data throughout the subcontinent and developing more sophisticated multivariable climate models to discern any changes in weather patterns. This regional initiative will need to be linked with work being done in other countries and the World Meteorological Organisation (WMO). Such joint scientific research must be accompanied by an even more complex study of the impact that changes in the monsoon patterns would have on the social and economic fabric of South Asian countries, and the methods that would enable adaptation to these changes. Given how critical the monsoons are to survival, it is imperative that a regional initiative is undertaken for mapping the monsoons. With its larger financial, scientific and technical resources, India will have to play a leading role in this endeavour. It has a well-developed satellite network to monitor weather patterns. Its meteorological department now has more sophisticated weather models and computing power, which it can share with South Asian neighbours.

SAFEGUARDING THE FRAGILE ECOLOGY OF THE HIMALAYAS

South Asia is home to the world's highest mountains, the Himalayas, which are sometimes described as the 'Third Pole' after the North and the South Poles, respectively, because of the massive quantities of permanent ice which lie embedded in its glaciers. Others describe the Himalayas as Asia's 'Water Tower', because many of the continent's perennial rivers, including the Indus, the Ganges, the Brahmaputra, the Salween, the Irrawady, the Mekong and the Yangtze (Chang Jiang) are born from these glaciers. These snow-fed rivers have, over millennia, sustained rich civilisations along their courses, as they wend their way to the oceans. Thus, the livelihood, in fact, the very survival, of these millennial civilisations, is dependent upon the health and sustenance of these glaciers. In South Asia, the entire Indo-Gangetic plain depends upon the perennial river flows that arise in the Himalayas. There is evidence that several of these glaciers are in stubborn retreat and losing mass not only due to environmental degradation, but also due to global warming. The melting of these glaciers would initially lead to an increased run-off in river systems but, eventually, their disappearance would turn perennial rivers into seasonal flows dependent upon the monsoons, which are themselves becoming more unpredictable.

As snows melt in the high mountains, glacial lakes are being formed which sometimes break their banks and flood areas downstream. There have already been several cases of storm surges and flash floods due to rapid snow melt in several parts of the Himalayas. These phenomena, known as Glacial Lake Outburst Floods (GLOF), are increasing in frequency in both Nepal and Bhutan. The Badri–Kedar disaster in 2013 was the result of a similar GLOF, combined with torrential rains.

The Himalayas represent a very unique ecology. There is a very wide variation in the flora and fauna in the Himalayan zone because of the very steep ascent in terrain over a very short distance. One moves from the subtropical, to temperate, to icy desert in a very short spatial distance, and this has created a very rich and rare biodiversity which is a veritable ecological treasure house. This is already being impacted by warming temperatures and melting glaciers as the already narrow habitat of the existing flora and fauna is being further eroded. There is very little reliable data on the health of the thousands of glaciers that make up the Himalayan

'Pole'. Much of our knowledge is anecdotal. The impact of glacial melt on river flows has not been studied properly. How this would affect the rich river flora and fauna is even less understood. For example, what would happen to fish populations in our rivers? On land, the behaviour pattern of both animal and bird life, and of the unique vegetation of the region due to climate change, needs to be monitored and analysed. There is not enough awareness that several South Asian countries, including Afghanistan, Pakistan, India, Nepal, Bhutan and Bangladesh, will all be deeply impacted from any changes in the fragile ecology of the Himalayas. There are other countries which will be impacted as well, particularly China. It is only when South Asia as a community is able to evolve a coordinated strategy will it be possible to engage China effectively, whether in safeguarding the Himalayas or preserving the health of the glacier-fed rivers on which their common survival depends.

The collaborative study of the behaviour of Himalayan glaciers and the impact on the flow of South Asian rivers must be sustained over a considerable period of time. To the extent that the problem is being exacerbated through environmental degradation, there needs to be an agreed code of conduct to help preserve this fragile mountain ecology. This may include norms concerning construction of roads and highways or hydroelectric power projects in the mountain zone. There needs to be some regulation over the spreading urban settlements in the zone, with little attention paid to waste disposal or sewerage. Unregulated tourism is leading to the contamination of water bodies and mountain lakes and the growing problem of untreated waste being dumped indiscriminately. The habitat for the rare and often endangered flora and fauna unique to the Himalayas is shrinking and without cross-border initiatives the ecological crisis will only get worse.

In this case, as in the proposed initiative on the monsoons, India must take the lead as it has the most advanced capabilities in the region. It has time-series satellite data on the entire Himalayan range which it can share with its neighbours. It needs their cooperation to carry out ground truth surveys in selected parts of the range. What would really make a difference is a joint collaborative project, perhaps in cooperation with the UN or other international agencies which have the requisite technical capabilities to methodically study the glaciers in the western, central and eastern

Himalayas, determine if, and to what degree, melting has been taking place, and what impact this is having on river flows and on weather patterns across the region. This must be accompanied by studies on the environmental degradation of the Himalayas and the cooperative measures required to arrest and reverse this trend.

THE REALM OF THE SEAS AND THE COASTAL PLAINS

The oceans, which embrace the subcontinent and the associated islands and island chains, play a critical role in sustaining coastal, island, as well as inland, communities. Coastal plains contain rich crop-growing areas, while fishing is a major source of food and livelihood. The oceans impact on weather patterns which, in turn, affect them and marine life. It is increasingly evident that climate change is leading to impacts which threaten all communities that draw their sustenance from the oceans and the coastal plains, and this is true across the region. Both India and Bangladesh have extensive low-lying coastal plains which support large populations. Both suffer from increasing coastal erosion and the rising salinity of soil due to salt water ingress. This takes place as a result of sudden storm surges, but also from longer term rising sea levels. The rise in sea levels is due to thermal expansion, or the increase in the temperature of water due to global warming, as well as due to the melting of large bodies of ice from permafrost areas, in particular, the Antarctica. A rise in sea levels would not only inundate low-lying coastal plains throughout South Asia, but also threaten the island countries of Sri Lanka and the Maldives. The Maldives is especially vulnerable as the numerous atolls which constitute the country are barely above sea level. Sea level rise may trigger large-scale population transfers, both intra-country as well as between countries, as affected communities seek to move inland or to higher ground. Such population movements may have serious economic and social consequences. This, in turn, may sharpen political tensions. We do not fully understand how climate change may affect ocean currents and marine chemistry which, in turn, will inevitably impact the rich flora and fauna in the seas around us. The impact on fishery resources may be significant and may exacerbate declining fish populations due to over-exploitation and marine pollution. There is an urgent need for the countries of South Asia to undertake a major study of how climate change will impact their shared marine ecology and the measures we need to jointly undertake to adapt to the changed marine environment. There is no doubt that irrespective of the climate change phenomenon, there are measures that could be adopted to regulate fishing in the region's shared ocean space, prevent marine pollution and put marine conservation high on the agenda for regional cooperation. As pointed out earlier, failure to control such degradation of the marine environment will inevitably exacerbate the impact of climate change. In this context, a South Asia Marine Commission may be a good platform to pursue a coordinated strategy.

Of particular urgency is the establishment of a sound regional capability to enable the early warning of impending maritime emergencies, such as the tsunami or cyclones. This must be accompanied by an efficient disaster response and management capability. India has set up a network of satellite-linked Automatic Weather Stations (AWS) along its coasts, which provide real-time weather data, and which is extremely useful for fishing communities and coastal populations. The network also enables early warning on extreme climatic events, so that populations can be moved to safer locations well in time, thus saving lives and property. The efficacy of such a network was apparent during the recent cyclone which hit the eastern coast of India. The network can be easily extended to cover the entire coastline of the Indian subcontinent. This has so far not been possible, mainly due to lingering suspicions and mistrust of India among some South Asian countries.

PRESERVING THE REGION'S BIODIVERSITY

South Asia is one of the most biodiverse regions of our planet, falling between two of the eight biogeographical realms: the Palaearctic and the Indo-Malayan. The region covers 19 of the 235 global ecoregions, a science-based global ranking of the planet's outstanding terrestrial, fresh water and marine habitats. Three of the 25 most significant biodiversity 'hotspots' of the world happen to be located in this region. Forests make up nearly 17 per cent of its land area, constituting an extensive and valuable carbon sink for the globe as a whole. These are invaluable assets and a shared pool of wealth for the countries of the region, but they lie astride most political boundaries. They cannot be sustained and allowed to grow and flourish unless the countries of South Asia recognise the inescapable need for nurturing this shared ecological space without which the life-sustaining systems, which bind the countries together, may break down irretrievably. The sad reality is that the region is living on an ecological overdraft; it is extracting more from its pool of natural wealth than nature can regenerate. This cannot continue without dire consequences for its already vulnerable populations.

Once it is accepted that sustaining South Asia's rich biodiversity is as integral to its productive capacity and economic well-being as are the monsoons, the Himalayas and the oceans, the logic for regional cooperation in this field, too, becomes compelling. What is needed is a regional plan for the preservation of regional biodiversity. One should begin with undertaking a region-wide inventory of biodiversity resources and establish a comprehensive regional gene bank. The wealth represented by the thousands of varieties of medicinal plants and herbs is presently being lost to outsiders because of the lack of information and shared knowledge. It is only through a well-structured regional initiative that such biodiversity loss can be prevented and the full benefit from the use of these resources can be derived by people of the region itself.

Some of the world's endangered species can only be found in South Asia. Tigers are one such class of animals. Rhinos are another. Their habitat ranges across national boundaries. These habitats are shrinking under the pressure of rising populations and expanding economic and industrial activity. climate change will also impact these habitats. For example, the retreat of glaciers is already shrinking the habitat for the snow leopard in the Himalayan zone. The countries of South Asia need to create cross-border biodiversity zones to protect endemic flora and fauna and ensure the survival of endangered species.

SOUTH ASIA AND THE GLOBAL CLIMATE CHANGE REGIME

The 16th SAARC Summit, convened at Thimphu in 2010, adopted ecological sustainability as its theme in a declaration entitled, 'Towards a Green and Happy South Asia'. This enabled the coordination of strategies in multilateral forums for addressing the challenge of global climate change. A significant step in this direction was the Common SAARC Position, which was presented at the 16th Conference of Parties to the UNFCCC in Cancun in 2010. The Common Position called upon developed countries to commit themselves to undertaking deep, and legally binding, reductions in their emissions of greenhouse gases within the time frame recommended by the IPCC. It emphasised the importance of mobilising new, adequate and additional resources, which are easily accessible, to address the full incremental cost of tackling climate change under the authority of the Conference of Parties (COP). The SAARC countries also stated that the adaptation needs of developing countries should be met by the developed countries through an allocation of 1.5 per cent of their GDP to be paid into the Adaptation Fund of the UNFCCC.

SAARC members identified a number of important regional initiatives as well:

(i) Work together to ensure access to adaptation finance for all developing countries, which are vulnerable to the adverse effects of climate change, with special reference to Least Developed Countries (LDC) and Small Island Developing States (SIDS).

(ii) Establish an International Centre for Adaptation Research and Training in the SAARC region as a platform for sharing experience and best practices in adaptation.

(iii) Provide adequate and full support for the conservation of forests as an integral part of the Reducing Emissions from Deforestation and Forest Degradation, or the REDD Plus mechanism under the UNFCCC.

(iv) Set up Technology Innovation Centres and Networks in the South Asian region and across the globe to promote the development and transfer of technologies addressing both adaptation and mitigation issues.

The world will make another effort to conclude a global climate change regime at the Climate Summit, scheduled to be held in Paris in 2015. As countries that are certainly going be impacted most by the consequences of continuing climate change, it is imperative that the countries of South Asia put across their perspective on this issue firmly and persuasively. The most persuasive argument would be the collaborative initiatives that they themselves are able to undertake not only to promote action on climate change, but also, at the same time, to contribute to our collective ecological security. One hopes that leaders of South Asia will demonstrate the wisdom and statesmanship that is required to deliver such initiatives.

◆

#This chapter was first published in 2015 in the *IIC Quarterly*, Vol. 41, Nos 3 and 4.

6

SOUTH ASIAN COOPERATION
Towards a Humane World

AKMAL
HUSSAIN#

THE DIALECTIC OF REGIONAL INTEGRATION: CONTENDING PARADIGMS OF STATES AND PEOPLE IN SOUTH ASIA

The gap between the commitment to regional integration by SAARC leaders and its actualisation signifies the dialectic between the aspirations of the people of South Asia and the practice of state power. The people seek liberation from mass poverty, deprivation of basic services, extremist violence and their vulnerability to extreme climatic events. In contrast, state structures locked in the obsolete paradigms of power, mistrust and suspicion are constrained from fulfilling the will of the people.

The current framework for the practice of state power conceives of national security in terms of building the military capability for mass annihilation of each other's citizens. The deadly nuclear dimension that since 1998 has been added to the India–Pakistan arms race is seen by the respective governments as the reinforcement of national security through a presumed 'deterrence'. It is not surprising that South Asia is the poorest and yet the most militarised region in the world (Haq, 1997). It contained 52 per cent of the world's poor in the year 2011.[1] Yet India and Pakistan have the capacity, even in a limited nuclear exchange, to kill more than 100 million people immediately, with many hundreds of millions more dying subsequently from radiation-related illnesses (Barry and Hirsh, 1998). With the stakes of catastrophic destruction as they are in the region, any non-zero probability of nuclear war should be unacceptable. Yet, as I have argued elsewhere, given the specific features of the India–Pakistan relationship, South Asia has a higher probability of an accidental or intentional nuclear war than any other region in the world (Hussain, 2010a and 2010b). As states in South Asia pursue national security through obsolete paradigms, in the new world that is now taking shape the influence of an emerging power will be determined not by the magnitude of destruction it can wreak on other countries, but by its contribution to enhancing life in an interdependent world.

The hopes of the people are drawn from the seismic change that has occurred in the centre of gravity of the global economy for the first time in three centuries from the West to Asia. If China returns to its high-growth trajectory and South Asia achieves economic integration to fulfil its great potential, then, by the middle of this century, China and South Asia could become the greatest economic powerhouse in human history. The possibilities of economic transformation are enhanced by the fact that societies in this region have a rich cultural tradition of experiencing unity in diversity through transcending the ego, of creative growth of the self through human solidarity and a harmony with nature. In bringing to bear these aspects of their shared core values, the people of South Asia could bring a new consciousness and new institutions to address the challenges of inequality, mass poverty, violence and environmental degradation that confront the world. In doing so, they could contribute to an Asian century that enriches human civilisation.

THE LOGIC OF ECONOMIC INTEGRATION

ECONOMIC INTEGRATION TO STIMULATE ECONOMIC GROWTH

Economic integration in South Asia could accelerate and help sustain economic growth in the member countries. This is because of the following factors: (i) Gains from trade emanating from comparative advantage; (ii) increased investment due to a large regional market; (iii) lower capital costs of projects due to availability of cheaper capital and intermediate goods through regional trade; (iv) a broader base of innovation; (v) efficiency gains through regional-level supply chains for intra-industry specialisation and (vi) an environment of greater competition through a free-trade regime. It could also help to stabilise food prices and provide cheaper consumer goods to lower income groups and thereby improve the distribution of real income.

The pursuit of improvement in the material conditions of the people of South Asia will have to give due consideration to the conservation of life support systems of the regional and global ecology. In this sense, the enterprise of economic growth cannot be done in terms of the aim of reaching the levels of luxury consumption prevailing in the West today, simply because it would be beyond the loading capacity of the life support systems of the planet. So the objective of overcoming poverty through economic growth would need to be conducted within a new relationship between humans, nature and forms of production.

ECONOMIC INTEGRATION FOR BUILDING PLURALISTIC SOCIETIES AND STRENGTHENING DEMOCRACY

Trade and investment across national boundaries in South Asia could create new constituencies of interstate peace that would not only bring material benefits to the people, but also enable the interplay of diverse cultures. Through such interaction, the syndrome of mutual demonisation and the resultant narrowing of the self could be replaced by experiencing the other as a vital fertilising force in the growth of a richer, more humane self. Such a process would make possible the rediscovery of unity in diversity which is part of the perennial wisdom of South Asian societies. These cultural concomitants of economic cooperation could strengthen the attempt by South Asian states to build pluralistic societies and sustainable democracies.

CONSTRAINTS TO ECONOMIC INTEGRATION

SAARC countries conduct trade with the rest of the world amounting to about USD 25 billion; although it has increased in recent years, intra-SAARC trade is still only USD 0.7 billion. This is because of the inadequate implementation of the SAFTA Agreement due to institutional constraints, pressures located in the power structures of Pakistan and India, and the vicissitudes of politics of the peace process.

The SAFTA Agreement[2] stipulates that member countries remove tariff barriers, non-tariff barriers and minimise the negative list of traded items. The constraints to implementation in terms of the Agreement itself lie in the fact that there is no enforcement mechanism to the stipulated actions to achieve free trade. This lack of an enforcement mechanism indicates the institutional weakness of the Agreement. The following are some of the consequent constraints to implementation:

(i) While there are timelines for the Least Developed Countries (LDCs) of South Asia (Bangladesh, Bhutan, the Maldives and Nepal) to achieve trade liberalisation by 2016, and the non-LDCs (India, Pakistan and Sri Lanka) to achieve full trade liberalisation by 2013, there is no enforcement mechanism within the terms of this agreement for achieving these deadlines, which is why the timelines of 2013 have not been achieved so far and the conformity to timelines for 2016 is uncertain. In Afghanistan, violence near the border on both sides for a landlocked country is the key constraint to trade.

(ii) A comparative analysis of the tariff structures of Pakistan and India indicates certain asymmetries which place Pakistan at a disadvantage and would have to be addressed when negotiations regarding the Most Favoured Nation (MFN) status and associated trade liberalisation are resumed. These asymmetries were pointed out in a recent study.[3] For example, the number of items in India's sensitive list of imports from Pakistan (1,753) is significantly greater than that in Pakistan's sensitive list of imports from India (1,577). The items in India's list are weighted towards agriculture and textiles, even though Pakistan has a comparative advantage in some of the subsectors of this commodity group. This apart, distortions in the relative prices on rice and wheat, created by prohibitive import duties placed by India on these imports from Pakistan (70 per cent and 100 per cent, respectively), are reinforced by the huge subsidies on agricultural inputs provided by central as well as state governments in India. These stand at 5.2 per cent of the GDP compared to 1 per cent in the case of Pakistan.[4]

(iii) It is now well established that non-tariff barriers, even in the absence of formal tariffs, can be a major constraint to trade liberalisation. The SAFTA Agreement has not adequately addressed this issue in terms of devising an institutional mechanism for eliminating them within a time bound framework. The Agreement merely stipulates that member countries 'inform' the SAARC Secretariat of all non-tariff and para-tariff measures, which should be reviewed by the SAARC Committee of Experts, and recommendations made to reduce such trade restrictions. Yet there is no binding commitment for countries within the terms of SAFTA to eliminate non-tariff barriers within a time frame. Specific measures need to be undertaken to identify the non-tariff barriers of various countries and arrive at binding commitments to eliminate them within the next three years.

While the lack of an enforcement mechanism generates constraints to implementation within the institutions of SAFTA, it does raise a question: What explains the absence of an enforcement mechanism in terms of the SAFTA Agreement, and why do the two largest countries, India and Pakistan, drag their heels in implementing it? The answer lies in the political economy of these states. In both countries, the national security paradigm is inimical to free trade and creates an adversarial conception of the neighbouring state which engenders mutual mistrust. The objective material interest of the two states of course lies in free trade, as is shown by a century of empirical and theoretical literature in economics. Yet ideology in this case often overrides economic logic.

CLIMATE CHANGE AND THE IMPERATIVE OF REGIONAL COOPERATION

THE ECOLOGICAL IMPERATIVE

South Asia has a highly integrated ecology with shared mountains, rivers and monsoons. Therefore, policy measures for addressing the socio-economic impact of climate change will have to be undertaken on the basis of cooperation between the nation states of South Asia. Let us briefly examine the vulnerability to, and impact of, climate change on the economy and society of this region.

The evidence is unmistakable: climate change is already occurring. South Asia, with its delicately balanced ecology, its heavy reliance on monsoons, its critical dependence on agriculture and persistent mass poverty, is one of the world's regions most vulnerable to climate change. Increased variability in the magnitude and timing of rainfall during the monsoons could increase the instability of agricultural production and add to the burden of the poor. The long and densely populated coastline with low lying islands, such as the Maldives, make the region vulnerable to rising sea levels associated with global warming. These rising sea levels along the low elevation, coastal regions of mainland South Asia are expected to salinise agricultural plains in these regions, resulting in the loss of livelihoods of 125 million people.

The Himalayas—containing the region's glaciers, source of its rivers and the key to the region's climate and economy—are highly sensitive to temperature increases. Leena Srivastava (2014) provides evidence to show that some Himalayan glaciers are melting faster than the global average. This could have a critical impact on the stability of water supplies and, thereby, on the economy and society of the region. R. K. Pachauri (2014) estimates that shortages of fresh water supplies will affect 500 million people in South Asia. At the same time, the Intergovernmental Panel for Climatic Change (IPCC) Report estimates that the effect of a 2.5° C increase in average temperatures is likely to reduce yield per acre of grain crops by up to 30 per cent in South Asia by the middle of this century.[5] Higher temperatures are also expected to increase year-to-year variability of monsoons (Giorgi and Bi, 2005, cited in Srivastava, 2014).

Climate change is also likely to have a significant impact on health. The increased frequency and intensity of heat waves could increase the incidence of heat stroke, cardiovascular, cerebrovascular and respiratory diseases (Hales, *et al.*, 2003, cited in Srivastava 2014). Furthermore, the increased frequency of floods could lead to an increase in the incidence of diarrhoea, dysentery, cholera, typhoid and rodent-borne diseases.

Managing population dislocation, natural disasters, the instability of water supply, food shortages and epidemics resulting from climate change will require a high degree of interstate cooperation in South Asia. The integrated ecology of South Asia, its mountains, rivers, forests and top soils constitute the basis of sustaining its economy and social life. The nation states of this region share this integrated life support system. They also share the risks posed to it by climate change. Therefore, cooperation amongst the people and states of South Asia is imperative not just for greater material welfare, but for their very survival. This cooperation would involve bringing to bear new institutions for undertaking adaptation and mitigation measures on the basis of their shared humanity and innovativeness. Cooperation, not conflict, is the key to building a better future for the people of South Asia.

The IPCC had predicted that global warming would increase the frequency and intensity of extreme climatic events.[6] The study by Cruz provides data to show that this is indeed happening in South Asia (Cruz, *et al.*, 2007, cited in Srivastava, 2014). For example, the frequency of intense rainfall events has increased during the last decade, causing floods and landslides in Pakistan, Bangladesh, Nepal, North-east India and Sri Lanka. Consecutive droughts in 1999 and 2000 in Pakistan and North-west India adversely affected agricultural growth, and the drought of 2002 in Orissa caused crop failures affecting 11 million people.

According to the IPCC, the increase in temperatures in South Asia in the decades ahead is likely to be above the global average. The adverse effect of temperature on heat-sensitive varieties of food grains could have a critical impact on agricultural production and accentuate the problem of food insecurity in South Asia.

WATER SCARCITY: THE DANGERS OF CONFLICT AND THE NEED FOR COOPERATION

The currently emerging water crisis in the Indus Basin River System and, in the decades ahead, in the Ganges–Brahmaputra–Meghna Basin, unless collectively addressed, could have major implications for the economies and societies of the region. Moreover, it has the potential of unnecessarily exacerbating interstate tensions between India and Pakistan.

The problem of water scarcity in the Indus Basin is predicated partly on the inherent limitations of water supply in the Indus River System and partly on the growing water demand associated with inefficient water use in the process of growth in the economy and population. Unsustainable developmental practices have exacerbated the problem with the intrusion of salinity into ground water, contamination of aquifers with harmful chemicals such as fluoride and arsenic, and pollution of surface water due to the lack of an institutional framework for the environmentally safe disposal of urban and industrial waste.

Declining river flows and increased water demand associated with growing populations and production have reduced water availability in the Indus Basin to only 1,329 cubic metres per capita per year. This is substantially below the generally accepted minimum per capita requirement of 1,700 cubic metres per year. In such a situation, instead of using scarce water more efficiently, the evidence suggests that the efficiency of water use in the Indus Basin is very low by international standards. The GDP per capita of water use in this area is only USD 3.34, while that of the five top food producers in the world (Brazil, China, France, Mexico and USA) is USD 23.8 per cubic metre.

The rational response to water scarcity by upper and lower riparian states is to cooperate in managing the water resources of the region for improved conservation measures and increased efficiency of water use. Failure to do so can potentially increase interstate tensions in the region.

NEW INSTITUTIONS FOR COOPERATION TO MANAGE WATER SCARCITY

The management of water scarcity in the Indus Basin requires sharing of information between India and Pakistan on water flows and best practices to achieve greater irrigation and water use efficiencies. Recently, the Stimson Centre, Washington, in collaboration with the Sustainable Development Policy Institute (SDPI), Pakistan, and the Observer Research Foundation (ORF), India, set up an International Working Group on the Indus Waters (IWG). Some of the suggestions made by the IWG for sharing information on water flows and best practices for managing the water scarcity include:[7]

(i) The exploration of ways to strengthen Article VI of the Indus Waters Treaty (IWT) on 'Exchange of Data'. In this context, the IWG pointed out that Article VI could be made more meaningful through new technologies, such as satellite-based remote sensing and GIS mapping, that could be used to develop joint environmental monitoring and measuring capabilities together with real time data collection and exchange on river flows and water quality.

(ii) Putting into effect Article VII of the Indus Waters Treaty on 'Future Cooperation' between India and Pakistan in the management of Indus waters. This could be done on the basis of generating joint water resources data and models for the temporal behaviour of rivers which could help India and Pakistan to take more efficient common decisions about 'siting, construction and operation of facilities for storage, hydroelectric power, flood control, habitat maintenance and environmental flows as well as the tradeoffs between these objectives'.[8] Data on water quality could also be built into digitised water resources models with computer screens for rivers in both countries to record changes in the volume of river flows in real time, and chemical compositions with respect to nutrients and pollutants. Such data could lay the basis for cooperation between India and Pakistan towards developing institutional mechanisms for cooperation in the reduction of water degradation and prevention of toxic chemicals from entering both surface water and ground water irrigation, and thence into the tissues of food crops and the life cycle. Toxic chemicals in irrigation water such as arsenic, mercury and lead can seriously damage human health and hence adversely affect productivity and economic growth. The proposed data generation and modelling technologies could give new meaning to Articles VI and VII of the IWT and 'lay the foundations for joint monitoring stations and telemetry platforms integrated to form an India–Pakistan collective Indus Basin Earth Observation System'.[9] This could play an important role in removing misunderstandings between the two countries about the volume of river flows at different times of the year and enable more efficient management of Indus Basin resources.

(iii) The promotion of possibilities for knowledge building and exchange as part of policy collaboration between

India and Pakistan. This collaboration could also take place at city-to-city, local and civil society levels. The Report argues that city governments in India and Pakistan face similar problems in managing the provision of municipal water and sanitation. Therefore, institutional mechanisms could be put in place to share best practices and policy lessons.

A SOUTH ASIAN SENSIBILITY FOR A SUSTAINABLE SOCIETY

The market is being currently apotheosised as the mythical space in which the individual can be free and yet provided with plenty by the hidden hand of the market. Yet, inherent to the capitalist accumulation process is the systematic inculcation of an insatiable desire to possess goods (Hussain, 2002). Writing in the 19th century, Karl Marx pointed out that 'the capitalist system not only produces goods that satisfy needs, but also the needs that these goods satisfy'. The subliminal language of advertisement does not *represent* goods, but rather *re-presents* them such that they appear to us in a *fantasised* form, not in terms of their material attributes, but as magical receptacles of such qualities as beauty, efficacy and power. Thus, qualities which we actually possess as human beings are transposed into goods, and the individual gets locked into an endless pursuit of acquisition (ibid.).

The culture of consumerism, which the market systematically inculcates, is inconsistent with conserving the environment. The life support systems of our planet cannot sustain beyond a certain limit the levels of global output growth despite any foreseeable development and adoption of green technologies. As Mahatma Gandhi said, 'There is enough in the world for everybody's need but not for everybody's greed.'

In South Asia, the interaction of diverse civilisations across millennia has brought to the surface certain fundamental features of each civilisation which, while being rooted in its specific linguistic, religious and cultural form, are essentially of a universal nature. Underlying the diversity of religious beliefs is a universal spiritualism of love, beauty and truth. Associated with this sensibility is a set of values of caring and sharing, of knowing goods to be merely useful rather than a means of enhancing a person's status and of experiencing nature not as a resource to be endlessly exploited, but as part of a sacred unity that sustains physical life—at the same time, its beauty enables a transcendent experience of truth. Thus, the peoples of South Asia over the millennia and across diverse religious beliefs have experienced the splendour of living simultaneously in the ephemeral and the eternal.

It can be argued that amidst its diversity, South Asia has shared civilisational propensities of transcending the ego as a means of fulfilment, of locating the need for goods in the context of human responsibility and of harmonising economic and social life with nature. It is this South Asian sensibility and the associated human values that could be brought to bear in building a new relationship between humans, nature and production to sustain life in the 21st century.

◆

#This chapter was first published in 2015 in the *IIC Quarterly*, Vol. 41, Nos 3 and 4.

NOTES

1. For my estimate, see World Development Report (2012: 394, Table 2).

2. This subsection is drawn from the author's presentation at the SAARC @ 25 Seminar at the India International Centre, New Delhi, 17 September 2010, and later published as an article. See Hussain, 'The Political Economy of SAFTA', *The Daily Times*, 2 October 2010.

3. The Beaconhouse National University's ongoing study was reported by one of the authors, Shahid Kardar. See Kardar (2013).

4. Ibid.

5. Inter governmental Panel for Climatic Change (IPCC), Climate Change 2007, Impacts, Adaptation and Vulnerability, Contribution of Working Group II to the Fourth Assessment Report of the IPCC, Cambridge University Press, New York, 2007, p. 471.

6. Inter governmental Panel for Climatic Change (IPCC), Climate Change 2007, Impacts, Adaptation and Vulnerability, Contribution of Working Group II to the Fourth Assessment Report of the IPCC, Cambridge University Press, New York, 2007.

7. Report of the Indus Basin Working Group, Connecting the Drops, An Indus Basin Roadmap for Cross Border Water Research, Data Sharing and Policy Coordination, Observer Research Foundation, Stimson and Sustainable Development Policy Institute (Mimeo), 2013, ISBN: 978-1-939240-02-6.

8. Ibid, p. 50.

9. Ibid.

REFERENCES

Barry, John and Michael Hirsh. 1998. 'Nuclear Letters', *Newsweek*, 8 June.

Cruz, R.V., H. Harasawa, M. Lal, S. Wu, Y. Anokhin, B. Punsalmaa, Y. Honda, M. Jafari, C. Li and N. Huu. 2007. *Climate Change 2007: Impacts, Adaptation and Vulnerability—Asia,* in M.L. Parry, O.F. Canziani, J.P. Palutikof, *et al.* (eds.), *Contribution of Working Group-II to the Fourth Assessment Report of the Intergovernmental Panel on Climate Change.* Cambridge: Cambridge University Press, pp. 469–506.

Giorgi, F. and X. Bi. 2005. *Regional Changes in Surface Climate Interannual Variability for the 21st Century from Ensembles of Global Model Simulations.* Geophys Res Lett 32:L13701. doi: 10,1029/2005GL023002.

Hales, S., S. Edwards and R. S. Kovats. 2003. *Impacts on Health of Climate Extremes,* in A.J. McMichael, D.H. Campbell-Lendrum, C.F. Corvalan, K.L. Ebi, A. Githelo, J.D. Scheraga and A. Woodward (eds.), *Climate Change and Human Health: Risks and Responses.* Geneva, Switzerland: World Health Organisation, Chapter 5, p. 87.

Haq, Mahbub ul. 1997. *Human Development in South Asia.* Human Development Centre. Karachi: Oxford University Press.

Hussain, Akmal. 2010. 'The Political Economy of SAFTA', *The Daily Times.* Lahore. 2 October.

———. 2010a. 'A Perspective on Peace and Economic Cooperation in South Asia', Chapter 1, in Sadiq Ahmed, Saman Kelegama and Ejaz Ghani (eds.), *Promoting Economic Cooperation in South Asia: Beyond SAFTA.* The World Bank. New Delhi: Sage Publications.

———. 2010b. 'The Challenges and Drivers of Regionalism in South Asia: The India-Pakistan Peace Process', Chapter 7, in Rafiq Dossani, Daniel C. Sneider and Vikram Sood (eds.), *Does South Asia Exist? Prospects for Regional Integration.* The Walter H. Shorenstein Asia-Pacific Research Centre. Stanford University: Stanford, CA.

———. 2002. 'Commodities and the Displacement of Desire', *The Daily Times.* Lahore. 28 November.

Inter governmental Panel for Climatic Change (IPCC). 2007. *Climate Change, 2007:Impacts, Adaptation and Vulnerability*, Contribution of Working Group II to the Fourth Assessment Report of the IPCC. New York: Cambridge University Press.

Kardar, Shahid. 2013. 'MFN Status for India Now', *Dawn.* Karachi. 19 February.

Pachauri, R. K. 2014. 'The Impact of Global Warming and the Imperative of Mitigation', in Akmal Hussain and Muchkund Dubey (eds.), *Democracy, Sustainable Development and Peace: New Perspectives on South Asia.* New Delhi: Oxford University Press.

Report of the Indus Basin Working Group. 2013. *Connecting the Drops, An Indus Basin Roadmap for Cross Border Water Research, Data Sharing and Policy Coordination.* Observer Research Foundation, Stimson and Sustainable Development Policy Institute (Mimeo).

Srivastava, Leena. 2014. 'The Environmental Challenges in South Asia: Regional Cooperation for Adaptation Strategies', in Akmal Hussain and Muchkund Dubey (eds.), *Democracy, Sustainable Development and Peace, New Perspectives on South Asia*. New Delhi: Oxford University Press.

World Development Report. 2012. *Gender, Equity and Development*. The World Bank. Washington DC.

◆◆

7
THE SIGNIFICANCE OF SAARC FOR BHUTAN

RAJESH
KHARAT#

INTRODUCTION

Small states, particularly in the Third World, are militarily weak and incapable of defending themselves without assistance. They are exposed to various threats of enormity such as socio-political instability, poverty, problems of national growth, vulnerable geographic location, underdevelopment, etc. Survival becomes even more difficult if these small states are landlocked. For instance, Bhutan and Nepal often face problems of accessibility and, naturally, their communication with the outside world becomes limited.

The Secretary General of the United Nations, in his *Annual Report 1966–67*, describes smaller states as 'entities which are exceptionally small in area, population and human economic resources'. By these parameters, Bhutan falls into this category with a very small area of 18,000 sq miles a population of about 742,000, and a population density of 19.3 per sq km. Consequently, its small population and territory leave it with inadequate human and natural resources. For instance, Bhutan is forced to invite labour and trained administrators from foreign countries such as India and Nepal.

Bhutan is a buffer state between two giant Asian neighbours—India and China—and landlocked; geostrategically, this isolates Bhutan not just from the rest of the world but also from within. Bounded by the Tibetan plateau in the north, on the southern side it is surrounded by the plains of the Jalpaiguri district of West Bengal, and the Golpara, Kamrup and Darrang districts of Assam. Bhutan is sandwiched between the Chumbi Valley of Tibet, Sikkim and Darjeeling in the west, and the Kameng district of Arunachal Pradesh in India, on the east. However, Bhutan maintains its relations and contacts with the rest of the world only through Indian territory.

With a low rate of industrial growth, Bhutan's economy is dependent upon other countries and international financial agencies such as the International Monetary Fund (IMF) and the World Bank. Thus, its geostrategic location influences its political and economic relations with other countries. According to the *World Bank Report* (2014), its Gross Domestic Product (GDP) per capita was last recorded at USD 2,037.16 in 2013.

As Bhutan is economically and militarily weak (with an army of only 10,000), it cannot defend its boundaries in a conflict situation. Under such circumstances, it has to look to other friendly neighbours, such as India, and also to other regional/international organisations such as SAARC, the Non-Aligned Movement (NAM) and the United Nations. This applies in the case of insurgencies as well.

Bhutan's state religion is Mahayana Buddhism which has a profound impact on the country's national life as Buddhism enjoys state patronage. In the domestic sphere, it maintains a separate identity, values and traditions, whereas at the international level, Bhutan is able to establish a cordial link with other Buddhist countries. As a result, although it is a small and weak state, Bhutan's religious identity has become an important asset in its external policy manipulation.

FOREIGN POLICY CONSIDERATIONS FOR BEING A PART OF SAARC

Since countries in South Asia maintain a geographical proximity, with the overlapping of colonial historical experiences, traditions, distinct cultural identities, common religious and linguistic features, there is a need to address the common problems of development such as poverty, unemployment, imbalanced growth, lack of infrastructure and backwardness in the industrial and agricultural sectors. In addition, the security perceptions of these nations are divergent. The politico-ideological thrusts are at times antithetical and, hence, within the region the foreign policies of various countries may occasionally conflict with each other. Therefore, an urgent need for South Asian regional cooperation for mutual advantage has been felt for a long time. Through this regional cooperation, neighbouring countries seek to develop cooperation in social, cultural and economic fields. There is also a growing realisation that a joint approach to major regional problems will be mutually beneficial for all the nations within the region (Muni and Muni, 1984). Altogether, this has led to Bhutan becoming a part of SAARC and its various activities as early as 1980 when the forum launched the Integrated Programme of Action (IPA) and regional self-reliance.

At the political level, Bhutan's major foreign policy consideration behind joining the SAARC forum was its strong desire to project itself internationally as an independent sovereign nation. Regarding foreign policy matters, Bhutan was bounded by Article 2 of the Indo-Bhutan Treaty of Friendship and Cooperation, signed in 1949, which put certain limitations on its independent foreign policy. According to Article 6 of this Treaty, Bhutan is permitted to import arms and ammunitions with India's assistance or approval. However, after joining SAARC, Bhutan began to gradually operate at the global level in an effort to diversify its foreign policy operations, in general, and its relations with India, in particular. At the regional level, too, Bhutan found SAARC to be a useful forum through which it could expand its foreign relations with South Asian neighbours without any adverse reaction or causing offence to India. In this way, Bhutan decided 'to increase its international contacts through the SAARC forum as one of the safeguards against the possibilities of external interference in its domestic situation' (Muni, 1984: 518).

From a strategic point of view, Bhutan harbours strong suspicions and apprehensions vis-à-vis its other neighbour, China. This is because, in 1959, China seized eight enclaves in western Tibet which were under Bhutan's jurisdiction for over 300 years. The Chinese military intervention in Bhutanese territory at the time of the Sino-Indian war of 1962 further increased Bhutan's fears. These incidents resulted in threats being posed to Bhutan's territorial integrity, internal stability and its political independence. Therefore, the diversification of diplomatic relations with other South Asian countries through SAARC was viewed by Bhutan as a useful means of counteracting these external pressures from a powerful neighbour.

Bhutan is an underdeveloped country, as may be seen by its low level of economic development. Industries are still in their infancy and most of these have been set up with Indian assistance. Contributions from European countries and other international agencies have so far been negligible and restricted only to the setting up of some industries, such as cement and wood pulp. Hence, it was in order to reap the benefits from a closer economic cooperation with the other SAARC countries that Bhutan joined this forum.

The expansion of trade has been an important objective behind Bhutan's active involvement in SAARC and it aims to develop its economic relations with Nepal and Bangladesh through SAARC in order to reduce the trade deficit with India. Therefore, Bhutan got involved in the activities of the IPA of SAARC and became the coordinator country of one of the working groups—postal services—probably because it was already earning foreign exchange through the sale of postal stamps. Moreover, on 13 and 14 May 1985, a meeting of the foreign ministers of SAARC countries was held at Thimpu in which Bhutan proposed that the President of Bangladesh, General Ershad, should host the Summit. This proposal was seconded by India and the Maldives. In the same meeting, the date of the first SAARC Summit at Dhaka was fixed and the final draft of the SAARC Charter was approved. At the Thimpu meeting, SAARC was envisaged as an 'Association' for the adoption of a new concept of collective self-reliance. Thus, Bhutan's contribution served as 'an influential and motivating factor which ultimately led to the unanimous consent of the member nations to form this regional alliance' (Bonn, 1988: 35). During his opening speech, on 13 May 1985, the then King of Bhutan, Jigme Singye Wangchuk, remarked that SAARC was a significant step in strengthening regional cooperation and pointed out that there was no other region in the world which required harmonious cooperation more than the South Asian region. The King called upon the seven founding member nations to forget their past differences and to shape their common future with courage and trust. Since then, Bhutan has engaged itself in every SAARC summit, actively making itself visible in order to register its voice on international and regional platforms.

SIGNIFICANCE OF SAARC FOR BHUTAN

When SAARC was launched, Bhutan introduced the New Citizenship Act of 1985. This was done to control the illegal migration of Nepalese into southern Bhutan; Bhutan was apprehensive about Nepalese immigrants who demanded the abolition of monarchy and the introduction of democracy. It is presumably a coincidence that the applause which Bhutan received for its contribution towards SAARC has culminated in a cautious domestic policy which restricted the further inflow of Nepalese immigrants. In subsequent years, Bhutan continued to be an active member of SAARC and, simultaneously, introduced policies such as *Driglaham Namzha* (a revival of traditional Bhutanese culture) and an ideology of 'One Nation, One People' in the 1990s, which led to the imposition of a code of conduct (the Drukpa language, religion and dress) for all Bhutanese citizens. The Bhutanese of Nepalese origin protested against this cultural domination and demanded the total abolition of the monarchy and asked for the introduction of democratic rights such as civil liberties, freedom of speech, among others. In response, Bhutan used SAARC as a platform to raise its voice against ethnic unrest in Bhutan and the other South Asian states to garner SAARC's support to justify its policies. Hence, during the 5th SAARC Summit at Male in November 1990, the King expressed his dissatisfaction with the disturbances in the peace and tranquillity of the region, which were mainly due to the rise of terrorist activities and ethnic crises in the region, and suggested that member states should give more time to informal meetings and discussion to promote mutual understanding. It would help 'to dispel misunderstanding[s] and apprehensions that may sometimes affect relations between member countries'.[1] Thus, he wanted to strengthen the confidence-building aspect of SAARC.

On 20 July 1998, King Jigme Singye Wangchuk handed over the reins of governance to the *Lhengye Zhungtshong* (Cabinet), stating that he would not be the Head of Government but would serve only as Head of State. He appointed the Chairman of the Cabinet to be the Head of Government on a one-year rotational basis among the elected Ministers. Lynpo Jigmi Thinely was elected as the first Chairman of the Cabinet and attended the SAARC Summit at Colombo (1998) instead of the monarch. This decision was viewed in the context of infiltration of the United Liberation Front of Assam (ULFA)–Bodo militants from Assam as a threat to Bhutan's survival and internal sovereignty. To do so, the Cabinet was empowered with full executive powers and was given the authority to fulfil the responsibilities that would ensure good governance and the development of the country. In other words, the Chairman's attendance at the SAARC summit as

Head of Government of Bhutan was an endorsement by the members of SAARC for Bhutan's shift to a new political system. One could also notice that the introduction of political reforms at the domestic level was designed to ward off the constant pressure from international organisations and donor agencies to hold bilateral talks with Nepal to resolve the crisis of the Bhutanese of Nepalese origin living in refugee camps in Nepal.

In the subsequent years, emerging democracies in and around South Asia might have prompted Bhutan to announce the 39-Member Constitution Drafting Committee on 30 November 2001 to incorporate provisions on organisations and governance, as well as fundamental rights of society. In addition, to strengthen the mechanism of checks and balances among the three branches of the government, Bhutan ordered the de-linking of the legislature from the executive on 1 July 2002. As a result, the first draft of the Bhutanese Constitution was prepared in March 2005 and the second draft was released in August 2005. Article 1 of the Draft Constitution states that the government would function as a Democratic Constitutional Monarchy and that sovereign power belongs to the people of Bhutan. It has also made provisions for Fundamental Rights, Fundamental Duties, Principles of State Policy among other provisions, which are expected in any democracy's written constitution. Moreover, there is a provision for representation in the National Assembly of two political parties registered with the Election Commission. The constitution describes the role of the ruling and opposition parties and provides that their structure, functions and sources of finances will be regulated by Parliament. In the following years, after enacting the Constitution of Bhutan in March 2008, the Bhutanese government conducted two General Elections—in 2008 and 2013—and on both occasions the international observers appreciated the political process in Bhutan as democratic, but at the same time different from its neighbours.

In the process of political developments in South Asia, the King of Bhutan might have come to the conclusion that drafting a written constitution was the only remedial measure available to it. It would have come to his notice that, all over the world, there is a clamour for more civil and political rights, and a demand for greater autonomy of economic and political institutions. This could be one of the reasons for the emergence of democracy and governance as new areas of cooperation within SAARC, and Bhutan too must have realised its importance, especially when all members of the association are democracies. Therefore, to reaffirm its commitment to democracy, Bhutan organised the first, and very successful, SAARC Conference on Media and Democracy in Thimpu in 2010 and became the host nation to the 16th SAARC Summit the same year.

ASSERTION OF AN INDEPENDENT FOREIGN POLICY

Bhutan is conscious of its inability to play a major role in the region because of its topography and untapped resources and, to some extent, because of the colonial legacy of the Indo-Bhutan Treaty of 1949, which was revised later in February 2007. Moreover, SAARC advocates the principles of non-interference in domestic and international affairs of other nations, and in unanimous decisions; it does not matter how small or weak a country may be. Bhutan has always favoured these principles, which are applied in its foreign policy strategy either in the United Nations or NAM. Hence, it has decided to use SAARC as a platform to enhance and diversify its foreign policy options without affecting India's interests.

For instance, on issues such as terrorism, Bhutan has always expressed its concern and fear of the various threatening developmental initiatives within the region. Therefore, in 1988, the Government of Bhutan ratified the 'SAARC Regional Convention on the Suppression of Terrorism' and also requested the other members to do so, as 'terrorism has become one of the growing threats to peace and stability in the region'. At the 7th Summit of SAARC, the King of Bhutan expressed serious concern about terrorism being one of the most serious impediments to economic progress in the region.

Referring to its own experience of terrorists' clandestine activities in Bhutan and on the Indo-Bhutan borders, the King said, 'Even a small country like Bhutan which has traditionally been a haven of peace and tranquillity has not been spared the depredation of terrorists who have been trying to subvert our country.' Unfortunately, this is a reality as, on several occasions, Bhutanese locals and businessmen were either killed or targeted by the Indian militants, viz., ULFA, National Democratic Front of Bodoland (NDFB) and Kamtapur Liberation Organization (KLO), who took shelter in Bhutan on the Indo-Bhutan borders. As a result, Bhutan's social and economic life was disturbed to the extent that Bhutan began to feel that its territorial integrity and sovereignty was being challenged. Therefore, whenever issues of terrorism appear on the SAARC forum, Bhutan insists on resolving the crisis. One could see Bhutan's grave concern towards terrorism when Thimpu hosted the Fourth Meeting of the SAARC Interior/Home Ministers in July 2010. To quote the then Prime Minister, Jigme Thinley:

> All our countries have been victims of terrorism and some of us have been an unwitting breeding ground for cross-border and international terrorism. No cause can be enhanced or served through acts of terror nor can any of it in any degree be deserving of sympathy and support. Yet, it receives nourishment and support from enough quarters to threaten our nations, communities and families alike raising the cost of providing safety to our citizens.

He also said, 'We believe that such interactions are essential to reducing bilateral and regional tension and contributing to regional security.'[2]

Bilateral issues have had Bhutan's support more often than not. For example, in June 1987, when India dropped 'relief' to Tamilians in Jaffna, Bhutan initially chose not to involve itself in this controversial issue. Pakistan and Sri Lanka were against this move, whereas Nepal and Bangladesh mutually supported this action. However, Bhutan later welcomed the Indo-Sri Lanka agreement and was in favour of its approval at the SAARC Summit at Kathmandu in November 1987. When the Kathmandu declaration failed to welcome the Indo-Sri Lanka Peace Agreement because of Pakistan's objection[3] to the discussion of bilateral political issues, the King of Bhutan said, 'We must keep in mind that the condition of our bilateral relations will affect the political environment of our region and determine the future well-being of SAARC.' Since then, Bhutan has consistently emphasised the strength of bilateral relations among the countries of the region at all SAARC summits.

In continuation of its adherence to bilateral issues, recently on 8 December 2014, during the Bangladesh visit, the prime minister of Bhutan expressed the need to make efforts to intensify relations for mutually beneficial cooperation in the areas of hydro-power, water resources management, trade and commerce, connectivity, climate change, tourism, culture, education, agriculture, and health and human resource development. In particular, Bangladesh had shown an interest in obtaining hydro-power from Bhutan and requested partnership in Bhutan's future power projects. The Bhutanese prime minister also agreed to work together with Bangladesh in this sector to enhance regional connectivity—bilaterally as well as subregionally. As a result, Bhutan became more active in other regional organisations and gatherings, such as the Bay of Bengal Initiative for Multi-Sectoral Technical and Economic Cooperation (BIMSTEC) and the Hindu Kush Himalayan region, to address pertinent issues such as accessibility to Landlocked Least Developed Countries (LLDCs) for the expansion of trade activities, environmental degradation and climate change.

One could also observe that, after hosting the 16th SAARC Summit at Thimpu in 2010, Bhutan became more assertive in its foreign policy so as to diversify its political and economic relations with countries other than India. For instance, it could diversify its formal and non-residential diplomatic relations with about 53 countries from all around the world. Its active participation in SAARC has also led to the creation of global public opinion in favour of Bhutan, as far as the Bhutanese refugee crisis is concerned. International humanitarian agencies and non-governmental agencies came forward to resolve the crisis when large numbers of refuges from Nepal's UNHCR (United Nations High Commissioner for Refugees) camps were resettled in Europe and America. This demonstrates how Bhutan has succeeded in muting criticism of the violation of human rights in Bhutan, and by the Royal Government of Bhutan. Second, Bhutan could use SAARC as a podium to internationalise its much debated and popular concept of Gross National Happiness (GNH). Initially, GNH was portrayed as a philosophy of Bhutan's development strategy but was later popularised by the government as an instrument of diplomacy. As a result, the philosophy of GNH became synonymous with Bhutan. Bhutan became a spiritual destination for many in the Western world, from which it also obtained economic assistance for its developmental programmes. Third, after joining SAARC in 1985, while attempting to move away from India's colonial legacy, Bhutan managed to persuade India to allow it to have independent bilateral talks with China. Although the talks between the two countries have not reached any conclusion despite 21 rounds, Bhutan is successfully maintaining politically correct relations with China and is able to receive Chinese assistance in the sectors of health, education and hospitality without any political strings attached.

BHUTAN IN REGIONAL INTEGRATION

Membership of SAARC proved to be a major milestone in Bhutan's foreign policy as it rightly took the decision to participate in its developmental activities in agriculture, rural development, forestry, tourism, communications, resource planning, trade and industry. It is expecting a joint exploitation of its hydro potential, natural and forest resources, large mineral deposits of limestone, marble, dolomite, graphite, lead, copper, slate, coal, talc, gypsum, beryl, pyrites and tufa, which are as yet unexploited and untapped due to the lack of infrastructural facilities.

The tourism sector shows great potential for Bhutan in terms of foreign revenue, and providing employment and income opportunities in rural areas. In spite of its policy of controlled tourists, Bhutan is increasing the number of Indian tourists and tour packages from the other SAARC countries. Bhutan is promoting 'Regional Tourism' under the umbrella of SAARC through the Bhutan Tourism Corporation (BTC). The BTC provides special discounts and concessions to students under 25 years of age, children and travel agents, as well as allowing tourists to use their own currencies in Bhutan, thus encouraging increasing numbers of tourists. The BTC has declared a special exchange arrangement for travel vouchers through the Bank of Bhutan. Under the same SAARC agreement, Druk Air offers a discount of 25 per cent to groups of 10 or more tourists organised by the BTC, travelling on a round trip, covering at least two SAARC countries. In addition, the Royal Government of Bhutan provides licenses to travel agencies to organise and operate tours under the guidance of the BTC. Consequently, tourists from SAARC countries can now visit Bhutan on tours organised by private agents.

In order to improve services and strengthen the tourism infrastructure, Bhutan established a new foreign committee under the South Asia Integrated Human Resources Development Programme. It has also established the National Tourism Human Resource Development Programme and the National Tourism

Human Resource Development Committee. As Bhutan lacks a formal training centre and facilities for tourism, this committee provides all the assistance to various tourist companies and tourism activity of Bhutan. In this way, despite its landlocked situation, Bhutan's participation in SAARC helps to promote its tourist industry and economy, as well as promoting its exposure to the rest of the world.

In South Asian Free Trade Association (SAFTA) meetings, Bhutan often takes a stand in the interest of LDCs and supports their demand to exempt the products of their export interest from their sensitive lists. Sensitive lists are the lists of products of special interest to individual member countries that are exempted from low SAFTA tariffs. The use of sensitive lists allows countries to protect growing domestic industries or important sources of customs revenue. However, the overuse of sensitive lists can make goods more expensive for consumers and reduce trade between countries. Therefore, the LDCs demand for the exemption of products of their export interest is justified and Bhutan, being an LDC, supported this cause.

Unfortunately, the member countries failed to reach an agreement on the formula and coverage of the revenue compensation mechanism. Despite this, Bhutan hopes to create mutual understanding in promoting trade, and the realisation of the objective of a free-trade area and SAFTA could help Bhutan promote and boost its produce and allow access to markets in the SAARC region. Lower import tariffs and other facilities provided under the SAFTA accord will, no doubt, broaden their scope for better trade in the long run—SAFTA being one positive step towards achieving a South Asian economic union.

However, some experts have declared that SAFTA may help in evolving a horizontal specialisation across the region to enable optimal utilisation of the synergies of member countries to their mutual advantage. Sri Lanka may well emerge as the region's hub for rubber-based industries, Bangladesh for energy-intensive industries, and Bhutan for forest-based industries, among others. Bhutan is looking for regional economic integration in South Asia, which could generate billions of dollars of new income, employment and trade, and could help the region in its fight against poverty. Moreover, Bhutan's domestic market is very small and it makes little sense to protect it. To Bhutan, SAFTA meant direct market access and was a significant step towards a deeper economic integration in the region.

Thus, Bhutan can now explore other markets for their products and gain automatic access. However, trade officials expressed an opinion that, while some products could have immediate benefits from the SAFTA agreement, Bhutan was most likely to fully reap the benefit only in the long run.

For instance, in December 2014, Bhutan and Bangladesh emphasised the need for enhancing trade relations for mutual benefit and a recognition of the huge potential they hold in bringing prosperity; the two sides agreed to diversify bilateral trade and take further trade facilitation measures for deeper market access. Bangladesh offered to export more products, such as readymade garments, pharmaceuticals, ceramics, jute and jute goods, and agricultural produce to Bhutan. Being aware of the huge potential of tourism, the two sides also agreed to further increase cooperation in this sector, as well as agriculture, and stressed the early commencement of work by the Joint Technical Committee. They also agreed to enhance collaboration in other sectors—education, health and human resource development. In addition, two agreements were signed between Bangladesh and Bhutan on 6 December 2014: (1) The Bilateral Trade Agreement and its Protocol (renewed for 10 years) and (2) Agreement on Allotment of Land to Bhutan for construction of its embassy premises at the Baridhara diplomatic enclave in Dhaka, as a token of friendship.

In conclusion, one could say that Bhutan's response to its own and South Asian regional issues opens up the possibility and necessity of its constructive role in the region. As a member nation with certain socio-economic and politico-cultural problems that are also being faced by the other countries of the region, we find that it consolidates SAARC as a forum to promote cooperation and the integrated development of the region.

◆

#This chapter was first published in 2015 in the *IIC Quarterly*, Vol. 41, Nos 3 and 4.

NOTES

1. See SAARC Supplement. *The Kuensel*. 21–23 November 1990.
2. Ibid. July 2010.
3. See *The Statesman*. 7 November 1987.

REFERENCES

Muni, S. D. and Anuradha Muni. 1984. *Regional Co-operation in South Asia.* New Delhi: National Publishing House.

Muni, S.D. 1984., 'Bhutan Steps Out', *The World Today.* London. Vol. 40, No. 12.

Bonn, Gisela. 1988. 'Jigme Singye Wangchuk: A Portrait of the King of Bhutan.' *Indo-Asia Special Edition. Techno-German India.*

◆◆

8

PEACE, SECURITY AND THREATS
A Balance Sheet

NIHAL
RODRIGO[#]

The inaugural first Summit of the South Asian Association for Regional Cooperation (SAARC) was held in December 1985 in Dhaka, Bangladesh. The Summit adopted the Charter and Provisional Rules of Procedure for the regional organisation. One of its provisions was that 'cooperation within the framework of the Association shall be based on respect for the principles of sovereign equality, territorial integrity, political independence, non-interference in the internal affairs of other States and mutual benefit' (Article ii). Of major political importance has been the clear indication that 'bilateral and contentious issues shall be excluded from the deliberations' in the Association, (Article x).

SAARC Summits were expected to be held on an annual basis. Yet, while 30 years have passed since the Association's establishment, only 18 summits have been held, the most recent in Kathmandu in November 2014.

As I indicated in an interview with the Foreign Policy Research Centre, New Delhi, the Declaration adopted at the Kathmandu Summit could be considered 'as a frank and practical balance sheet of sort', incorporating some realistic proposals based on sensible grounds for the future. For example, the Declaration proposed that SAARC Summits need not be held on an annual basis. Paragraph 34 of the Kathmandu Declaration, quite practically, given the complex dilatory negotiations on settling dates for each Summit, 'agreed to hold henceforth the Summit meetings every two years'. In practical terms, instead it would be the SAARC Council of Ministers that would meet annually and settle thorny issues as far as possible. I understand that it was at that level that a tentative decision was taken on the venue of the next Summit. The Kathmandu Summit Declaration 'welcomed the offer of the Government of the Islamic Republic of Pakistan to host the Nineteenth Summit of SAARC' (paragraph 6).

In considering South Asia's contemporary political situation since the establishment of SAARC, particularly with respect to the region's peace, security and threats posed by terrorism on which this chapter concentrates, it is helpful to look back on past centuries as well.

Currently, SAARC consists of eight independent member states: Afghanistan, Bangladesh, Bhutan, India, the Maldives, Nepal, Pakistan and Sri Lanka. In his book, *A Decade of Confrontation: Sri Lanka and India in the 1980s*, John Gooneratne, a former colleague in the Sri Lanka Foreign Service, writes:

> Recorded relations between Sri Lanka and India are reckoned in terms of over two and a half millennia, covering the spectrum of political, cultural [and], religious interactions. They go to form the historical memory of Sri Lanka. Some memories are cherished and greatly revered, such as the introduction of Buddhism to Sri Lanka, during the period of Emperor Asoka's reign in the second century B.C. Other memories are not so pleasant, such as the prolonged depredations of the Anuradhapura and Polonnaruwa kingdoms of ancient Sri Lanka by the armies of the different kingdoms of South India (p. 1).

Dr Gooneratne referred to India of the 2nd century, which is now Nepal, the birth place of the Lord Buddha. Pakistan and Bangladesh are now separate states that are no longer part of India.

In contemporary times, violent separatist tendencies have also been part of the South Asian scene. Sri Lanka has battled with the so-called Liberation Tigers of Tamil Eelam (LTTE), an ethnocentric terrorist group, which was supported, even financed, by India for a brief period. India's then Prime Minister Rajiv Gandhi was eventually assassinated by the LTTE following his negotiations with Sri Lanka's late President, J. R. Jayewardene, to assist Sri Lanka's ethno-terrorism. Subsequently, the LTTE killed Sri Lanka's Prime Minister, Ranasinghe Premadasa. Even Sri Lanka's Foreign Minister, Lakshman Kadirgamar, himself a Tamil, was shot dead by the terrorist group.

Terrorism still continues to be a threat in South Asia owing to perverted theories of religions, particularly in Pakistan where, recently, over a hundred children were mercilessly slaughtered in Peshawar.

Apart from domestic aspects, such as ethnic conflicts and perverted versions of religions, South Asia, located in the Indian Ocean Region, needs also to contend with security threats from globalised criminal cartels in which some of South Asia's citizens are also complicit. The Indian Ocean Rim Association for Regional Cooperation (IORARC) has identified the following main characteristics of the Indian Ocean, which borders five of the eight SAARC countries. It is the third largest of the world's oceans in extent; the people living off the ocean account for about 40 per cent of the world's population; its ports, including South Asia's Mumbai, Gwadar, Colombo, Hambantota and Chittagong, handle over 30 per cent of global trade; around 60 per cent of sea-borne oil trans-shipments cross the ocean and it is estimated to contain about 40 per cent of the world's gas reserves. The IORARC also provides connectivity to underworld criminal cartels involved in human smuggling, drug-trafficking and gun-running.

Sri Lanka itself is located virtually at the centre of the Indian Ocean, which gives it strategic advantages and economic benefits, but also poses certain dangers. As far back as the 15th century, the Chinese navigator Zheng He visited the island of Ceilao (as Sri Lanka was then known) to establish a convenient transit point for trade. Chinese products much in demand then in the West were silk and porcelain, cherished by the elites in European society. A theory of the Australian historian, Gavin Menzies, was that China's Zheng He even visited the Eastern coast of what is now the United States as his ships were far larger and more seaworthy than the *Santa Maria* of Christopher Columbus. Given the contemporary potential for East–West connectivity across the Indian Ocean, China has been working to build secure transit/link points across the IORARC. Ports and harbours have been enlarged/upgraded in Bangladesh (Chittagong), in Gwadar (Pakistan) and in Hambantota (Sri Lanka). India had expressed some concern but, eventually, did not strongly oppose the development of Hambantota. Traffic into Mumbai, north of Hambantota, has been hampered. In fact, Shyam Saran, a former Special Envoy to the Indian prime minister, and a contributor in this volume, had assessed that over 50 per cent of shipping to and from Indian ports could have been handled by the port of Colombo, and that a great deal of Indian break-bulk was being also handled in Colombo. Hambantota could, therefore, be seen as taking some of the pressure off Colombo.

The Booz–Hamilton–Allen security think tank in the United States projected that the ports/harbours being developed in Gwadar, Hambantota and Chittagong all amounted to a 'string of pearls' being designed by China to 'restrict', even strangle, India's rise in the Indian Ocean. It seemed linked with the US 'pivot to the Indo-Pacific'. The former Indian Army Chief, J. J. Singh, at a Conference held in 2013 at Punjab University ridiculed the theory, given the major importance of ensuring security cooperation among SAARC countries to ensure closer cooperation in the Indian Ocean Region.

Sri Lanka has since hosted an annual Conference called the Galle Dialogue to secure better coordination against terrorism and other criminal activity amongst all countries frequenting the Indian Ocean. At the most recent meeting of the Galle Dialogue held in December 2014, amongst the 36 participants were defence officials and diplomats from Australia, Bangladesh, China, France, India, Indonesia, Iran, Japan, Kenya, Malaysia, the Maldives, Nigeria, Oman, Philippines, Qatar, Russia and South Korea. The keynote address was delivered by the Indian National Security Advisor, Ajit Doval. He called for cooperation amongst the participants, in particular amongst India, the Maldives and Sri Lanka, stressing 'the need for maritime security for prosperity'. Bilateral discussions between India and Sri Lanka also took place on reports of the presence of a Chinese nuclear submarine off the island's coast.

The US Representative at the Dialogue, Robert Boggs, Professor of South Asian Studies at the Near East & South Asia Studies in Washington (who had also served as a diplomat in the US Embassy in Sri Lanka) dealt also with environmental aspects that pose threats to the Indian Ocean. He stressed the need for coordinating humanitarian assistance and disaster response. This included the dangers of excessive exploitation of fisheries resources.

The Rise of the Asian Century is now very much part of current broader global economics as well. China has replaced Japan as the second largest economy in the world after the United States. China is now also engaged in projecting the 'Twenty-First Century

Silk Route of the Seas'. This has been supported by Sri Lanka. The Asian Development Bank (ADB), and even the World Bank, predicts China's eventual ascension as the largest economy in the world during this century. China, however, does not wish to be in competition with India, or any other SAARC country, preferring coordination. In September 2014, a Joint Communique signed by China and India sought to disclaim rivalry and competition. Despite Booz–Hamilton–Allen's economic astrology, the two will work together, which would eventually augur well for South Asia, too.

◆

#This chapter was first published in 2015 in the *IIC Quarterly,* Vol. 41, Nos 3 and 4.

REFERENCE

Gooneratne, John. 2000. *A Decade of Confrontation; Sri Lanka and India in the 1980s.* Sri Lanka: Stamford Lake (Pvt.) Ltd.

◆◆

9
POLITICS IN PAKISTAN TODAY
The Challenge of Securing Democracy

RASUL
BAKHSH
RAIS[#]

INTRODUCTION

The countries of SAARC have a number of common features that provide the background and much of the potential for promoting, strengthening and sustaining cooperation on a broad range of issues. Geography and history stand out as the most important commonalities, along with strands of language, culture and civilisational heritage among people of mixed ethnic groups straddling the state boundaries of the South Asian states (Muni, 2010). Ethnicity is itself a major common element between sets of any two neighbouring South Asian countries. True, religion, territoriality and the post-colonial state and nation-building processes have thrust upon them fundamentally diverse national identities. That was, and perhaps is today, the necessity of being a state that they must establish themselves as different by connecting the present with an imagined or real past through the respective narratives of national identity.

With the exception of Afghanistan, the troubled periphery of the Empire, all other South Asian countries share three very important characteristics—common colonial power, the British, the political economy of imperialism, and the institutional structure of the state. The state building process under the Empire included the establishment of the bureaucracy, military, law, judiciary, constitutional schemes and elections. The emergence of several streams of social, religious and political movements culminating in nationalist movements created the historical and social landscape for democratic development at the time of independence of India and Pakistan. The regions comprising the two states were endowed with a favourable colonial heritage for inaugurating representative forms of government. The same is true of other South Asian states with the exception of Afghanistan that was not ruled directly by the British. Every shade of nationalism had a strong streak of democratic aspirations that may be defined as self-rule, empowerment and representation. After decades of struggle, bouts of confrontation with the colonial power and conflicts within the communities, it was expected that national leaders would form responsive governments rather than rule and take decisions that would improve the social and economic conditions of the people. Nationalism, in many ways, ushered the new states into an age of optimism, as much as it plunged them into communal conflict, large-scale forced migration of communities, settling refugees and conflict over territories. While those painful years and many decades of uncertainty are behind us, some of the countries in the region, like Pakistan, continue to confront serious challenges of building a secure and stable democracy and a peaceful society.

In every South Asian country, democratic politics remains an evolutionary process, procedural in nature with mixed elements of tradition, hierarchical social structures, representation and authoritarianism (Jalal, 1995). The historical experience of mature democracies of Western Europe is no different. It took them effort, time and many economic and social transformations—modernisation—for democracy to become the 'only game in town'. Making the transition from procedural or political democracy to substantive democracy and sustaining democratic rule would require more than the consensus of political actors or elite pacts of the constitutional framework. Economic development with a focus on providing basic needs of the people in South Asia would provide legitimacy to the elite. There is a fair amount of literature on democratic transitions which suggests that there is a positive relationship between modernisation in the wider sense and democratic durability. Democratic endowment and the level of participation and institutionalisation of democracy varies from state to state in the region, with common streaks of authoritarian and traditional structures posing many challenges to political stability and democratic substance in each of the SAARC countries. Even with many visible resemblances, each South Asian country presents a different case of political evolution, if not unique in explaining democratic constraints, sources of political instability, violence in society and political development.

Pakistan is one of the exceptional cases of democratic instability. Democracy collapsed four times after independence in 1947. With the breakdown of democracy due to serious political crises of legitimacy and popular uprisings, the military stepped in, taking complete control of the state and restructuring political order according to its vision of political stability and order in society. This chapter situates Pakistan in South Asian history, its cultural landscape and similar social structure to address several questions about the revival of democracy for the third time since 2008. First, what role do political forces and social change play in the restoration of democracy in Pakistan? What are their strengths and weaknesses? What are the challenges Pakistani democracy faces in consolidating itself? Finally, how important are civil-military relations in stabilising democracy? The central argument is that the dominant political elite structure in Pakistan lacks democratic essence in its party organisations. Its dynastic hold over the parties, personalised rule and considerable control over entry into leadership ranks has kept 'democratic' politics confined to inter-elite political relations, which has remained closed and exclusive. This raises serious questions about the representative nature of the assemblies and political executives that rule in the name of democracy. Monopolistic elite-oriented power politics can no longer operate effectively or smoothly in the vastly changed social environment of Pakistan. The emergence of civil society, free media and the middle class continuously question the democratic character, competence, leadership quality and style of decision-making of the dynastic elites. Inefficiency and ineffectiveness of governments further compound the legitimacy of the 'representative' elites of Pakistan. Furthermore, rising frustrations of the citizens about failures in realising social and economic rights, threatening internal security challenges—terrorism—create a large space for the military to play a visible or not-so-visible role in the 'democratic' politics of Pakistan.

SIGNS OF DEMOCRATIC HOPE

Pakistan has seen extraordinary political events with the military seizing power four times, a parliament completing its tenure

(2008–2013) for the first time ever, and power being transferred from one political party to another. The completion of tenure marks a new political beginning, a big step towards democratic transition. What made it possible and what does it mean for the democratic future of the country? Pakistan's current phase of democratic stability or continuity rests primarily on the national consensus among the political elites of the country, disregard for their ideological leanings, size of popular support and the regional base of their influence. Elite consensus on the framework of the polity, the form of government and general rule of political games is the first, most essential step towards a constitutional democratic process. The next steps towards democratic transition become simpler, and political disputes along the way are more easily resolved within the larger consensus of the system. Democratic politics in unstable, security-deficient countries with low levels of economic development are messy because they involve perpetual conflict of interest among many competing political, regional and religious groups, parties and players. In polarised societies such as Pakistan, which is going through painful transitions socially and economically, the peaceful accommodation of divergent interests and play of politics within the normal range of norms and institutions remains somewhat troublesome. Never has the development of democratic culture, institutions and politics been a linear path, at least not in the case of Pakistan. Pakistan's political story is a mix of progress, severe setbacks, resilience and perpetual challenges, and stubborn legacies of the long years of military rule.

The democratic power transition is a sign of hope that democracy may achieve a degree of stability, but just hope and a single peaceful transfer of power may not account for the energy needed for democratic continuity, a point we will elaborate in the latter part of the essay in discussing challenges to democratic consolidation. At this point, there is more than one reason for democratic optimism. First, let us elaborate on what has brought about the elite compact on saving democracy from direct or indirect disruptions by the military. As always, it is self-interest in making the choice of a system that would ensure that the elite remain the main players. After aligning with the military or playing games in pulling down a rival party government, major sections of political elites, if not everyone, believe that democracy with all its flaws is a better option than military rule.

They wish to put power plays of the past behind them when their factional feuds and power rivalries weakened the political class and greatly damaged their standing with the people. Confrontational politics opened up a space for the military to intervene as a power-broker behind the scenes. Consequently, political elites lost power, legitimacy and credibility to govern effectively. The transition to democratic rule that started in 1988 remained shaky. It was after many losses that major factions of the political elites realised the futility of confrontation and began to comprehend the value of political cooperation both for the restoration of democracy and its sustainability. It was in this spirit that despite many openings and opportunities, the Pakistan Muslim League Nawaz (PMLN) refused to be part of any power play that would pull down the inept and inefficient government of the Pakistan Peoples Party (PPP). There appears to be a wider understanding between these two major parties and their smaller political allies that they must demonstrate democratic solidarity and recognise and respect the political mandate of other parties. There appears to be better clarity about the rules of the political game that is demonstrated by this consensus among the elites in Pakistan. It is an important step forward, but the elite-compacting is not a sufficient guarantee of democratic stability (Burton and Higley, 1987). It will require opening up their ranks to recruite leaders from non-elite sectors of society. This may accommodate the aspirations of the new social forces in the country and make them stakeholders in the system. They will have to go beyond constituency-driven patronage politics to delivering on governance and providing better security, law and order. The elite-oriented politics of Pakistan may slowly gain the genuine confidence of the people by performance legitimacy.

Second, although the public trusts the military more than the political elites, a national consensus on democracy weighs heavier today than ever before, and the trust in the national government, though less than in the military, has improved since the transfer of power from the PPP to PMLN in 2013.[1] This sentiment is likely to grow with a similar transfer of power in future. Occasional clamouring for military intervention from political actors that have benefitted from military rule by serving their surrogates has not earned either respect or public support. Contrary to such views, civil society across the provincial boundaries, regional parties and national leadership believe that the solution to fragile democracy lies in improving and sustaining it—not uprooting it. There is wider agreement among the observers of Pakistani politics that military regimes have generated multiple problems for society, state and democratic institutions. With the exception of the first military rule of Ayub Khan (1958–69), they have repeatedly failed to address the structural problems of the country and lay the foundation for economic development (Ziring, 1971). The country did develop at an economically faster rate than any other comparable country at that time. But, his rule also sowed the seeds of the destruction of Pakistan by alienating the peoples of its eastern wing, now Bangladesh. All the military generals left the political scene in worse condition, and with more complex and stubborn problems than before. To consolidate and sustain their personal rule, they fragmented political parties, and divided society by ethnicity and religion. The country continues to face some of the unintended consequences of their rule in many forms—Islamic radicalism, religious bigotry and politics of hate and confrontation. The lessons of their failures have convinced every thinking politician that living with a noisy and clamourous democracy is better than living under the forced calm of military dictators.

Third, there is growing ownership of democratic rule in terms of popular participation.[2] At the grass-roots level, the people are more comfortable with their elected leaders with whom they can relate more comfortably than with those who are imposed from above. People have demands at the local level. They want developmental projects such as natural gas, power lines, roads, sewerage, schools and social services. Popular demands have an electoral connection in every democracy, whether mature or evolving as in Pakistan. Even the brief periods of democratic rule in the past have strengthened political bonds between the electorates and the elected representatives through grass-roots politics. Starting with the post-1985 elections, rural development and greater allocation of funds have become a constituency-driven political norm. With the villages of Pakistan developing, though at a much slower pace than desirable, the urban–rural divide is narrowing. Over time, development-oriented patronage politics has introduced democracy at the grass-roots level by creating a demand–response nexus. Failure to address local problems means electoral failure, compelling the next elected member to do better. In many elections, in many constituencies and many times, electorates have defeated absent, no-shows and less-concerned members of assemblies and national parliament. This explains the routing of the PPP from three provinces, including the Punjab, the largest in the 2013 elections, and also that of the Awami National Party (ANP) in the Khyber Pakhtunkhwa. It is another mark of democratic development when people elect party candidates on the basis of performance rather than primordial connections. This has happened several times in Pakistan, and in many constituencies.

Finally, the rise of new social forces—middle class, media and civil society—strengthen the hope that democracy will stay and even get better. One thing that emerges from historical and sociological research on the middle class is that it is a sign of great progress, as its existence reflects a change in the condition of poor sections of society to a more comfortable economic and social position. Second, material changes—economic development, industrialisation and urbanisation—create conditions for the transformation of classes, redefining their association with social structures and broadening their world outlook. For this reason certain cultural traits and values are associated with classes—rich, poor and the middle class. There is a positive link between the rise of the middle class and demands for substantive democracy—rule of law, fair elections, good governance and accountability. A visible dissatisfaction of the middle class with 'bad' democracy drives it toward protest movements, as is evident from the participation in the anti-Musharraf movement in 2007 and, more recently, support to *dharnas* (sit-in) and rallies organised by Imran Khan and his Pakistan Tehreek-e-Insaf (PTI, the movement for justice) against the alleged rigging of the 2013 elections. The expansion of media and civil society in Pakistan has its roots in the expansion of the middle class and these forces have tended to reinforce one another's strengths.

The emergence of the PTI as the second largest party in the 2013 elections is a reflection of the power of new social forces and new political trends that question the credibility of traditional political parties. Growing urbanisation and the gradual unhinging of social groups moving into district towns and major cities are bound to turn the politics of Pakistan away from the domination of traditional elite families to new leaders and movements.

The challenge to the traditional parties that Imran Khan and his PTI present is not the final contest between old and new politics, but the beginning of a process that would eventually bring substance to Pakistani democracy by raising questions about accountability, performance and responsiveness to the needs of the citizens.

CHALLENGES TO DEMOCRATIC CONSOLIDATION

Even with these hopeful signs, no transitional democracy, much less Pakistan which has seen four military interventions and considerable support for military rule, can be considered safe. Fragility, threats and challenges to Pakistani democracy abound: ineffective governance, political polarisation, violence and the pattern of civil-military relations. Even a limited democracy in procedural form must perform some basic functions to keep its promise. When people elect their governments, expectations are always high. One of the basic problems of democratic consolidation is that representative governments in the past have failed to deliver on economy, governance and better law and order. By every measure, their performance has been poor. This has always presented a problem for the further development of democratic norms and institutions. Why has this been an issue in Pakistan? It is the questionable personal qualities of the 'democratic' leaders and poor institutional capacity to deliver on the lofty promises they make during the elections.

There appears to have emerged a social disconnect between the power elites of Pakistan and the general public. The leaders of civil society, public intellectuals and media question democracy in its present form and argue that this is nowhere close to what they understand of democracy. The past three tenures of the elected governments produced a distorted view of democracy for bad governance, widespread corruption and neglect of difficult issues. Rightly, some sections of society feel disgusted at the way dynastic leaders have promoted private interests at the expense of the public and the republic. Countering their arguments against democracy is as hard as telling the 'democratic' leaders that democracy is more than getting elected or forming majorities among the electable class. The claims of legitimacy only through forming majority coalitions and ruling in traditional ways rather than governing to promote public interest are shallow. The elites get elected even with poor performance because elite families have a strong hold over their constituencies, and when one family is defeated another replaces it. There is something missing in the political culture of Pakistan, and that is strong and consistent civic engagement, i.e., people taking responsibility for things not done, or done badly, by the governments. No power group, party or leader can behave responsibly until citizens present him or her with a real challenge. That requires the development of civil associations, culture of peaceful protest and civic solidarity. In all these respects, Pakistan is better today than it ever was but still has to go a long distance to capture the real spirit of democracy.

Political polarisation among the political groups and parties, both at the regional and national levels, often takes the form of confrontation, forcing out the group in power. This not only destabilised democracy but also further promoted multiple political conflicts (Amin, 1995). Gradually, the PPP and the PMLN, the two feuding rivals of the past, have realised that cooperating for democratic sustainability serves their interests better than confrontation that weakened and expelled both from power. If that appears to have abated, been diffused or somewhat settled, another has emerged—confrontation by the PTI against every other party taking to the streets in 2014. In this the coherence, cooperation and consensus that the political elite required to change the balance of power in favour of the civilian regime was lost. Rather, three opposites of what would keep the political order stable— fragmentation, confrontation and conflict—have defined the post-2013 election scenario in Pakistan.

One may argue that in an ethnically plural, populous and complex country with a history of political violence and declining institutional capacity to govern, fragmentation is a natural outcome. It is true to a certain degree. But such challenges are exactly what politics is all about, and democratic politics, in particular, is about building consensus, resolving conflicts and moving forward together. The real reason, in my view, is that the rules of the political game are not firm. The PTI and some others question the fairness of the 2013 elections and continue to boycott the assemblies until a judicial commission is formed with the power and the mandate to conduct a full inquiry into election 'fraud'. The electoral process, the voters' list and the role of judicial and other officials who conduct the elections remain unsettled. On these crucial issues, Pakistan's politics is stuck in an unending impasse. Majoritarian politics on the one hand and confrontation on the other have always weakened democracy, and they continue to do so. Compromise and conciliation, the two political virtues that stabilise democracy, had not sunk deep into the political thoughts and practice of the political class.

The role of Islam in politics remains a highly emotional and destabilising issue for society as well as for the democratic construction of the Pakistani state. The basic question is: What is the place of Islam—is it in society or in the state? There is a liberal–religious–conservative divide. The political parties never take a clear position on this brittle issue and prefer to stay in the grey area. Their ambiguity and expediency have allowed the extremist clerics and their followers to capture the street. That apathy has morphed into a bigger problem of religious militancy. Many of the conflicts Pakistan confronts today, from Taliban insurgency to sectarian violence and terrorism, are rooted in this neglect. Furthermore, a cynical and selective use of religion and the employment of religious groups as informal allies in the pursuit of foreign policy goals towards Afghanistan and India have generated boomerang effects in society.

Although religion as a political route to power has so far failed, the proliferation of religious networks, organisations and movements, often conflicting with one another, have bred intolerance, extremism and violence. In some ways, the proliferation of electronic media that Pakistan celebrates as one of its democratic achievements has served a greater purpose for religious movements than for the political world. While the political class, for good or bad, faces many questions about what they do or fail to do, firebrand clerics get away with their frequent hate speeches and even inciting people to violence. The good part of the story is that public opinion has turned against religious movements, parties and organisations. The public does not vote for religious parties in the numbers that they once did. Their collective vote bank has shrunk to about 6 per cent in the 2013 elections from their highest at 22 per cent in the 1970 elections. This is due to the apologetic stance of the religious parties towards sectarian and Taliban groups. Recent moves by the military and the government to defeat Taliban insurgency has popular support and may further push religious parties to the margins of Pakistani politics. But they have been on the margins many times and for many decades. As long as secular, modernist and democratic forces in the country remain as weak as they are, and the political parties fail to resolve the issue of Pakistan's destiny, religious parties and groups may continue to pose a serious political challenge to democracy, and the political and social stability of the country.

Finally, civil-military relations and how they create harmony and agreement between the PMLN government and the security establishment hold the key to democratic stability in the country. Prime Minister Nawaz Sharif has had troubled relations with the security establishment since his invitation to former Indian Prime Minister Atal Bihari Vajpayee in 1998 and for taking an independent route to explore an 'out-of-the-box' solution to the Kashmir issue. He firmly believed that the imbalance in civil-military relations was an issue and had to be corrected by civilians asserting their authority. He did act with considerable assertion but soon found himself humiliated, removed, imprisoned and exiled for a decade. Interestingly, when assuming office for the third time in May 2013 as prime minister, he began to pursue an identical agenda. He was unforgiving of Musharraf and used his authority to have the latter indicted on grounds of treason for imposing emergency in November 2007. Sharif resumed back-channel diplomacy with India on the Kashmir issue, and pushed forward the case for granting India Most Favoured Nation status for trade. Against the assessment of the military and popular sentiment against negotiations with the Tehreek Taliban Pakistan (TTP) or making any concessions to them, the prime minister took a different line. He was persuaded, some might say forced, to back off on every step he took on these issues.

The security establishment protected their former Chief Pervez Musharraf and prevailed on the prime minister to backtrack on moving towards India. Prime Minister Narendra Modi's attitude towards Pakistan and the deteriorating situation on the border was not helpful to Sharif. The military under its new chief, General Raheel Sharif, decided to launch a massive operation in north Waziristan in June 2014, ending Sharif's negotiation option. After the TTP massacre of school children on 16 December 2015, the pendulum of civil-military relations has swung towards the security establishment. Apparently with the consent of the civilian government, the military has placed itself in the driving seat in redefining the country's war on terror and forcing some fundamental shifts in policy, law and institutional roles. A moratorium of about

10 years on the execution of condemned prisoners has been lifted and has facilitated the hanging of terrorists. Parliament has unanimously passed a constitutional amendment allowing the establishment of military courts to try terrorists for the next two years. More importantly, it appears that the civilian government has lost control over critical choices in foreign and national security policy. One Pakistani analyst has termed the evolving political order a 'hybrid' one, a mix of civilian-military informal partnership (Rizvi, 2015). This type of civil-military interaction is the outcome of a national crisis—terrorism and low civilian capacity to lead from the front. Civilian leaders both in the government and opposition parties realise that terrorism poses the gravest threat to national survival. At this stage, they believe that giving a free hand to the armed forces is a national emergency. This may be a more comfortable position than losing everything to the military. The upshot of all these developments is that civilian supremacy remains as unsettled an issue as it ever was. It may eventually find a new equilibrium and stability around it, but when it happens and where it settles is an issue on which one can only speculate.

CONCLUSION

Politics in Pakistan over the past several decades presents an exceptional case of democratic instability or breakdowns. It has seen four direct military interventions since independence and much indirect involvement in which the security establishment played a role in changing governments. Pakistan's inability to hold on to democracy begs more serious questioning of the political elites, the ruling group, the party system and leadership than has been done in scholarly comments on Pakistani politics. The democratic breakdowns have been explained mainly in terms of 'civilian-military imbalance', security or the 'garrison state' syndrome, 'over-development of the state' and other propositions. The problem with approaches using the military as a push factor is that they are static in their analysis and fail to capture the changes in politics, society, or in the orientation of the military as a dynamic organisation. Transitions from military rule are not one event or incident, but long processes that mature when civilian leadership captures the public and social space through efficiency and effective governance.

As previously discussed, there are many factors that make Pakistan's democratic transition incomplete and its consolidation quite uncertain. The most important one is elite politics and power that keeps the economic and political power circulating within limited sections of society. A 'democratic' system functions under the personalised rule of dynastic party leaders, remains closed to new social forces, and has many inner contradictions that increase its vulnerability to the military's direct role or involvement behind the scenes.

At best, Pakistani democracy has crossed one important threshold—the peaceful transfer of power from one party to another. It is an important part of democratic transition but no more than that. While the constitutional means to construct power are in place, the political environment is competitive, elections do take place and new social forces have emerged, the democratic process faces many challenges. Chief amongst them are the crisis of governance, declining capacity of state institutions, poor law and order, political violence and multiple polarisations.

◆

#This chapter was first published in 2015 in the *IIC Quarterly,* Vol. 41, Nos 3 and 4.

NOTES

1. http://www.pewglobal.org/2014/08/27/a-less-gloomy-mood-in-pakistan/ (accessed 27 February 2015).

2. Measured in terms of voter-turnout, participation has increased substantially from 44.23 per cent in the 2008 elections to 55.2 per cent in the 2013 election. *Express Tribune* (Lahore), 21 May 2013.

REFERENCES

Amin, Tahir. 1995. 'Pakistan in 1994: The Politics of Confrontation', *Asian Survey,* Vol. 35, No. 2, February, pp. 140–46.

Burton, Michael and John Higley. 1987. 'Elite Settlements', *American Sociological Review*, Vol. 52, pp. 295–307.

Jalal, Ayesha. 1995. *Democracy and Authoritarianism in South Asia: A Comparative and Historical Perspective.* Lahore: Sang-e-Meel Publications.

Muni, S.D. 2010. *Emerging Dimensions of SAARC.* Delhi: Cambridge University Press.

Rizvi, Hasan Askari. 2015. 'The Civil-Military Hybrid', *Express Tribune*, 23 February.

Ziring, Lawrence. 1971. *The Ayub Khan Era; Politics in Pakistan, 1958–69.* Syracuse: Syracuse University Press.

◆◆

10
NEPAL'S POLICY TOWARDS SAARC

SANGEETA
THAPLIYAL#

The South Asian Association of Regional Countries is in its 30th
year of inception, with Nepal holding the position of Secretary
General for a term of three years. Although the country is
engaged in writing its new constitution, the 18th SAARC Summit
was successfully hosted in Kathmandu in November 2014. The
Summit's emphasis was on 'Deeper Integration for Peace and
Prosperity' in which the SAARC framework agreement for energy
cooperation (electricity) was signed. While the member states
emphasised regional cooperation in 'trade, investment, finance,
energy, security, infrastructure, connectivity and culture, and
the implementation of projects, programmes and activities in a
prioritised, result-oriented and time-bound manner', the Summit
was in the news more for its intent to engage the observer states
as dialogue partners in 'project-based cooperation in priority areas
as identified by the member states'.[1] According to media reports,
Pakistan, Sri Lanka and Nepal wanted to include China as a member
state, but some in Nepal argue that this was the media's creation as
it was not discussed or raised officially. However, the Chinese press
also reported that Nepal's leadership wanted China to have a more
'influential role in SAARC'.[2] These two issues had garnered more
public attention than those far more serious that were discussed in
the forum, highlighting the continuation of the discourse on how
smaller countries use extra-regional powers, including China, as a
balancer to India in the region, or the role they play in regional or
international organisations to pursue their national interests.

Membership to international or regional organisations confers
an identity, a voice and platform to states and, more importantly,

to smaller states to present their point of view to the international community. For small, landlocked countries like Nepal, membership to international organisations becomes important as it gives a voice and presence amidst the dominance of its larger neighbours. Nepal's geographical proximity to India and China has been a major influence in its foreign policy.

CHINA AS A BALANCER

The land-link of the eastern, western and southern borders of Nepal with India has led to socio-cultural, political and economic linkages. This geographical complementarity was emphasised in the special relationship between the two countries from 1950 onwards. With changes in time, context and decision-makers, relations have evolved over the years from special relations to cordial and friendly ties. Apprehending Chinese forces near its northern borders, Nepal signed treaties with India with regard to peace and friendship, and trade and transit. Nepal's relations with Communist China had begun with suspicion arising from developments in Tibet in the 1950s, but the emphasis later shifted to balancing neighbours with the policy of non-alignment and peaceful coexistence from the mid-1950s onwards. Subsequently, Nepal developed diplomatic relations with China in 1955.

A major influence in the foreign policy of Nepal has been the exposition of King Prithvinarayan Shah in his Divine Counsel, where he described Nepal as a yam between boulders, with reference to its two neighbours. Too much reliance on any one country brings about fears of dependence. Landlocked between India and China, Nepal felt the need for regional cooperation, more so because of its economic dependence on India. Since the 1950s, India had been Nepal's biggest aid donor, helping to develop its transport and infrastructure networks. The need grew manifold after political changes occurred in north Nepal. India's aid mission in the Indian Embassy handled projects on modernising education, health, agriculture, power, irrigation, horticulture and veterinary medicine, among others. This economic dependence, along with India's alleged political interference in Nepal, enhanced feelings of vulnerability. For instance, Indian economic assistance was criticised for being channelled through the Planning Commission and not through the External Affairs Ministry, thus placing Nepal on par with other Indian states (Joshi and Rose, 1966: 75–76).

The quest for power between parties, the monarchy taking centre stage in Nepali politics and later banning pro-democratic political parties in the early 1960s, brought in changes in Nepal's foreign policy with an emphasis on non-alignment and equidistance between its neighbours. The change in actors, from democratic forces to the monarchy, was one variable for such a change in emphasis.

Nepal's policy of equidistance between its neighbours was evident in its proposal declaring itself a zone of peace in 1975. The proposal became the major foreign policy objective with the third amendment to the constitution in 1980. However, it was dropped from the new constitution drafted by the democratic government in 1990. In addition, the change in government, from the panchayat to multiparty democracy, changed the tone and tenor of Nepal's foreign policy, from the policy of equidistance to friendly ties with India.

Steeped in its apprehension of submergence with its bigger neighbours, especially with the socio-cultural and economic domination of India, Nepal pursued its policy of independence with caution. Nepal's apprehensions of being denied a fair deal with India on water-sharing emanated from its experience with Kosi and Gandak. With this in mind, Nepal made an attempt to bring the discussion on water from the level of bilateral to regional. In fact, Nepal is the first country in South Asia which proposed regional cooperation on the utilisation of its water resources for hydro-power. While addressing a gathering of foreign delegates to the 26th Colombo Plan Consultative Meeting in Kathmandu in 1977, King Birendra said,

> It is our conviction that if cooperation can be called for, especially, cooperation of Asian countries such as Nepal, India, China, Bhutan, Bangladesh, Pakistan, Sri Lanka and all other regional countries, a vast resource of bountiful nature can be tapped for the benefit of man in this region....Given genuine friendship and mutual cooperation, I declare in the name of my people and my government that Nepal is willing to co-operate in such a joint venture, a venture that will lead not only to 'Planning Prosperity Together' but also

emphasise our independence through interdependence (King Birendra, 1982: 178).

In his statement, the King not only spoke about cooperation with South Asian countries, but also included China, Nepal's northern neighbour. The King laid emphasis on independence through interdependence. The statement had come soon after Nepal had declared itself a zone of peace, an initiative which also emphasised the policy of equidistance. In fact, China and Pakistan had accepted the proposal soon after its announcement. The equation of regime security with national security led Nepal to change its foreign policy. The Nepalese government was apprehensive that the democratic forces challenging it were being supported from India. This led to a shift in Nepal's foreign policy from the special relationship with India to the policy of equidistance, which meant distancing itself from India and developing relations with China. This policy of independence also led Nepal to call attention to regional cooperation.

Bangladesh had floated the idea of a regional organisation in 1980. Nepal accepted Bangladesh's proposal for setting up SAARC. Khosla (2014) writes that Nepal enthusiastically supported the idea of regional cooperation, and its foreign secretary visited Bangladesh, Bhutan, Pakistan and Sri Lanka to lobby for an early summit. Nepal hoped that its zone-of-peace proposal would garner support from regional actors in the new forum.

> Nepal undoubtedly hoped that a regional forum would support its 'Nepal as a zone of peace' proposal, reduce its heavy dependence on its two large neighbours and enlarge the scope for 'balanced interdependence', create solidarity among the smaller countries of the region (presumably against Indian dominance) and eventually, hopefully, include bilateral issues, meaning India-Nepal issues, and thereby act as a pressure point on India (ibid.: 167).

India was apprehensive that regional countries were trying to collectively contain it to the region and isolate it on global issues. In addition, the enthusiasm shown by the Western countries, especially after the Soviet military intervention in Afghanistan, made India cautious about the regional grouping. Indian Prime Minister Indira Gandhi had expressed concern over the involvement of extra-regional power in the regional organisation. At the inaugural meeting of foreign ministers in New Delhi in 1983, Mrs Gandhi said, 'We want to be friends with all on a footing of equality. We should be ever vigilant against the attempts of external powers to influence our functioning' (ibid.: 166).

The SAARC Charter was adopted by regional actors on 7–8 December 1985, with the objective of promoting the overall welfare of South Asians by providing an opportunity to live in dignity and allowing them to realise their full potential, which would help in accelerating the social progress, economic growth and cultural development of the region. There was a common objective in promoting collective self-reliance among the member countries. However, such cooperation had to be consistent with bilateral and multilateral obligations of the member states.[3] SAARC was formed in 1985 to accelerate the process of socio-economic development in the region through the cooperative endeavour of member states on agreed areas. Its main objective was to cooperate positively for regional betterment and not be bogged down by contentious bilateral issues affecting members, which did not need regional discussion.

This Association was Nepal's preferred choice in order to shift from the bilateral mode of cooperation to a regional framework. In 1988, King Birendra once more reiterated that 'Nepal is willing to cooperate in any venture for the multipurpose development of her water resources, bilaterally, trilaterally, or multilaterally, for the mutual benefit of the people of the region'.[4] In the interim, Nepal had bought arms from China in 1988, and tariff concessions to Chinese products made them cheaper than Indian products. These went against the letter and spirit of the treaty of peace and friendship (1950) and the arms assistance agreement of 1965. King Birendra's statement, made to involve international players in harnessing water resources, was timed with domestic compulsions, when his authority was challenged by democratic forces within the country.

Nepal's proposal to include China as a SAARC Observer Member, or Dialogue Partner, followed India's proposal to include Afghanistan as a SAARC member. King Gyanendra had dismissed the democratically elected government and assumed the reins of power in 2005. Not finding a favourable response from India, and in order to balance the Indian influence, he tried to bring in China into SAARC (Baral, 2010: 262). The King was dethroned after the Maoists and the Seven Parties alliance came together, and the dismissed parliament was reinstated in 2006. It was the King's opinion that his endeavour to include China in SAARC at the Dhaka Summit in 2004 did not find approval with India and, as a result, it was with Indian support that the political actors within Nepal dismissed the monarchy from power.

NEPAL'S INITIATIVE TOWARDS SUBREGIONAL COOPERATION

In order to avoid dependence on its neighbours, regional tensions and hiccups to development, Nepal proposed a move towards subregional cooperation. On realising that regional organisation and cooperation was not progressing, Nepal proposed subregional cooperation instead amongst Bangladesh, Bhutan, India and Nepal in December 1996. An Approach Paper was presented in the SAARC Council of Ministers meeting on the feasibility of subregional cooperation in the form of growth polygons, which was defined as 'localised economic cooperation zones where countries with different economic sizes, socio-cultural patterns and political systems have sought to integrate parts of their territories for mutual gains'.[5] Nepal proposed the creation of production complementarities, built around natural resources, for the subregion. The Approach Paper emphasised cooperation in water, energy, environment, transportation, transit, communications, tourism, trade and investments.

Subregional cooperation was discussed by SAARC, and at the Colombo Summit (1998), SAARC members encouraged the 'development of specific projects relevant to the individual needs of three or more member states under the provisions of Articles VII and X of the Charter'.[6] Article VII of the Charter states that 'The Standing Committee may set up Action Committees comprising member states concerned with implementation of projects involving more than two, but not all, member states.' Hence, instead of subregional cooperation, where many developmental projects are required to be undertaken, specific projects under the Action Committee can be submitted to the Council of Ministers of SAARC, which has to approve it on the basis of unanimity, as stated by Article X of the Charter. Thus, the question of isolating any specific country of the region does not arise because all countries, as members of the Council of Ministers of SAARC, have a say in the approval of the specific project.[7]

The idea of the subgroup was to ensure a faster pace of development. It was an additional measure, rather than a substitute for bilateral, regional or multilateral cooperation. Developmental activity in any area within a subgroup would have a spillover effect on other developmental areas within the subgroup and outside the group. Ultimately, subgroup activity would be linked to the entire region, which would ensure the long-term objective of collective self-reliance amongst member states.

Landlocked Nepal faces certain constraints, such as a poor physical infrastructure, weak institutional and productive capacities, small domestic markets, remoteness from world markets and greater vulnerability to external shocks. Hence, Nepal had shown particular interest in cooperation through project-based modes in the areas of infrastructure and energy cooperation, environmental and climate change, especially of mountainous countries.

Nepal's initiative towards subregional cooperation was endorsed by regional actors in the SAARC Summit in the Maldives in 1997. Subsequently, Bangladesh, Bhutan and Nepal requested the Asian Development Bank (ADB) for assistance in facilitating their economic cooperation initiative. This request led to the implementation of the South Asian Subregional Economic Cooperation (SASEC) programme in 2001.

The Asian Development Bank (ADB) serves as Secretariat to the SASEC Programme. ADB supports SASEC countries in strengthening regional ties for growth and promoting cooperation and provides financial and technical support to improve connectivity, strengthen institutions and trade links, and expand human capital.[8]

Energy and power, transport linkages, trade and investment are some of the main areas identified by SASEC.

However, the subregional approach was unsuccessful. Bangladesh and Nepal had approached the ADB without taking India into confidence. The trust deficit on regional cooperation and the attempt made by neighbours to bring in extra-regional players did influence India's perception of SAARC.

The progress and development of SAARC could not dispel the apprehensions of the member countries about each other and about the organisation. In accordance with the SAARC Charter, bilateral and contentious issues are not discussed, although they have been discussed outside the SAARC forum and sometimes attract more attention than SAARC summits themselves. However, power politics persist within SAARC. King Gyanendra's attempt to bring in China as an observer state in the Dhaka Summit in 2004, India's endeavour to bring in other observer states such as Australia, China, the European Union, Iran, Japan, the Republic of Korea, Mauritius, Myanmar and the US, highlight power play and the attempt at balancing forces within the forum.

In the 18th SAARC Summit, China displayed its interest in elevating its role in the forum. Speaking to the press, the Chinese foreign ministry spokesperson Hua Chunying said, 'We value the role played by SAARC and stand ready to elevate our partnership with it so that together we can play a greater role and contribute constructively to the region'.[9] China has been trying to play a bigger role in the region. Since the pro-Tibetan demonstrations in Nepal in 2008 during the Beijing Olympics, China has been increasing its presence through economic-aid packages, investments in defence and infrastructure. 'As of July 2012, 428 projects under Chinese investment came [in] to operation in Nepal with [an] investment of ₹7,860 million which helped create 26,651 jobs'.[10] Nepal is emerging as a tourist destination for Chinese nationals. In 2012, the number of tourist arrivals was 42,518 which had increased to 89,509 in 2013.[11]

Within this context, China too would like to play an increased role in SAARC and this is clear by the statement made by the Chinese representative at the Kathmandu Summit. China's Vice Foreign Minister Liu Zhen Min said, 'China has put forward a series of initiatives (including) increasing trade between South Asia and China to 150 billion US dollars and investment to 30 billion US dollars in the next five years.' The latter sum would go towards road construction, he further said. In its endeavour, China finds Nepal, along with Pakistan and Sri Lanka, as a willing partner. 'SAARC may be neither India-centric nor India-driven but is, in the view of these members, India-dominated. With China on board, these countries assume that the balance of power would shift in their favour' (Shastri, 2014). If India–Pakistan tensions, or regional politics, still influence SAARC proceedings, then power play by giving China a bigger role in the regional body would affect the cooperative spirit further.

These political issues have overshadowed economic interests in official corridors. In 30 years, SAARC has not achieved the desired results, whether it is India–Pakistan relations, or the suspicions of smaller countries, or free trade due to political hurdles, such as Pakistan's refusal to extend the Most Favoured Nation status to India despite both being members of the World Trade Organisation (WTO). In addition, technical committees of integrated programmes of action have failed to move towards actual critical areas, which can make this cooperation tangibly effective and sustainable (Lama, 1998: 43). This makes SAARC an institution that merely identifies areas for cooperation without effectively putting words into action.

Since India is the largest country in the region sharing boundaries with all its neighbours, 'it is condemned to be both the necessary engine as well as the likely obstacle in the fulfilment of SAARC's potential' (Rajan, n.d.). India's economic relations with South Asian countries, at best, are at the bilateral level. Neighbouring countries are aware of India's growing economy and would like a share in it as well. With an emphasis on good neighbourhood policy, Prime Minister Modi, during his visits to Nepal, spoke of the need for economic cooperation, and linkages in highway, information and technology. At the SAARC Summit, Modi said,

> Infrastructure is my greatest priority in India. And, I also want to set up a Special Purpose Facility in India to finance infrastructure projects in our region that enhances our connectivity and trade. We speak of ease of doing business in India. Let's extend this to our region. I promise to ensure that our facilities at the border will speed up, not slow down, trade.[12]

In fact, in the first week of February 2014, representatives from Bangladesh, Bhutan, India and Nepal met in New Delhi to discuss subregional cooperation for working out a model for power trade and inter-grid connectivity (Gilani, 2015). The efforts to bring in economic cooperation through bilateral or regional/subregional cooperation would help Nepal refurbish its economy that had suffered due to years of political instability. The motto of the 18th SAARC Summit—'Deeper Integration for Peace and Prosperity'— best illustrates the manner in which individual and regional concerns of member countries may be addressed. In order to achieve this, member countries should make an effort to bring economic cooperation back on the rails rather than fritter away energies on power play.

◆

This chapter was first published in 2015 in the *IIC Quarterly*, Vol. 41, Nos 3 and 4.

NOTES

1. Kathmandu Declaration. 2014. Eighteenth SAARC Summit. Kathmandu. http://www.saarc-sec.org/userfiles/Summit%20Declarations/Kathmandu-18thSummit26-27Nov2013.pdf (accessed 18 December 2014).

2. 'Nepal Leaders, Experts Call for China's Active Role in SAARC' . Xinhuanet.com, 23 November 2014. http://news.xinhuanet.com/english/china/2014-11/23/c_133808733.htm. (accessed 19 February 2015). Also check 'Nepal Leaders, Experts Call for China's Active Role in SAARC'. Chinadaily.com.cn. 24 November 2014. http://www.chinadaily.com.cn/world/2014-11/24/content_18965934.htm

3. Charter of the South Asian Association of Regional Cooperation. 1985. http://saarc-sdmc.nic.in/pdf/charter.pdf (accessed 29 January 2015).

4. Statement by His Majesty Birendra Bir Bikram Shah Dev, King of Nepal. Fourth SAARC Summit. 29–31 December 1998. Islamabad, Pakistan.

5. 'Approach Paper for Subregional Cooperation in SAARC: Executive Summary', presented by Nepal in the Council of Ministers' Conference in New Delhi, 18–19 December 1996.

6. Declaration of the 10th SAARC Summit. Colombo. 31 July 1998. http://www.saarc-sec.org/userfiles/Summit%20Declarations/10%20-%20Colombo%20-%20 10th%20Summit%201998.pdf (accessed 29 January 2015).

7. Charter of the South Asian Association of Regional Cooperation. 1985. http://saarc-sdmc.nic.in/pdf/charter.pdf (accessed 29 January 2015).

8. SASEC. http://sasec.asia/index.php?page=what-is-sasec (accessed 11 December 2013).

9. 'China Says it Wants to Elevate Partnership with SAARC.' *The Economic Times.* 25 November 2015.

10. Bilateral Relations (Nepal–China). Kathmandu. Ministry of Foreign Affairs, Government of Nepal. http://www.mofa.gov.np/en/nepal-china-relations-78.html (accessed 10 January 2015).

11. Ibid.

12. Text of Prime Minister's speech at 2014 SAARC Summit in Nepal. 26 November 2014. http://www.narendramodi.in/text-of-prime-ministers-speech-at-2014-saarc-summit-in-nepal/ (accessed 18 December 2014).

REFERENCES

Baral, Lok Raj. 2010. 'A Nepali Perspective', in S.D. Muni (ed.), *The Emerging Dimensions of SAARC*. New Delhi: Foundation Books.

Gilani, Iftikhar. 2015. 'SAARC Subregional Group Kicks Off.' *DNA*. 4 February. http://www.dnaindia.com/india/report-saarc-sub-regional-group-kicks-off-2057994 (accessed 5 February 2015).

Joshi, Bhuwanlal and Leo E. Rose. 1966. *Democratic Innovations in Nepal*. Berkeley: University of California Press.

Khosla I.P., 2013. *How Neighbours Converge: The Politics and Economics of Regionalism*. New Delhi: Konark Publishers.

King Birendra, H.M. 1982. *Proclamations, Speeches and Messages, 1972–81*. Kathmandu: His Majesty's Government Press.

Lama, Mahendra, P. 1998. 'SAARC Integrated Programme of Action: Towards More Effective Cooperation', *South Asian Survey*. Vol. 5. No. 1.

Rajan, K.V. 'Renewing SAARC'. www.alternative-regionalisms.org/wp-content/uploads/2009/.../rajan.pdf (accessed 20 December 2014).

Shastri, Ramachandran. 2014. 'China in SAARC: Time to Weigh the Pros and Cons.' *DNA*. 23 February 2014. http://www.dnaindia.com/analysis/column-china-in-saarc-time-to-weigh-the-pros-and-cons-1964516) (accessed 2 February 2015).

11
BANGLADESH IN SAARC
Identity Issues and Perspectives

SANJAY K.
BHARDWAJ[#]

INTRODUCTION

In the 21st century, the world as a whole has been experiencing enormous change as the forces of liberalisation and globalisation are leading to its transformation into a global community. The intensity of development in South Asia has also been accompanied by sustainable economic growth. Consequently, the majority of South Asian states are now expanding their strategies to take advantage of the nascent opportunities of development. India and its neighbours are either reaching out to other countries for their developmental needs and defence requirements, or nurturing the possibilities of strengthening their regional institutional framework. Nevertheless, with China's relative rise and its expanding footprint in South Asia, new questions are being raised about Indian leadership in the region. New challenges are fast emerging, with neighbours vociferously demanding China's induction as a member of SAARC. These challenges are taking place at a time when India's foreign policy is assuming a new dimension under the leadership of Prime Minister Narendra Modi.

The landslide victory of the Bhartiya Janta Party (BJP)-led National Democratic Alliance (NDA) has, in more ways than one, broken the stranglehold of coalition politics in India. It now provides the requisite space and framework to reflect on and analyse several trends: first, in India, the focal point of the election shifted from the primitive agenda of religious majority–minority interface and regional–nationalistic stratification to a more modern school of thought, i.e., development and transformation which is all-inclusive; second, the invitation extended to the heads of governments of SAARC states to attend Narendra Modi's oath-taking ceremony was viewed as an emphasis on policy by India on its neighbourhood; third, the prime minister's first foreign visit to Bhutan, followed by Nepal, and the foreign minister's visit to Bangladesh, were applauded as steps towards a more friendly, peaceful and economically integrated South Asia in which extra-regional powers would have less influence. The implications of the present dispensation of India and responses by neighbours might contour the regional developmental politics of the region.

Nonetheless, many South Asian states are still focused on their national identities (inclusive/exclusive), which implicitly impede the process of regional integration. Despite significant common characteristics in terms of traditions, culture and language, they have built a hostile nationalistic base. This is evident through the increasing voices and patterns of the ethno-religious (Pakistan), religious-cultural (Bangladesh) and ethno-lingual (Sri Lanka) identities among these states which are becoming the basis for their respective national constructs. These are contested not just at home, but also at the regional level. The secular-democratic strand (India) has also come under attack from fascist-dictatorial regimes in the region.

Within this context, and taking Bangladesh's dispensation in SAARC, this chapter is an attempt to understand how far the battles over the nationalistic identity constructs within the state and the region have adversely impacted the efforts of the regional integration process in South Asia. What are the factors responsible for its slow progress? What does it take to initiate a regional organisation like SAARC? What are the requisites for its success?

SOUTH ASIA AS A REGION

The South Asian region is a cluster of geographically proximate countries that share common historical bonds, cultural and social affinities, economic, political and strategic interests. In terms of sheer numbers, SAARC certainly does not fail to impress with eight members and nine observer countries. A compact geographic expanse covering the whole of the South Asian subcontinent, ranging from the Hindu Kush in the north to the Maldives in the

South, a total of 1,980,992 square miles and 1.6 billion people make it the largest regional organisation (population-wise) in the world (De, 2013). However, these characteristics appear to be less impressive while examining the negative political and socio-economic developments in the region. The post-independent states of South Asia have suffered from a number of 'mutinies' and incidents in which democratically elected governments were toppled. At the regional level, too, the countries do not exhibit a strong desire to live in harmony and cooperation.

Geographically, India shares its border with almost all South Asian states, causing neighbours to feel 'India Centric'. However, Bangladesh lies along the Bay of Bengal, with a limited land border with Myanmar in the south and south-east. In fact, these geographical conditions cause Bangladesh to feel 'India locked'. The two Himalayan countries, Bhutan and Nepal, are also 'land locked'. Furthermore, there are vast geographic, economic and military disparities between India and other South Asian states, in which the former dominates the region, while the latter suffer from what may be termed as small-state fear psychosis. This small state insecurity syndrome vis-à-vis India has been demonstrated by the religious-cultural constructs of their interstate relationship.

IDENTITY AND REGIONAL COOPERATION

Katzenstein has observed that in scholarly analysis, domestic politics often works as a determinant of the making of foreign policy: 'the main purpose of all strategies of foreign economic policy is to make domestic policies compatible with the international political economy' (1976). However, from the perspective of regional integration, Deutsch (1957) and Haas (1958) have examined the influence of parties and interest groups on regional integration. In the same vein, Putnam (1988) observes that liberal democracies are always influenced by two level games: one at the domestic level and the other at the international level in the negotiation process. Decision-makers cannot neglect either while making policies. At the national level, domestic groups pursue their interests by pressurising the government to adopt favourable policies, and politicians seek power by constructing coalitions among those groups. At the international level, national governments seek to maximise their own ability to satisfy domestic pressures, while minimising the adverse consequences of foreign developments. Neither of the two games can be ignored by the central decision-makers, so long as their countries remain interdependent, yet sovereign (ibid.).

Most South Asian states inevitably allow domestic sensitivities, and regional interdependence and vulnerability in bilateral relations and regional cooperation. However, the problem becomes even more acute when developing states, such as Bangladesh and Pakistan, with their fragile democratic institutions, attempt to survive in an international regional system. Religious nationalistic discourse, small-state insecurity and counterbalancing strategies have been used for political discourse as well as to meet the crisis of legitimacy in these states. The conflicts of economic, strategic and social interest have tended to reinforce regimes to practise anti-Indian strands of nationalism. Indian policy-makers have also worsened the situation by the inept handling of such conflict spillovers. These strategies have been scrutinised within the framework of Bangladesh's dispensation in SAARC.

BANGLADESHI IDENTITY IN REGIONAL CONSTRUCTS

In post-independence South Asian states, anti-colonial tendencies faced multifarious problems of ethnicity, religion and region. With the disappearance of the 'other', which was the colonial master, the veneer of glue that welded these disparate communities precariously into a national movement began to yield to numerous fissiparous tendencies. Consequently, many post-independent states plunged into the vortex of either military dictatorships, or religious resurgence, or ethnic backlash. This happened primarily because of the erosion of the anti-colonial nationalistic hegemony and the crisis of legitimacy, which was tackled either by invoking primordial appeals such as religion, ethnicity and language, or harbouring anti-neighbour constituencies, or by resorting to the discipline and repression of military dispensations or, most often, by all the above factors working in concurrence.

The birth of Bangladesh was an epoch-making event in the history of South Asia which arguably negated the 'two-nation theory'. It clearly demonstrated that religion alone is not sufficient to exhaust the factors that constitute the forging of a nation. Bangladesh was the product of linguistic nationalism, or 'Bengali nationalism', rearing its head against religious hegemony. Understandably,

'Bengali nationalism' was inherently secular in nature, and this trait of the liberation struggle helped found the nation, based on the four pillars of secularism, socialism, democracy and nationalism.

Nonetheless, Bangladesh has had the distinction of having undergone two national movements—in 1947 and 1971. Having been put to mutilation twice has impacted the fashioning of identities in a peculiar way—perhaps it is the confusing situation of the old being dead and the new not yet being born; and, in the interregnum, national space being initially occupied by muffled constructions of secularism, socialism and democracy, only to be replaced later by military dictatorships coupled with a strident Islamic hegemony (Bhardwaj, 2011).

In fact, the post-independent ruling elites in Bangladesh have shaped the distinct nationalistic political discourses within the 'liberal-secular-cultural' and 'religious nationalistic tendency with Islam at its core'. These distinct national political leanings have been used, time and again, for legitimacy and counterweight strategy by military and democratic regimes.

The general trend was that when the Awami League (AL), along with progressive left-wing political parties, formed the government in Bangladesh, it usually maintained cordial relations with India. However, when the Bangladesh Nationalist Party (BNP),[1] along with other religious right-wing political parties, came to power it generally maintained an attitude of mistrust towards India and developed religious-strategic ties with Pakistan and China, respectively. The latter alliance has constantly adopted an anti-Indian foreign policy stance as a counterbalancing strategy. Indeed, this construction in Bangladeshi politics had paved the way for the initiation of SAARC as a regional organisation, and even after its foundation, meetings and issues of discussions were influenced by the type of political power in place. These forces in Bangladesh have striking characteristics, functionalities and idiosyncrasies, and can be separated into three distinct strata: liberal, radical and rational.

LIBERALS, RADICALS, RATIONALISTS

Liberals are identified by their belief in the principles of mutual respect, coexistence, brotherhood, and friendly ties with neighbours with whom they share linguistic and cultural bonds, and historical legacies. As the moderate and educated class with shared values, they proposed the ideas of democracy and regional cooperation and stood by one another in the hour of need. It is their firm belief that India helped Bangladesh in the Liberation War of 1971; they consider India their ally, look forward to amicable ties and are desirous of living in peace and harmony with their bigger neighbour.

As may been seen by rhetorical proclamations, India's unintended, but stray, attempts to emphasise its common ethnic and cultural affinities with its neighbours and foster cooperation was misconstrued and eventually backfired as this was supposedly perceived to threaten the status of their hard-earned national identity. Thus, at the other extreme are radical forces which construct the exclusive nationalist discourse in state and foreign policy formulation. These forces possess and promote the sentiments of religious fanaticism and carry a heavy baggage of the memories of 1947's partition of India, based on the two-nation theory. They maintain an anti-neighbour, ethno-religious nationalistic posture for political discourse. Old Muslim Leaguers bear these ideals, both in Bangladesh and Pakistan (an Islamic state).

After 1975, Bangladesh came to resent India's overpowering presence in the region, and India, in course of time, became one of the central issues around which its domestic politics revolved. India-baiting came to be one of the most effective ways of burnishing one's nationalist credentials in neighbouring domestic politics, and political parties made full use of this tactic. Apart from engaging India in a collective manner at the regional level, this section of the ruling elite forwarded their alliance with China, Pakistan or Saudi Arabia for political mileage to counterbalance India in the region. They are hegemonic fundamentalists and promote religious extremism by their actions. For long, Bangladesh has been an ardent supporter of China's inclusion in SAARC. China's comparative military edge over India and their mutual hostilities after the 1962 border war strategically favoured many South Asian states, particularly Pakistan and later Bangladesh, both with a common interest of containing India in the South Asian region.

In between these two poles of liberals and radicals is an educated, moderate, neo-institutional and development-centric young generation which could be called the rationalists. This generation considers education, trade, healthcare, infrastructure and economic liberation as the core of all political and diplomatic action.

They believe in better lifestyles, employment opportunities and are inspired by the spectacular growth of industries such as Information Technology and Information Technology Enabled Services (IT, ITES) in India and other parts of the world. Rationalists believe in resolving all outstanding bilateral issues on the principles of parity and equity. At the same time, they are also strong critics of any unilateral action in dealing with issues of transnational importance. This generation is keen to be a partner in the process of economic growth and development, and is also not sceptical about an alliance with extra-regional powers. It is this young, educated, middle class that has created a proactive force in the region, including in India, by channelising its strengths towards the broader objectives of political and economic cooperation and not merely the myopic aim of promoting the cause of ethno-religious forces.

This generation had given a massive mandate to the Awami League-led alliance in the 2008 general election of Bangladesh, based on the promises of development and cooperation. With a similar agenda, the Modi-led BJP had also recorded a phenomenal victory in the 2014 elections. Thus, in today's political scenario, rationalists have become the key determinant of regional integration and cooperation in areas of mutual interest amongst neighbours. A paradigm shift of mindsets at almost all levels of government in both countries has been witnessed regarding regional/subregional cooperation, following their long-held obsession of bilateralism. It has been realised that there are some issues about which countries need to think beyond the bounds of bilateralism, and the two prime ministers have signed the historic 'Framework Agreement on Cooperation for Development'. It was perhaps at the 37 Joint Rivers Commission (JRC) meeting in Delhi where India, for the first time, had agreed to discuss water issues beyond the bilateral parameter by bringing Nepal into the fold in a bid to work out a sustainable strategy for ensuring water security for the region.

SMALL-STATE STRATEGY AND BANGLADESH'S REGIONAL CONSTRUCT

In real terms, a small state is always guided by the 'constraint of inefficiency' in the international sphere. This has certain implications on foreign policy-making towards powerful neighbours. Owing to the asymmetry in size, economy and military power, a small state looks forward to reliable options to strengthen its bargaining edge vis-à-vis its powerful neighbours. It attempts to survive in the international system rather than to play a dominant role (Afroze, 2005). If its real potentiality remains inadequate, it generates the 'insecurity syndrome', which further influences the state's behaviourial pattern.

The smaller states of South Asia have generally adopted three strategies to deal with India. Pakistan, for instance, has strategically collaborated with extra-regional powers. Bhutan, on the other hand, has developed positive collaborations with India as the big neighbour with enormous opportunities. Bangladesh, Nepal and Sri Lanka believe in developing positive engagement through multilateral institutional frameworks for situational benefits, the approach determining the fate of these frameworks. Thus, structural constraints are the most important determinant of a state's behaviour in international politics, with the smaller states soon 'balancing' against Indian preponderance in the region.

On the flip side, regional power also evolves as an efficient regional institutional mechanism in handling critical issues emanating from immediate neighbours. A multilateral or bilateral device thus develops in the exploration of opportunities in the region which tackles the critical politico-security and economic challenges that emanate as a result. Time and again, confrontations with neighbours took place with the intention of minimising the increasing influences of extra-regional powers. Consequently, India signed certain principled institutions, agreements and treaties with its neighbours and has also played the role of a responsible regional power by unilaterally donating funds for developmental programmes in the region (Dixit, 1996).

Bangladesh is a small South Asian state with limited military and economic capacity; its potential mismatch with India has generated the small-state fear psychosis. The country's inability to protect its sovereignty and developmental interests had constrained it to initiate a regional organisation. A multilateral regional forum was part of its small-state strategy to ally itself with other small states in the region in order to engage India collectively. It was assumed that this would empower better negotiations to counter the fear of a big and powerful neighbour on the regional platform. In fact, the problems and concerns of these smaller states are peripheral rather than global.

After the assassination of Sheikh Mujibur Rehman, Bangladesh's bilateral relations with India were strained. The comparative inferiority complex and the compulsion to deal with India in bilateral discourse and diplomatic negotiations motivated the then military regime headed by General Zia-ur Rehman to consider a regional platform (Bhasin, 2003). Salamat Ali (1980) describes it as an attempt to create a forum in which the waywardness of one member could be corrected by the combined pressure of the others. Later, the viewpoint that members respect 'the principles of sovereign equality, territorial integrity, national independence, non-use of force and non-interference in the internal affairs of other states and peaceful settlement of all disputes' was also incorporated in the SAARC Charter.[2] This declaration was to assure an independent role for small states. In fact, Bangladesh initiated the SAARC process with two intentions, the first being the outcome of Bangladesh's fear of lack of potentiality (system affecting states) to counter India at the negotiation table. The second was to attract the sympathy of regional communities and to impose multilateral regional pressure on India. Thus, Bangladesh's strategy was to counter India's ability to negotiate on bilateral problems.

At the initial stage, India was also apprehensive about the formation of such a regional organisation. As J. N. Dixit stated:

> India had reservations initially about the establishment of SAARC when President Zia-ur Rehman proposed such an association in 1980. Indira Gandhi's anticipatory perception was that such a grouping would serve as a forum for countries such as Bangladesh, Sri Lanka and Pakistan to exert collective pressure on India on issues on which they differed from India (1996: 383).

As the small neighbour of a regional power, Bangladesh has always been paranoiacally fearful of Indian domination, and the efforts towards more superpower engagement in the region are an attempt to address this fear. Bangladesh's desire to create SAARC was to build a South Asian collective forum to regionally engage India (Sabur, 2000). Thus, the strategic dimension behind Bangladesh's initiative was to dilute the so-called *India doctrine*.[3] Later, Bangladesh often used SAARC as a platform to raise bilateral problems and has never hesitated to work 'in tandem with Pakistan on issues affecting India' (Dixit, 1996).

CHINA AS A COUNTERWEIGHT STRATEGY IN SAARC
China is keen to integrate with SAARC with Bangladesh's help. The intention behind Bangladesh's support is to counter India's domination in regional matters. Chinese back-up has provided Bangladesh with more bargaining capability at the international level against India. During Sheikh Hasina's China visit in March 2010, both Bangladesh and China decided to deepen cooperation in the South Asian region and praised each other's role in SAARC, expressing their appreciation of the active efforts made to promote regional cooperation. The two sides agreed to strengthen communication and coordination in regional cooperation (Bhardwaj, 2014). However, 'market-led economic reforms' have also been promoting the region as vitally economic and the cynosure of trans-regional cooperation. At present, China enjoys observer status in SAARC. Greater Chinese involvement with SAARC will widen the economic scope of the region while simultaneously increasing Chinese influence.

This strategy of courting China is not yet typical of Pakistan and Bangladesh's foreign policy, but other states in the region—including both Sri Lanka and Nepal—have frequently used it to counterbalance India. True to its hegemonic overtures in the region, China has been more than willing to play the role of a 'counterbalancer' in SAARC as it not only strengthens Beijing's influence in South Asia as a subregion, but also keeps India distracted in regional affairs by creating obstacles in its efforts to become a significant player in the region and, by implication, globally. Thus, China has emerged as the most feasible option and containment force against India in South Asia. China has notably collaborated with the non-India friendly regimes of South Asia and assured them economic and defence assistance. Therefore, it has been noticed, time and again, that Bangladesh has pushed the Chinese quest to become a member of SAARC.

CONCLUSION

While regional cooperation in general has been successfully initiated and implemented in most regions of the world, South Asia remains 'the least integrated region in the world'. SAARC was started three decades ago, but it has achieved little so far. Meetings are held regularly, though not always; when sudden tensions crop up, cooperation with regard to trade and development slows down. Efforts to develop person-to-person contact are numerous, but limited success has been achieved in terms of developing a sense of common identity. One obvious problem has been the acute hostility between India and Pakistan, along with other rivalries over the years. We are yet to learn to look beyond these.

South Asian countries may learn from the countries of the European Union (EU), a pioneer example of regional integration since early 1950s, which have also faced multifarious problems in the 20th century. This regional institution, conceived by visionary politicians such as Robert Schuman of France and Konrad Adenauer of Germany, envisaged a new form of politics based on the supranational 'community method' rather than the traditional balance-of-power model (Cameron, 2010). Despite many problems, the leadership, generated by Paris and Berlin (the Franco-German axis) has been, and remains, the driving force behind European integration. EU member countries have deliberately foregone parts of their state sovereignty and adopted a common currency, working together in matters of security under the umbrella of the Common Foreign and Security Policy (CFSP) and the Common Security and Defence Policy (CSDP).

In South Asia's case, India and Pakistan may shed their baggage and lead the process of regional integration in which smaller states such as Bangladesh may contribute their efforts to strengthen SAARC. South Asian countries have consistently been voicing their concerns and persistently underlining their expectations for cooperation in a host of areas including connectivity, security, migration, trade and commerce. There are a number of framework agreements in the areas of food and energy security, terrorism, human trafficking, maritime security and piracy, natural disasters, global warming, poverty and sustaining economic growth, which are included in SAARC. Its members should implement these joint declarations and conventions with complete commitment and sincerity. The recently held 18th SAARC summit in Kathmandu has emphasised the need for cooperation to integrate the South Asian region. In the declaration, heads of states or governments expressed their strong determination to deepen regional integration for peace, stability and prosperity in South Asia by intensifying cooperation, inter alia, in trade, investment, finance, energy, security, infrastructure, connectivity and culture, and implementing projects, programmes and activities in a prioritised, result-oriented and time-bound manner.[4] However, to strengthen the implementation aspect, SAARC has to be equipped with a good number of skilled staff and sufficient funds.

In fact, linguistic–cultural bonds and religious linkages have not given the neighbours an impetus in maintaining enduring warm relations; rather, these connections have been turned into a fear factor—the 'India factor'—that determines the fate of regional cooperation. Integration ventures have been stalled by narrow politico-strategic interpretations. In reality, any cooperation among the South Asian states implies the sharing of national control over natural resources, even physical and social infrastructure. For the Westphalian state, the abandonment of national control over natural resources involves the loss of national sovereignty. This element brings fear psychosis into play amongst smaller states leading to reluctance, and precipitates a withdrawal syndrome from the process of regional cooperation. For example, tackling perceptions with regard to national sovereignty on natural resources (energy, connectivity and trade corridors, etc.) are major issues among the states of South Asia (Lama, 1999). However, on the security issue, it has implications for India as well. The cross-border movement of violent non-state actors has ruined the regional environment, while battles over territorial and border disputes have also stalled regional cooperation.

A glaring feature of contemporary South Asia is the non-existence of a peace and cooperation constituency. Non-military Confidence Building Measures (CBMs) are very critical to the enhancement of cooperation among South Asian states and those built by economic stakeholders have mostly sustained themselves. It is critical to consider measures by which commonalities are stressed, since this could contribute to a greater understanding. Education could play a key role in this area. SAARC University is a resource that could be developed, but we also should think in terms of programmes that can easily be administered in the area as a whole, with both staff and students coming together for pedagogical purposes. Developing common publications for all levels of the educational system can also help. If the governments genuinely want to address the economic and security concerns of this region, they have to act as responsible, committed actors/leaders in the region. 'Constructive Unilateralism' may resolve many of the irritants with neighbours.

◆

#This chapter was first published in 2015 in the *IIC Quarterly,* Vol. 41, Nos 3 and 4.

NOTES

1. BNP was founded by the then military regime of General Zia-ur Rehman in 1979, who initiated the creation of SAARC.

2. SAARC, Charter of the South Asian Association for Regional Cooperation [Online Web] Accessed 5 March 2015 URL:http://saarc-sdmc.nic.in/pdf/charter.pdf.

3. India Doctrine is the South Asian version of Monroe Doctrine and reflects India's view of the entire region as a single strategic unit and herself as the sole custodian of security and stability in the region. See Sabur (2000: 639–42).

4. Kathmandu Declaration, Eighteenth SAARC Summit 25–27 November 2014, http://www.mea.gov.in/Uploads/PublicationDocs/24375_EIGHTEENTH_SUMMIT_DECLARATION.pdf)

REFERENCES

Afroze, Shaheen. 2005. 'Small States in Global Respective: In Search of a Role Model in Regional Stability', in Mohammad Humayun Kabir (ed.) *Small States and Regional Stability in South Asia.* Dhaka: University Press Limited.

Ali, Salamat. 1980. 'The Multilateral Session', *Far Eastern Economic Review,* Hong Kong: 32.

Bhardwaj, Sanjay. 2014. 'Policy Options for India in Bangladesh: An Agenda for the New Government', Institute of Peace and Conflict Studies, Issue Brief, No. 251.

Bhardwaj, Sanjay K. 2011. 'Contesting Identities in Bangladesh: A Study of Secular and Religious Frontiers.' ARC working paper No. 36, LSE, London http://www2.lse.ac.uk/asiaResearchCentre/_files/ARCWP36-Bhardwaj.pdf

Bhasin, Avtar Singh (ed.) 2003. *India-Bangladesh Relations: Documents 1971–2002, V-I,* New Delhi: Geetika Publishers.

Cameron, Fraser. 2010. 'The European Union as a Model for Regional Integration', Council on Foreign Relations. January 2015.

De, Prabir. 2013. 'Connectivity, Trade Facilitation and Regional Cooperation in South Asia', http://ris.org.in/images/RIS_images/pdf

Deutsch, Karl W. 1957. *Political Communities in the North Atlantic Area: International Organization in the Light of Historical Experiences*. Princeton: Princeton University Press.

Dixit, J.N. 1996. *My South Block Years: Memories of a Foreign Secretary*. New Delhi: USB Publishers Distributors Ltd.

Hass, Ernst B. 1958. *The Uniting of Europe: Political Social and Economic Forces, 1950–1957*. Stanford: Stanford University Press.

Katzenstein, Peter J. 1976. 'International Relations and Domestic Structure: Foreign Economic Policies of Advanced Industrial States', *International Organization*, 30, Winter, pp. 1–45.

Lama, Mahendra P. 1999. *Energy Cooperation In South Asia: Issues Challenges & Potential*. New Delhi: South Solidarity.

Putnam, Robert D. 1988. 'Diplomacy and Domestic Politics: The Logic of Two-Level Games', *International Organization*, 42(3), pp. 427–60.

Sabur, A.H.M. Abdus. 2000. 'Foreign Policy of Bangladesh: Challenges in the 1990s', in Virinder Grover (ed.) *Bangladesh: Government and Politics.* New Delhi: Deep and Deep Publications.

12
NEPAL, SAARC AND SOUTHASIA

KANAK
MANI DIXIT#

There are certain advantages that accrue to being the oldest nation state in the subcontinent, and Nepal enjoys them. In a country which was established nearly two-and-a-half centuries ago through the unification drive of King Prithvi Narayan Shah, society developed a resilience that can only come from a shared and continuous history, outside the colonial embrace. It is true that nation building in the nation state is an incomplete project, and the marginalised communities of mountain, hill and plain are crying foul against the Kathmandu Valley-centric state. But Nepali, the link language, oils the political discourse and the resulting earthiness gives the polity an edge that is not available to the colonised parts of Southasia where the English-to-vernacular emerges as a sharp class divide, also impacting the practice of politics.

Nepal is also the only subcontinental country that has a historically evolved land frontier (with India), rather than being carved out at the hands of the departing *saheb*. This has also meant that the border is open, even as elsewhere Partition generated inter-capital animosities that foisted closed borders and harsh visa requirements that continue to this day. Because of various historical factors and the lack of obvious 'enemies' in the neighbourhood, plus its touristic orientation in the modern era, Nepal has the most liberal visa regime in the region. Citizens from all over the subcontinent, except Afghanistan, get visa-on-arrival in Kathmandu, and this also holds true for arrivals from much of the rest of the world.

As a country, there is a particular public attitude evident to most visitors to Nepal—that the country is 'friendly'. This seems to help the growth of tourism as an industry, which has prospered since the 'opening' of the country in the 1950s, not only because of the natural wonders of Nepal, but also the openness to outsiders exhibited by the population. This is not a romantic notion meant for the tourism brochures, but has actually to do with the national demography. The national population is the cumulative total of many small communities, with the largest caste/ethnicity being no larger than 17 per cent. There is no one big numerical majority or a significant minority group, which makes Nepal a country only of minorities, though of course there are those communities which are privileged and others that have been marginalised. The micro-communities are required to be open to each other for the sake of economic survival, which is what gives Nepal that particular flavour of social harmony, a reading that is based on sociological rather than fanciful notions.

Nepal has geographical centrality between the nation states of the northern half of the subcontinent, where in fact the bulk of the Southasian population lives—more than 700 million in the catchment and plains of the Brahmaputra, Ganga and Indus. Nepal is thus accessible both by visa regime and geographical placement, with an open border linking it to the largest country of the subcontinent in terms of economy, population and geopolitical prowess. The lack of bilateral animosity linked to the fallout of Partition makes Nepal a country that is acceptable to all. This is also the reason why Kathmandu was the obvious choice for the establishment of the Secretariat of the South Asian Association for Regional Cooperation (SAARC).

AREAS OF DISSONANCE

While history, geography and demography thus allow Nepal to emerge as an important hub and meeting place for a Southasia that seeks to prosper through regionalism and cross-border contact, there are nevertheless weaknesses in terms of Nepal's ability to engage with Southasia and utilise its centrality for the sake of regional peace and prosperity. In particular, there are some incongruous factors in relation to Nepal's relationship to big neighbour India. The most important factor which would challenge Nepal's image as well as engagement with Southasia is the fact that Nepali citizens were in the Indian military as part of the Gorkha regiment and other units. This is a historical legacy dating back to the British military's use of

Nepal's citizenry as soldiers through formal bilateral agreement. This formal relationship was extended to India after 1947, when there was a division of what was then the 'Gurkha' regiments between the UK and the Indian republic. This incongruous situation sits heavily on Nepal as a member of SAARC, and is also something deliberately ignored by all members of the regional organisation for the sake of general amity. And the reality is that, in its continuing state of economic distress throughout the modern era, Nepal is not in a position to pull out of the arrangement, given the important income Gorkha service brings to the 'martial tribes' and to the national economy as a whole. However, there is no denying the dissonance when it comes to the reality of a sovereign country of Southasia allowing its citizens to fight for another (against a third country).

How does the incongruous situation arise—of a sovereign country in the modern era that seeks regionalism to also allow its citizens to fight for a neighbour against another neighbour? The answer lies in the anti-democratic system and subsequent political chaos which have acted like a cap on the polity and economy throughout Nepal's modern-day existence, sapping the genius of the people while preventing economic growth and equity. As a result, among other things, Nepali society has no recourse but to continue with the recruitment of its citizens into foreign armies.

Indeed, the economic distress that has dogged Nepal is the result of the continuing political turmoil and democratic challenges that the country has faced throughout its modern era, which started in 1950 with the end of the Rana family oligarchy. The political turmoil continued through the autocratic panchayat regime (1960–1990), the Maoist 'people's war' period (1996–2006), and the peace process and political transition thereafter. This ongoing instability has first and foremost impacted the lives and livelihoods of the Nepali citizenry, to such an extent that they lack the ability to exploit the plentiful natural resources with which the country is blessed. Therefore, the poorest continue to migrate out—to India, the Gulf, Malaysia and elsewhere—for subsistence and survival. Besides the resolute inability to rise from the 'least developed country' category to the 'developing country' category, Nepal has been rendered diplomatically weak, unable to carry out the activities of a proud and sovereign nation state in the international and regional/subcontinental arena.

There was a fleeting moment in the late 1950s and early 1960s when Nepal did attain stature in the international arena under the leadership of the social-democrat leader Bisweshwor Prasad Koirala. He stood shoulder-to-shoulder with the greats of the global South of the day, from Gamel Abdel Nasser to Jawaharlal Nehru to Chou En-Lai, both because of his personal capabilities and Nepal's emergence in the 1950s as a promising young democratic nation. Koirala's government was able to take several initiatives both regionally and internationally, but the coup by King Mahendra placed it in the ranks of autocracies and the pride and positioning of the country was affected.

The Panchayat autocracy was followed by a parliamentary democracy, where social change, economic growth and equity became a priority. Political pluralism and economic growth were a requirement for the people to finally be freed from the curse of history, but also for the country to take its place of pride among the regional nation states. However, the national momentum as well as socio-economic advance were derailed when the Maoists went underground and started a 'people's war' in 1996, a conflict that was to last till 2006. Society was scarred, and the positive international image of Nepal suffered, with the idyllyic image replaced by one of a country with 'killing terraces'. Even after the conflict ended in 2006, Nepal has not been able to bounce back because the peace process and the political transition have dragged on for a decade, even as the country converted to a republic, became constitutionally secular, and was declared as 'federal' (with the definition of federalism left pending).

With turmoil within, during the conflict and transition, Nepal became preoccupied with internal affairs, leading to neglect of both international and regional relations. Even ambassadorial appointments became less important, also due to inter-party horse-trading in an unstable polity, to the extent that Nepal did not have an ambassador in its most important international outpost, New Delhi, for nearly four years between 2011 and 2015. Nepal's politicians succumbed to the directorial hand of donor and diplomats, and even unaccountable 'operatives' of India, and it became even more subdued than earlier in its dealings with Beijing. The international donor community in Nepal, more powerful than in any other country of the subcontinent, rather like a bull in a china shop, got involved in a myriad of sensitive areas during a time of constitution writing, including on federalism and inter-community affairs. This led to additional polarisation and a weakening of the democratic parties.

HELPING SAARC

Thus, over the 1990s and 2000s, Nepal has become a scarecrow of its former self when it comes to international relations. On internal affairs, it has become much more susceptible to international pressure, especially from the two powerful neighbours. Nepal suffers as ambassadors in Kathmandu engage most undiplomatically in domestic political affairs. The constitutional debates are constantly jostled by real and perceived positions of Beijing and New Delhi. Amidst the internal preoccupations, there has been neglect of international affairs and a resultant weakening. This is evident in Kathmandu's inability to have its army generals appointed to command positions in the UN's peacekeeping units, even though it is the fifth largest contributor of peace-keepers. It is not able to negotiate important treaties and agreements with its neighbours because of populism that is rife at home, and the capacity of diplomats and bureaucrats to engage internationally in myriad areas, from climate change to money-laundering and security of labour migrants, is severely compromised because the political class is too distracted.

Thus it is that Nepal, a country with great potential to contribute to Southasian regionalism due to its history and placement, is unable to take the required initiative within SAARC or without. Kathmandu, as mentioned, is the location of the SAARC Secretariat which has a core group of directors from each of the member countries, and which helps in consultations and negotiations on topics ranging from surface transport agreements to cross-border spread of infectious disease. In 2015, the constellation of forces would also seem to be in favour of Nepal's proactivism within SAARC, given that Nepal has the current chairmanship of SAARC following the 18th Summit and the current Secretary General of SAARC happens to be a Nepali diplomat.

Given Nepal's broad-based acceptability among the eight member countries, and the particular coming together of the Secretariat, chairmanship and secretary generalship in one place, in theory, Nepal is ideally placed to shake SAARC from its stupor. It is not that there is a lack of ideas for the improvement of SAARC; what is needed is their being activated. The extant suggestions include strengthening the staffing of the Secretariat, increasing its autonomy and funding, making the SAARC agenda less beholden to the consensual dictate of eight foreign ministries, rationalising the activities of the organisation, encouraging independent scholarship on SAARC and Southasian matters, and helping conceptualise visions and concepts of Southasia as a region that go beyond the straitjacketed nation state formula of SAARC.

In a different time, Nepal could certainly have aspired to play such a proactive role, but its internal crisis for the moment does not allow it that flexibility. The concentration and motivation is lacking among the spectrum of politicians, intelligentsia and civil society. But we need also to consider whether it is possible for any country, howsoever dynamic, to try and shake up the SAARC organisation. The sad reality is that nation-statism, and its strident sibling ultra-nationalism, define the national ethos of each country of Southasia, even the oldest nation state (Nepal) which should have over time attained some maturity in these matters. In the newly formed post-1947 nation states, in particular, the national elite of the capitals have so defined nationalism that the resultant populism flattens all who seek different paths in international and regional engagements.

The sharp-edged ultra-nationalism is what SAARC was meant to counter. Fortunately, at every summit, at the very least the heads of states/government do voice their commitment to regionalism, but that seems to be about as far as it goes. Even as the countries profess commitment to SAARC, there seems now to be a subtle shift in the wind, and a trend away from SAARC's eight-country regionalism to other formulae. These include bilateral attempts at cohabitation (such as with two-way Most Favoured Nation status and free trade agreements) and subregional groupings within South-asia as well as with parts of other regions, especially South-east Asia. The most public articulation of this willingness to move away from SAARC regionalism came from India's Prime Minister Narendra Modi, who said in his speech at the 18th Summit in Kathmandu: 'The bonds will grow. Through SAARC or outside it. Among us all or some of us.'

In the context of what SAARC set out to do, unfortunately, six decades (in the case of much of post-Partition Southasia) seems too little a timespan for a mood of regional camaraderie to upend the ultra-nationalism that mires each country. In particular, the India–Pakistan rivalry is so all-consuming that it crops up at all times, including at SAARC summits, much to the exasperation of the other countries who would want to set a new threshold for debate. The lock-hold of nationalism over regional relations in each nation state of SAARC leads to the conclusion that there is little possibiity for Nepal to use its position to bring about a transformation of regional relationships—at least for now.

ECONOMIC CONNECTIVITIES

The clarion call to cultural continuities and shared histories as a means to invigorate regionalism in Southasia has proved inadequate, not having the strength to tackle shrill ultra-nationalism in each country. To create long-lasting and beneficial regionalism, this stridency has to be whittled down through other means, and the best method seems to be creating cross-border commercial stakeholders. This is probably the arena where the nation states of SAARC should concentrate in the coming decade in order to develop a regionalism that is both healthy and practical. The goal would be to develop stakeholders that would protect the gradual growth of camaraderie across the borders. The opening of economic and infrastructural connections would help in creating, as far as possible, the conditions that existed before 1947, or even 1956, when there was still relatively easy passage across the frontiers. Thus, the goal would be to help in concretely promoting connectivity all over Southasia—through highways, railways, water navigation, airways, the Internet, customs procedure rationalisations, electricity transmission lines, visa regimes, and so on.

During the time of its chairmanship of SAARC, even as its own internal political situation begins to normalise and stabilise with the writing of a new constitution, Kathmandu is required to activate itself on the Southasian agenda through SAARC and outside SAARC. In doing so, it must take a realistic position on what is practically feasible and what is merely visionary. It must see how its positioning can be used in promoting the connectivities already mentioned. It could start by publicising the historical open border with India, as an exemplar for other frontiers of Southasia, and ensure that Kathmandu itself is better connected with the rest of the region in terms of air connections, transmission lines, visa regimes, etc. This is also the time to take advantage of the evident personal interest of India's Prime Minister Modi in better engagement of India with its immediate neighbours.

To become an effective player to promote the re-engagement of Southasia with itself, however, first Kathmandu must emerge from the morass of overt and covert interventionism in which it is mired. The primary blame for this is to be borne neither by the two immediate neighbours to the north and south, nor the overseas 'diplo-donor' community, but by Kathmandu's political class and the intelligentsia which has allowed matters to come to such a pass. It is this political class that must wake up to the possibilities of Nepal and of Southasia.

However much Nepal may stabilise and its intelligentsia rise to the occasion, there may be little that Kathmandu can do to open the door to Southasian dialogue. The SAARC train is a slow one, and Nepal may not be able to do much within the organisation. On the other hand, Nepal is ideally placed to create a niche for itself in Southasia in a manner that it can be an exemplar. More than any other arrangement, the open Nepal–India border stands out as livewire example of what we seek for the rest of Southasia, where the borders are locked by barbed wire, halogen lamps, guard dogs or maritime surveillance. There are many other areas where Nepal, with its relatively small size but with 'sovereign dynamism', can act the way many of the other neighbours cannot.

Further, Southasian regionalism need not only be defined as 'SAARC regionalism' of eight countries working in unison. Indeed, a region as complex, diverse and vast as Southasia should not be straitjacketed into one kind of regionalism based on the conglomeration of individual nation states. Beyond the declared SAARC agenda, there are numerous areas where Nepal could promote Southasian regionalism. To name just a few, tourism could be the glue for regionalism, leading the campaign to connect Southasian capitals and cities across borders by air, being the entrepôt country between China and Southasia through the Himalayan corridors, seeing how the slow-starter South Asian University can be energised, how to make 'subregionalism' a Southasian agenda, and so on.

Beyond the 'SAARC definition', there can be several other ways to define the regional conglomeration that is Southasia—a coming together of sovereign nation states and sub-entities of similar size, the collaboration between border regions across soft frontiers, the division between North Southasia and South Southasia, linguistic groupings (such as Bengal–Bengal, Punjab–Punjab), and so on. Any country of the SAARC region can experiment with one or more of these various regions, but perhaps it is easiest for Nepal.

Given the knotted history of the modern era of Southasia, the bilateral animosities, the power of the capital elites and a host of other ills, Nepal is a country whose 'good intentions' are the least in doubt. It may not be able to do much for Southasia, but it can contribute by evolving as an exemplar nation state, where there is high economic growth as well as guarantee of equity, where ultra-nationalism is held back, and where democracy and development is 'inclusive', tackling age-old marginalisations and the sense of being left behind by so many communities. Nepal could utilise its size, sensibility and sovereignty to convert the Westphalian nation state into a workable formula for itself, a format and formula to be useful for Southasia as a whole.

◆

This chapter was first published in 2015 in the *IIC Quarterly,* Vol. 41, Nos 3 and 4.

13

INDIA, PAKISTAN AND 'SOUTHASIA'

BEENA
SARWAR#

The most reported on, commented on, or photographed moment at the 18th South Asian Association for Regional Cooperation (SAARC) summit in Kathmandu, Nepal, 2014, may well have been the smile and handshake between the Prime Ministers of India and Pakistan, Narendra Modi and Nawaz Sharif. This moment overshadowed, in terms of media limelight, all the other discussions between the eight heads of states from around South Asia who participated in the event on 25 and 26 November 2014, from Bangladesh, Bhutan, India, the Maldives, Nepal, Pakistan, Sri Lanka and Afghanistan.

Despite being backed by these eight governments, SAARC has had little success in integrating the region economically or politically in the 30 years since its formation. South Asia, the world's most populous region with a total of some 1.62 billion people, is also home to half the world's poor.

And it is the continuing sour relations between the two largest member states of SAARC, Pakistan and India, that prevent it from being successful like other regional associations, such as the European Union (EU), or the Association of South east Asian Nations (ASEAN). So much so that what should have been a routine meeting and interaction grabs all the attention.

Obviously, a handshake and a smile between the representatives of these countries, no matter how unexpected, cannot change any ground realities unless the gesture is accompanied by sustained diplomatic moves. However, it speaks for the significance that India and Pakistan's bilateral relationship holds for other countries of the region that not only the representatives of the host, Nepal, but also the President of Afghanistan Ashraf Ghani tried to ensure that the handshake took place and tried to 'bring closer the minds of the two leaders'. In fact, all SAARC leaders made the effort collectively, as Nepal's Foreign Minister Mahendra Bahadur Pandey said later.[1]

This is because at every SAARC meeting, it becomes clear that it is relations between India and Pakistan that continue to hold back regional development and cooperation. To put it bluntly: 'SAARC remains largely ineffective, hostage to the political polemics of member-nations, particularly India and Pakistan,' as Bangladeshi professor Imtiaz Ahmed of the Department of International Relations of Dhaka University observed. Dr Ahmed was one of the 5,000 or so delegates who attended the parallel 'People's SAARC', held in Kathmandu alongside the official event in 2014 (Tariq, 2014).

The People's SAARC, formed in 2007, is just one of the several cross-border organisations in the region that the formation of SAARC has catalysed over the years. The very notion of a South Asian regional association, however ineffective it may have proved to be, has opened doors for more interaction and groupings along these lines, as intellectuals and activists saw the opportunity to push for greater regional peace and cooperation, in general, and better bilateral relations between Pakistan and India, in particular.

The formation of SAARC, launched after several regional meetings over many years, affirmed the notion of a South Asian region beyond narrow national identities. And, for all its setbacks and weaknesses, it continues to progress, if excruciatingly slowly, towards the advancement of its goals. One of these is the formation of the South Asian University (SAU) in New Delhi, an international university established jointly by all eight SAARC member nations that started operating in 2010.

SAU offers postgraduate and doctoral programmes in various disciplines. Aiming to establish 11 postgraduate faculties and a faculty of undergraduate studies, it attracts students from all the SAARC member nations. Each nation also recognises the degrees awarded by SAU. This is the only university in the region with student representation from all eight SAARC countries. The students from the other SAARC countries are given a special multiple-entry SAU visa that also exempts them from 'police reporting'. Normally, Indians and Pakistanis are allowed only single-entry visas for short periods of time, and have to report to the police within 24 hours of arrival and departure to the city for which the visa is valid.

So far, the Pakistani students have not had too much problem on the visa front, says Prahlad Aheibam, Public Relations Officer, SAU. However, there have been 'a few hiccups with certain cases' that the university administration has raised with the relevant authorities and managed to resolve.

Given a general lack of awareness about SAU in Pakistan, and the hesitance of many Pakistani families to send their children across to the 'enemy country', the Pakistani quota of 10 per cent students remains underutilised. The average intake from Pakistan to SAU over the last couple of years has been around 12, although the university currently has about 20 students from Pakistan. The Pakistani students, who have attended the university, give glowing testimonials about their experience. In fact, 'witnessing the camaraderie that exists between the students of our university is something that never fails to warm our hearts,' says Aheibam.

Alauddin Mohammad, a Bangladeshi postgraduate student of Development Economics at SAU comments:

> The visa, travel and trade constraints that exist between the countries of South Asia make it the world's least connected region. Political insurgencies, fragile democratic institutions, fundamentalism, terrorism and ethnic conflicts all threaten regional peace and prosperity.

'How do we address these problems? Where is our starting point? What are our priorities, and on what basis?' he asks in an article published in the *Aman ki Asha* page of *The News International* in 2014.[2] Citing figures about income inequality, poverty levels and infant mortality in the region, Mohammad makes a compelling argument for the governments of the regional countries to make a commitment towards three major public expenditures—increase allocations for education and health and decrease military allocations in their respective budgets.

More people-centred policies are also on the agenda for the People's SAARC. As its Declaration[3] released in Kathmandu on 25 March 2007 states, 'the official SAARC failed to fulfil the promised goals of a better South Asia', and, instead, the 'economic policies pursued by ruling classes and parties of the region created conditions of exclusion and marginalisation, denial of rights, justice and democratic freedom in the different countries of the region'.

The Declaration further states that the people of South Asia:

> declare that we are not enemies of each other, that we do not want war against each other, that we do not want to be armed into starvation. We further call upon all the governments of the different countries in the region to cease all covert and overt hostilities, to resolve all disputes through amicable dialogue to immediately reduce tensions, to decrease the militarisation of the borders and to take urgent steps to bring about total disarmament in the region.

The People's SAARC demands ease of travel for 'people across the region by guaranteeing the notion of visa-free South Asia', as well as the strengthening and institutionalising of 'democracy, human rights and justice, and proportional participation of women at all levels of state and civil society institutions' in countries of the region.

The long list of demands includes demilitarisation and denuclearisation, the promotion of 'communal harmony within and between communities, societies and states', combating religious, ethnic and gender-based violence, environmental sustainability and the protection of indigenous peoples and their resources, gender rights, food security and the independence of the judiciary.

Other common concerns across countries of the region, outlined by the People's SAARC, include the issues of refugees and internally displaced people, the right to information and media freedom, as well as the states' responsibilities to provide health, education and basic needs, and more.

Whatever its weaknesses, the launch of SAARC did catalyse the formation of various other regional organisations and initiatives as intellectuals and activists saw the opportunity to push for greater regional peace and cooperation and, within that, better bilateral relations between Pakistan and India.

It was at regional seminars in the 1980s and the 1990s focusing on women, environment and development that many Indians and Pakistanis initially connected. In fact, it would be fair to say that even as the boundaries drawn after the departure of the

British in 1947 have grown more rigid, particularly between India and Pakistan, and also India and Bangladesh, there has been greater interaction between people's organisations. But, worryingly, it has become even more difficult for 'ordinary people' to make cross-border visits, even to see relatives, due to increasing visa restrictions. As a result, there is a growing distance, particularly among the younger members of families that once lived jointly together.

The rigid definitions we see today of what it means to be a Pakistani, Indian or a Bangladeshi, a Nepali or a Sri Lankan, are relatively recent. We need, as Kanak Mani Dixit, editor of *Himal Southasian*, the pioneering Kathmandu-based magazine, says, 'more complex self-identities'. Why can a person not be a Sindhi and a Pakistani, or a Keralite and an Indian, while also being South Asian?

The term 'South Asian' is relatively new and originated not in South Asia, but in Western, particularly American, academia and strategic studies departments, as Dixit notes. In any case, he does not find it very satisfactory. 'It is not a term that is "felt from the inside"', as he puts it. And the earlier name for the region, 'Hindustan', now has religious connotations, although it was drawn from the River Sindhu or Indus that runs through what became Pakistan after Partition in 1947.[4]

Dixit's alternative is the term 'Southasian', used as one word, in an attempt 'to restore some of the historical unity of our common living space', as the introductory note in the *Himal Southasian* puts it. 'The aloof geographical term "South Asia" needs to be injected with some feeling. "Southasia" does the trick for us, albeit the word is limited to English-language discourse.'[5]

The vision of a common future for Southasia is based on certain basic joint objectives reiterated by the eminent Bangladeshi lawyer and former Foreign Minister Dr Kamal Hossain at a seminar held to commemorate the birth centenary of noted late journalist Nikhil Chakravartty, in New Delhi, on 3 November 2014. To quote Dr Hossain:

> Clearly, the first on the list must be peace and stability in our region in [the] interests of the poor and the deprived in each of our societies. Development, in this context, must mean sustainable human development that must be sensitive to environment[al] and

social concerns. A sound test of a people-centred development is how it improves the conditions of the bottom 50 per cent of our populations.[6]

It was the prescient Nikhil Chakravartty who wrote nearly a quarter century ago that it is time that we ourselves—the people—forced our governments to let us cross over to each other's homes and establish a bond of unbroken amity. 'Why should we be scared of restrictions? If we come forward in hundreds and thousands, the governments in our two countries are bound to respond,' wrote Chakravartty in a visionary article.[7]

Chakravartty was one of the founders of the South Asia Dialogue series started in 1991, a yearly conference of scholars that aimed to meet annually in each country for five years, with the stated objective of pushing for 'Peace, Development and Cooperation'.

Several other like-minded intellectuals and activists were involved in the initiative, including giants such as the late Dr Eqbal Ahmad and Dr Mubashir Hasan. Well-known retired foreign secretaries, ambassadors, governors, government secretaries, ministers and judges have participated in the series, besides lawyers, journalists, doctors, educationists, artists, businessmen and women, trade unionists and students.

The connections made by participants of the South Asia Dialogue series spawned other regional and bilateral initiatives. Some took place at the bilateral level, such as the Pakistan–India People's Forum for Peace and Democracy (PIPFPD), formed in 1994, while others, like the Women's Initiative for Peace in South Asia (WIPSA), established in 1999, were at the regional level.

A consistent refrain at these citizens' meetings over the past few decades has been the critical need to resolve India–Pakistan relations as a prerequisite to any progress at the regional level. At meeting after meeting, seminar after seminar and conference after conference, intellectuals, business people, analysts and politicians from around Southasia, as well as at bilateral meetings, have called for India and Pakistan to ease bilateral visa and trade restrictions, and resolve all outstanding issues through dialogue.

Another demand that has been increasingly heard over the past few years is the call for something along the lines of a South Asian Union or a South Asian Federation. If France and

Germany, countries that were sworn enemies for centuries, can be part of the European Union, why can India and Pakistan not be part of such a grouping, is the question that people are asking. And, of course, there are multiple reasons, but at least the voices are being raised to express a thought that was unthinkable not so long ago (Sarwar, 2013).

Since 2010, the business community has been a part of these efforts, starting with the first India–Pakistan economic meeting in New Delhi, May 2010, organised by Aman ki Asha, the ground-breaking peace initiative jointly launched by the Jang Group in Pakistan and The Times of India group in India on 1 January 2010. Aman ki Asha focuses on India–Pakistan relations, but implicit in the initiative is the dream of regional peace. One way of doing this is through boosting bilateral trade and economic relations.

Three bilateral business meetings have been held so far, two in Delhi and one in Lahore. Participants have discussed mutually beneficial ideas and projects including:

(i) A South Asian energy grid, an integrated electricity network allowing cross-border trade in electricity, as well as oil and gas pipelines running through South Asia (Pakistan being the transit country linking Central Asian oil and gas resources, and Tajik and Afghan hydro-power to South Asia).

(ii) A South Asian multi-modal transport corridor linking Central Asia to South-east Asia, connecting all the regional economies.

(iii) Leveraging India's capital markets and private sector-led global footprint for the rest of South Asia.

(iv) Liberalisation of key service sectors, including education, health and information technology.[8]

The joint declaration at the very first Aman ki Asha meeting noted with concern that South Asia remains the world's least economically integrated region, and urged India and Pakistan to take steps to realise the tremendous potential of regional trade and commerce.

'The reality is that Pakistanis are friendly and full of warmth. We should not let radical groups shadow the future of 1.4 billion people of India and Pakistan,' commented Mumbai-based businessman Rajendra Pratap Gupta after the second Indo-Pak economic meeting in Lahore, 2012. 'Together, India and Pakistan can bring a new dimension to the politics of South Asia.'[9]

Unfortunately, both countries remain too caught up in their constructed narratives of 'the other' as 'the enemy' to move forward. India is too focused on forging ahead economically, while Pakistan remains embroiled in internal turmoil brought on by decades of military intervention in politics and flawed policies with regard to the insertion of religion in politics. So much so that an agreement signed by India and Pakistan in 2012 that would ease visa restrictions and allow people-to-people contact has yet to be implemented in full. A few clauses have started being implemented, such as visa-on-arrival to senior citizens at the Wagah–Attari border. But such is the level of distrust that most people, especially if they are elderly, are understandably reluctant to take the risk of going to the border and trying to obtain a visa there at the last minute.

What is needed is a paradigm shift, to look at the region as a penumbra, suggests Kanak Mani Dixit.[10] This would allow the identities to merge and emerge viewed through the lens of this poetically scientific term that refers to the soft shadow cast by the moon. A Southasian penumbra suggests a fluidity that is denied by sharp-edged nationalisms that are becoming more rigid even as the Internet and digital technology-enabled social media and smartphones allow people to connect virtually.

An emerging factor that is blurring these boundaries is rising expatriate populations of Southasia in different countries. Migrants to countries like the United States often subsume their narrow national identities into a larger identity—'pan-nationalism'—positioning themselves as 'Latinos' or 'Hispanics', rather than as Spaniards or Argentinians or Portugese, or in the case of people from the Indian subcontinent, as 'South Asians' or 'desi', rather than Bangladeshi, Sri Lankan or Pakistani.

By taking on these broader identities, they counter the presumption that people can be neatly categorised, observes developmental economist and social scientist, Dr Daniel Naujoks. This can shape the narrative further, because migrants help influence policies in their home countries.[11]

Such an approach at a broader level would help people in the region to cope with the sheer, overwhelming size of India—with eight times the population of South Asia's next most populous country, Pakistan. Looking at the larger picture rather than at manufactured, narrow national identities would allow various parts of the region to interact as equals and let Southasia, in all its diversity, begin to flourish. India can itself play a positive role by allowing federalism to develop and not closing off its borders, suggests Dixit.

A good example of the kind of borders that would help relations in the region is the open Nepal–India border—a great, bustling, heavily trafficked Southasian marketplace in stark contrast to the heavily fortified India–Pakistan border with its few sanitised truckloads of goods. This is also in keeping with the long-term vision of SAARC.

'A federal India would mean the ipso facto success of a Southasian Union,' says Dixit. 'The two Punjabs are already interacting directly. Why can Sindh not talk directly with Gujarat, or Chittagong with Mizoram…?'

Why not indeed? The region has everything to gain with such an inclusive and overarching approach, and nothing to lose except narrow national identities that only lead to jingoism and tensions. What comes in the way, of course, is realpolitik—the actual situation on the ground rooted in histories shaped by animosity and mistrust.

The people of Southasia, in their personal interactions with each other and in reaching out to each other at every opportunity, have repeatedly shown that they can rise above this historical baggage. The question is whether, despite their smiles and handshakes, the leaders of our countries can do that.

◆

#This chapter was first published in 2015 in the *IIC Quarterly*, Vol. 41, Nos 3 and 4.

NOTES

1. Aman ki Asha is a joint initiative of the two largest media groups in Pakistan and India, Jang Group and The Times of India, respectively, launched on 1 January 2010. www.amankiasha.com. I have been working as Editor, Aman ki Asha, Jang Group, Pakistan, since January 2010.

2. 'Wanted: A Democratic Policy Regime in South Asia', Allauddin Mohammad, Aman ki Asha, *The News International*. Pakistan. 23 April 2014. http://amankiasha.com/detail_news.asp?id=1346

3. People's SAARC Declaration, Kathmandu, Nepal, 25 March 2007. http://peoplesaarc.blogspot.com/

4. 'Desis, Southasians, and the Rest of Them', talk by Kanak Mani Dixit at Columbia University, 16 January 2014, organised by the South Asian Journalists Association.

5. I have been editorially associated with *Himal Southasian* since its launch in 1997.

6. 'The Mark of a Journalist', Humra Quraishi, 9 November 2013. http://www.themetrognome.in/columns/enough-said/mark-journalist

7. Chakravartty, Nikhil. 1990. 'Walls Must Come Down'. *Mainstream*. 4 August, quoted by Dr Mubashir Hasan, in his keynote address 'Walls Must Come Down' in memory of Nikhil Chakravartty, India International Centre, New Delhi, 3 November 2003.

8. Joint Declaration, Aman ki Asha Economic Meet, New Delhi, 18–19 May 2010.

9. Aman ki Asha, 2012. 'Exchange of Friendly Missives', 16 May. http://amankiasha.com/?p=2664

10. 'The Southasian Penumbra', Beena Sarwar, *The News*, 28 March 2014. http://www.thenews.com.pk/Todays-News-9-240710-The-Southasian-penumbra

11. Daniel Naujoks, keynote address, 'Borders, Nations, and Peace in South Asia: Social Norms and Diverse Societies', honouring the Nobel Peace laureates Malala Yousufzai and Kailash Sathyarti, New York, 25 October 2014. Quoted in 'We Owe it to Our Future Generations', by Beena Sarwar, 'We Owe it to Our Future Generations', Aman ki Asha page in *The News*, 29 October 2014. http://www.thenews.com.pk/Todays-News-14-280962-We-owe-it-to-our-future-generations

REFERENCES

Sarwar, Beena. 2013. 'A Southasian Vision', *The Friday Times*, 27 September–3 October, Vol. XXV, No. 33.

Tariq, Farooq. 2014. 'Nepal: People's SAARC Challenges Regional Elite's Agenda', *Green Left Weekly*, 6 December https://www.greenleft.org.au/node/57959

❖❖

14
ANXIETIES OF SAARC
An Experiential Reading through South Asian University[1]

SASANKA
PERERA[#]

APPROACH

The South Asian Association for Regional Cooperation (SAARC) celebrates 30 years of existence in 2014. It is an opportune time to explore its relevance, take stock of its present status and ponder over its future. This essay proposes to pose these broader questions by taking an approach quite different from what is usually adopted by scholars of international relations and politics. My interest is to explore the regional manifestation of two kinds of imaginations and explore what these imaginations mean for SAARC. These two imaginations are: the imagination of the nation state on the one hand, and the imagination of the multilateral collective on the other. Each country, including the eight that make up South Asia, inevitably expresses an imagination of the state in the manner in which it deals with itself, as well as each other. And the imagination of the multilateral collective should manifest itself in the manner in which an entity such as SAARC is ideally expected to work. In this context, what would the implications of these twin imaginations be for SAARC in the midst of relentless globalisation at the present moment of the 21st century, particularly if these imaginations play contradictory roles?

To think about these two imaginations, I propose to take the readers on a journey through three specific experiences of my own, as well as my students and colleagues at South Asian University (SAU). This will be my point of departure. The selection of this somewhat peculiar vehicle for exploration has very clear reasons. After all, every individual who works for South Asian University is a citizen of one nation state or another in the region, while all of them work or study in an entity created with the agreement of all eight nation states that constitute the region, channelled and realised through SAARC. Besides, the university, in its present form, is a metaphor for the region's aspirations, its hopes, its successes, its geopolitical realities and its anxieties. Crucially, lived experiences of individuals are a reliable measure to gauge how perceived ideals and rules actually work on the ground. These experiences are located in the intersections of the two imaginations to which I referred earlier, which, in real terms, is a grey zone in international relations. More clearly, this area of intersection is a kind of regulatory Bermuda triangle, where the shadows of the nation states' imagination of themselves and the imagination of the multilateral collective, which in this case happens to be SAARC, are cast on each other in an enduring discourse of relative confusion and liminality.

In its most ideal and basic form, nation states are supposed to be independent entities with a clear sense of their borders and a pronounced sense of their sovereignty, irrespective of the fact that these sensibilities might at times be contested. When a multilateral collective, such as the European Union (EU), Association of Southeast Asian Nations (ASEAN) or SAARC, is formed, that collective can work only if the nation states that constitute the collective can achieve the following three basic preconditions:

(i)   Their ability to pragmatically redefine some of the ways in which their own sense of statehood is generally defined, and allow for the personality of the collective to manifest and emerge on the ground.

(ii) Their ability to halt bilateral issues from becoming a hurdle in the workings of the collective. Without making undue comparisons, EU is clearly the best recent example of this ideal kind of political arrangement, which has become very successful despite long histories of war and mutual distrust.

(iii) The availability of adequate political will and wisdom among political leaders to surpass locally and bilaterally contentious issues, and political parochialities, to work towards the greater good of the collective without compromising national interests, including security.

If we cannot address these issues successfully, it is quite likely that the imagination of the nation state and its rituals of statecraft will shackle the collective from realising its potential. Perhaps it is in such a context that *The Hindu* described SAARC prior to the 18th Summit as 'bursting with potential, burdened with disappointment'.[2] The experiences of my students and colleagues, and my own, that I want to narrate, can also be broadly located within this untapped potential and its relentless disappointments.

EXPERIENCE 1

In 2011, in preparation for coming to Delhi to start work at South Asian University, I applied for what is known as the 'SAU' visa. It is a special category of visa that the Indian state, in its wisdom to move towards better realising the ideals of SAARC, had created for the benefit of South Asian citizens who were likely to come to SAU to either work or study. This was essentially done on the basis of the provisions elaborated in the following three documents: (1) Agreement for Establishment of South Asian University signed between the foreign ministers of all SAARC countries on 4 April 2007; (2) South Asian University Act, 2008, No. 8 of 2009, passed by the Parliament of India and (3) the Head Quarters Agreement signed between the Secretary General of SAARC and the Secretary of the External Affairs Ministry of the Government of India on 30 November 2008. The actual creation of this visa shows the ability, when necessary, for a nation state to work towards the benefit of the collective by changing some of the ways in which it usually works.

The SAU visa was conceived as a hassle-free long-term residency permit with a number of privileges. For me, however, it became like any regular long-term visa due to two restrictions imposed on it: (1) mandatory registration with Foreigner Regional Registration Office (FRRO) and (2) an entry restriction of three times per year into India. Taken in the general scheme of long-term residency visas, none of these conditions are out of the ordinary. But according to the agreements that were in place, both restrictions should not have been imposed on my visa. The FRRO registration was not so much of an issue, except that it required considerable time and patience. However, Article VI C of the Head Quarters Agreement notes clearly that such registration is not needed. Despite that, the entry restriction was a very serious problem. As a foreign national,

I had to plan carefully as to which family and personal obligations had to be given up, and which official or intellectual assignments I could attend and those that had to be sacrificed. The personal and professional impact of this imposition was quite pronounced for me as well as for others in similar circumstances. Naturally, it is not easy to deal with the demands and challenges of building an international university with such debilitating restrictions haunting one's routine activities. But, analytically speaking, this was a simple case of the nation state's shadow eclipsing the personality of the collective.

EXPERIENCE 2

In 2013, the Department of Sociology at South Asian University, having looked at the ongoing and planned activities of the SAARC Cultural Centre in Colombo, thought that it would make sense for the two entities to collaborate with each other. After all, both were created by the same parent organisation. Besides, some of the activities of the Cultural Centre seemed quite interesting. More significantly, it appeared that a number of departments in SAU could positively contribute to these activities. These included numerous conferences, research programmes, and photography and art competitions. As a faculty, in particular, and as a university, more generally, we were well placed intellectually and in terms of what might be called a South Asian sensibility, to collaborate in these events because they were very close to our research interests and personal passions. At the time, in the Faculty of Social Sciences alone, there were scholars from four South Asian countries with research interests in at least five of these countries. Colleagues in the Cultural Centre were open to collaboration. But they indicated that SAU academics from different SAARC countries had to apply for participation in various events through the respective External Affairs Ministry in their countries. Even the photographs for a SAARC-wide competition had to be channelled through this route. These were very time-consuming rituals of statecraft. In this situation, it was quite evident that one SAARC entity simply could not collaborate with another directly, without having to go through the rituals of power generated by the stately imagination of itself by each country in the region. Again, the imagination of the nation state was self-evident in this situation, while the imagination of SAARC, the bilateral collective to which both our organisations formally belonged, could not be seen, could not be perceived and could not even be sensed.

EXPERIENCE 3

All students who come to SAU from other countries in the region are supposed to get SAU student visas for the period of their study. Despite some difficulties, this seemed to work from 2010 onwards when the university initially started operations. But from 2014 onwards, students from Pakistan who came to SAU were given SAU visas for 730 days with pre-defined entry and exit points. More significantly, the visa restricted them to Delhi during their stint at the university. Under routine circumstances, there is nothing unusual in these kinds of restrictions. Often, when Indian citizens travel to Pakistan for specific reasons and when Pakistanis come to India, most of them get city-specific visas. So, this is a taken-for-granted practice regularly utilised by the nation states of India and Pakistan in their bilateral dealings. But how does this make sense when taken in the context of collective interests of the multilateral collective? As a university of SAARC with the mandate to offer knowledge without borders and to create a South Asian consciousness, it becomes very difficult to uphold these lofty ideals if a group of our own students is restricted to Delhi during its tenure as students and is deprived of learning from the vastness of experiences that India so readily offers. As of this year, many other students from Sri Lanka, Bangladesh and Afghanistan were getting very different kinds of visas, instead of the SAU student visa for different durations which required regular renewal that was both time-consuming and expensive. I am sure there must be official reasons to explain this. But for an academic community, this does not help. It impacts on our sense of collective identity, and on our teaching, while creating an unhelpful sense of anxiety and unease.

Pakistani colleagues, even if they get the special SAU visa, cannot open a bank account in India. They have to resort to pre-modern and unsafe practices of informally storing their salaries, which becomes a problem when they attempt to take their savings back to their home country. Again, it appears this also has to do with unresolved bilateral issues and is a matter of reciprocity. But it is indeed quite sad that a mainstream SAARC organisation cannot resolve such fundamental issues despite the multilateral agreements through which the university was established.

INTERPRETING EXPERIENCES

The common feature in these three experiences indicates how the aspirations of a multilateral organisation, and the dreams of individuals who subscribe to these ideals, get curtailed because the very strong imagination of the nation state continues to impact negatively upon the evolution of the ideals of the collective. This happens despite the existence of overarching agreements among these countries designed to prevent such outcomes. As we know quite well, the imagination of the collective did not suddenly emerge from an unknown universe, disrupting the nation state. Instead, it evolved carefully and over time, with the consensus of the contributing states. It is this state of affairs that Dr Subramanian Swamy, Chairman of BJP's Strategic Affairs Committee, articulated at the Lalith Atulathmudali Memorial Lecture in Colombo on 26 November 2014.[3]

> First, SAARC is off and on in a limbo. Thus, the first issue is this: how to grapple with SAARC's uncertain future and how to put it back on the rails again, and not permit in the future, international political changes affecting the functioning of SAARC.

> Second, SAARC has to resolve whether essential economic cooperation in an increasingly globalised world economy can be achieved despite continuing political conflicts. The issue is whether political differences—beyond vital national interest issues—can be set aside by each member country while a more harmonious environment is created through healthy economic cooperation.

> Third, is SAARC so fragile that it cannot survive if bilateral controversial political questions are raised in its deliberations without undermining its utility?

It seems to me that Dr Swamy has captured the centrality of the same issues I have tried to explain with regard to my own circumstances, but with particular reference to economic cooperation. As in this case, political leaders often understand quite well what needs to be done with SAARC. However, these analyses seldom get translated into tangible outcomes on the ground. It appears that countries in our region are so deeply drowned in the intoxicating imagination of the nation state that they cannot imagine the collective as a viable, empowered and necessary political reality. The gradual pace at which SAARC has generally evolved, as well as its inability to come to terms with most of the anticipated agreements in the recently concluded 18th Summit, clearly places this unenviable situation in the larger context. This is what Prime Minster Narendra Modi meant when he observed in the 18th SAARC Summit: 'As SAARC, we have failed to move with the speed that our people expect and want'.[4]

CONCLUDING COMMENTS

In the context of the experiences narrated, as well as the history of SAARC itself, which is now part of South Asia's larger corpus of general knowledge, we may ask what the relevance of SAARC is in the context of the relentless globalisation that typifies our global existence. It is self-evident that SAARC is nowhere close to realising its potential. Many of the hurdles in achieving SAARC's ideal goals have come about due to its inability to get out of the shadow of the nation state and embrace the imagination of the collective.

In the context of what I have outlined so far, let me make two propositions to conclude my thoughts. If I am to be self-reflective, I would admit that SAU has many issues that need resolution. Even so, despite its many lapses, it is a much better model for SAARC itself to emulate. And I say this with a serious degree of responsibility. After all, no one asked me or any of my colleagues what our citizenship was when we applied for employment. We were also not asked to apply through the Ministry of External Affairs or other government entities in our respective countries. We were not asked to bring letters of introduction from the prime minister, the president or an MP in our countries. We approached the university as individuals, and were recruited only on the basis of training and competence. Since our inception in 2010, we have done our best to admit students from all SAARC countries despite considerable difficulties. Students from outside India now constitute nearly 50 per cent of our student body, although some countries like Pakistan, Sri Lanka, Bhutan and the Maldives remain under-represented. It is this relative success to which the SAU anthropologist, Mallika Shakya from Nepal, refers in the following words in a recent essay:

'My current employer South Asian University (SAU) is partly Nepali. The class I teach at SAU is also partly Nepali, but more importantly, it is only partly Indian, while being also partly Afghan, Bangladeshi, Bhutani, Maldivian and Sri Lankan. I am a lot more at home with this class than I would have been if it was just one of any of these nationalities.'5

But we have not been as successful in maintaining this sense of balance in the recruitment of faculty and support staff. Of 55 regular faculty members, only six come from countries other than India. This is a serious issue which obviously needs to be addressed in all future recruitment drives. Even so, by regulations and by taking into account the existing pattern of employment of senior administrators, the university is obliged to recruit its Director of Finance from a country other than India. In 2014, it had one Deputy Registrar from Pakistan, Bhutan and India each, while the Registrar was from India. Its librarian was from Bangladesh, while his assistants were from India. It had one Assistant Registrar from Nepal, while the other was from India. It had an architect from Sri Lanka and an IT specialist from India. Rule 6.1 of the university mandates that at any given time, the president and vice-president of the university must be from different countries. All these suggest that SAU is far more serious in terms of rules, and often in practice as well, to work towards an imagination of South Asia beyond the shadow of the nation states that fund the university, so that a more humane and reasonable South Asia might be imagined and hopefully achieved. This does not mean, however, that in the minds of students, colleagues and officials, the shadow of the nation state does not exist. In fact, it often does as rhetorical articulations of competing nationalisms. But this is to be expected given the almost natural emergence of nationalism in human consciousness. What is important, however, is that such sensibilities are not given official or formal recognition. However, the inability of SAARC to achieve its larger goals and to evolve its multilateral sensibility in the long term, might also spell a bleak future for an institution like ours, though it is clearly one of SAARC's very few success stories. In real terms, given the university's wider signification of South Asia in numerous ways, its lack of success in the long run, or its eventual collapse, would essentially signal the end of SAARC as well.

My second proposition is the restating of an obvious fact, even though it is often lost in the formal and official discourses on South Asia. That is, SAARC is not the only discourse in, and on, South Asia. For me, SAARC is simply one of the many platforms and discourses on South Asia while it might be the official, more audible and more visible of these. In this context, there is a need at the level of our collective perception and discursive practices to de-link South Asia from SAARC when necessary. As all of us know, there are other histories, memories, discourses, networks and efforts in the region that have allowed for a more humane, more equitable and more reasonable imagination of South Asia to emerge, unshackled from the shadow of the nation states and the debilitating non-movement of the multilateral collective itself. I have in mind the networks of writers, filmmakers, scholars and artists who are actively engaged in creating cohesive networks of international relations across the region, but often away from the public gaze.

Take, for instance, the South Asian Network for the Arts, which came into existence at the beginning of the present millennium. It created a viable network of artists from across the region. These artists met regularly in different countries and engaged in art-making and artistic experimentation, which placed in context issues of local relevance as well as matters that cut across the region and beyond within the discursive practices of these emerging trends of art. As a result, I strongly believe that South Asian art today is a serious discourse on the region's ongoing political and social transformations. The point I want to make is that these networks have emerged precisely because SAARC's own were not available or were not viable.

Many of us have dreamt of a better-integrated, more connected and a more humane South Asia for a very long time. In my case, this has been going on for at least a decade and a half before my formal association with South Asian University. Scholars and thinking people in our region, such as Ashis Nandy and Shiv Visvanathan from India, Imtiaz Ahmed from Bangladesh, Kanak Dixit from Nepal, Zia Mian from Pakistan, just to mention a few, have contributed immensely to this self-reflective and out-of-the-box thinking on the region. Some political leaders have taken this thinking to a more visible political level. It is in such a context that India's former Prime Minster Dr Manmohan Singh in January 2007 publicly articulated his dream of a South Asia where he could have breakfast in Amritsar, lunch in Lahore and dinner in Kabul.[6] But we know quite well that that dream was never realised. It is this existing, unenviable ground reality that Narendra Modi very subtlely articulated in the recently concluded SAARC Summit when he noted: 'Nowhere in the world are collective efforts more urgent than in South Asia; and, nowhere else is it so modest'.[7]

I think it should be axiomatic where exactly SAARC stands at the global stage today. For me, until SAARC comes of age and decides to reinvent itself away from the discomforting shadow of the nation state, the future is elsewhere. And that is in the consciousness and goodwill of the region's people, and their ability to imagine and create their collective space beyond the limitations of both the nation state and SAARC.

◆

This chapter was first published in 2015 in the *IIC Quarterly*, Vol. 41, Nos 3 and 4.

NOTES

1. This essay is an edited version of the presentation made at the panel discussion on 'SAARC in a Globalizing World' organised by the South Asian University on 8 December 2014 at India International Centre, New Delhi.

2. http://www.thehindu.com/opinion/blogs/blog-suhasini-haidar/article6632431.ece (last accessed 27 November 2014).

3. http://www.thehindu.com/opinion/lead/a-case-for-saarc-reforms/article6630591. ece?homepage=true (last accessed 5 December 2014).

4. http://www.narendramodi.in/text-of-prime-ministers-speech-at-2014-saarc-summit-in-nepal/ (last accessed 5 December 2014).

6. http://archive.indianexpress.com/news/amritsar-breakfast-lahore-lunch-and-a-kabul-dinner/20468/ (last accessed 5 December 2014).

7. http://www.narendramodi.in/text-of-prime-ministers-speech-at-2014-saarc-summit-in-nepal/ (last accessed 5 December 2014).

◆◆

15

DEVELOPING A REGIONAL HUMAN RIGHTS MECHANISM

AISHATH
VELEZINEE[#]

FOUNDING SAARC

The South Asian Association for Regional Cooperation (SAARC) was initiated in 1985 by the leaders of seven countries[1] with specified objectives[2] to:

   (i)   promote the welfare of the peoples of South Asia and improve the quality of their lives;

  (ii)   accelerate economic growth, social progress and cultural development in the region and to provide all individuals the opportunity to live in dignity and to realise their full potential;

 (iii)   promote and strengthen collective self-reliance amongst the countries of South Asia;

 (iv)   contribute to mutual trust, understanding and the appreciation of one another's problems;

  (v)   promote active collaboration and mutual assistance in economic, social, cultural, technical and scientific fields;

 (vi)   strengthen cooperation with other developing countries;

(vii)   strengthen cooperation amongst themselves in international forums on matters of common interests; and

(viii)   cooperate with international and regional organisations with similar aims and purposes.

The principles for regional cooperation in SAARC as agreed were, 'respect for the principles of sovereign equality, territorial integrity, political independence, non-interference in the internal affairs of other States and mutual benefit'.[3] A major theme of the SAARC Charter is non-interference in the internal affairs of other states; other states here meaning the states within the organisation itself.

The driving force, it appears, was a reluctance by the then South Asian leaders to be left behind, as the rest of the world reorganised under regional organisations such as the European Union (EU), North American Free Trade Agreement (NAFTA), Latin American Free Trade Association (LAFTA), Economic Community of West African States (ECOWAS), Association of Southeast Asian Nations (ASEAN) and Asia-Pacific Economic Cooperation (APEC) (Mehrotra, 1997).

SAARC IN THIRTY YEARS

Thirty years on, SAARC has expanded territorially with the addition of Afghanistan as a full-fledged member, but has failed to reach its full potential by any measure, the greatest barrier to its own success being, arguably, SAARC—or the SAARC Charter—itself.

SAARC leaders have failed to uphold the pledge in the Charter for the Heads of State or Government to meet 'once a year or more often' counting just 17 SAARC Summits in 30 years, a fact often remarked on by observers and analysts when SAARC is in the news.

The common reason for cancelled or delayed summits is the on-off tensions emanating from the historical and continued dispute between India and Pakistan on the issue of Kashmir, a matter that remains far from resolved.

Non-interference in internal affairs has meant that SAARC has been unsuccessful as the forum both to address and debate regional tensions, or for peace negotiations; instead, its leaders opt to abstain at times when dialogue is most essential. As Maass wrote,

> If one arranges the various regional groupings in a ranking list, the European Community, on account of its high degree of integration as well as economic and political cooperation, would be on top, while SAARC in its present stage would only be placed at the bottom (1999: 40–62).

Little has changed in SAARC in the years since this observation.

DEMOCRATISATION IN THE SAARC REGION

What has changed in the SAARC region, though, is the shift from despotic rule in some countries to a declared commitment to greater democracy at the domestic level. The 2009 SAARC Charter of Democracy may be viewed as a recognition of this shift.

Democracy in practice, however, remains at varying levels among SAARC countries. Till now, the SAARC Charter of Democracy[4] which, by its phrasing, opens SAARC to engagement in the 'internal affairs' of member states for the greater purpose of consolidating democracy in South Asia and the protection of the human rights of the South Asian people, has not translated into meaningful engagement, or changed the approach of SAARC as an organisation to events in member countries that directly impact on democracy in South Asia.

A case in point is the response to the controversial change of government in the Maldives on 7 February 2012. While other regional organisations, such as the EU, were concerned by the questionable circumstances of the transfer of power which brought an end to the first-ever democratically elected government in the Maldives, SAARC, as an organisation, remained silent. India, the largest democracy in the world, meanwhile, was too quick to accept the transfer of power. Ironically, the SAARC Secretary General at the time, a Maldivian, had actively joined in bringing down the democratic government, a shameful affair that SAARC simply ignored. The facts of the matter, and the threat of legitimising undemocratic transfers of power, either by direct endorsement or indirect acceptance through silence, hit home quickly when the new post-coup government drove out the largest Indian business investment in the Maldives, revoking the GMR Group's airport deal without legitimate reason or respect for the rule of law.

SOUTH ASIAN PEOPLE IN THIRTY YEARS

Meanwhile, the people of South Asia have moved forward much faster than their governments, seeking an opportunity for greater integration and common prosperity. A notable change over these years has been in the movement of people, the high increase in regional migration, with the smallest country in South Asia, the Maldives, offering employment opportunities to much larger populations in other South Asian countries.

With negligible numbers of regional migrant workers in the Maldives in 1985, today they form a third of its total resident population, the majority from South Asia. Bangladesh accounts for the highest number, often exploited with low pay and difficult working conditions. India, Sri Lanka and Nepal, too, have significant migrant workers in the Maldives. Conversely, large populations from the Maldives live in Sri Lanka and India, mainly for medical care or education.

Regional tourism has expanded in all countries, leading to the greater exposure of South Asian peoples to one other, although visa and other bureaucratic measures still hamper travel between some South Asian nations locked in a historic dispute. Greater movement, and especially the movement of migrant workers, has not always been smooth, and the absence of a SAARC regional mechanism to protect the human rights of all South Asian people has perhaps never been felt more acutely.

Human rights, however, has remained a subject from which South Asian leaders have systematically shied away.

PEOPLE'S SAARC

The People's SAARC, a civil society movement of South Asian people lobbying to bring the people's perspective into the SAARC bureaucracy, has, however, continuously raised 'soft issues' as opposed to the official limiting of discussions to trade and economic matters. This exposes the chasm between SAARC and the people of South Asia.

The most recent People's SAARC Declaration, adopted in parallel to the Kathmandu Summit in November 2014, raised 32 subject areas of critical concern spanning:

  (i)   Poverty eradication
  (ii)   Rights of women
  (iii) Inclusive democratic governance
  (iv)   Respect for human rights
  (v)   Food sovereignty and security
  (vi)   Environmental conservation and climate justice
  (vii) Promotion and protection of indigenous and traditional knowledge

(viii) Rejection of monolithic, neoliberal developmental models

(ix) People-centred regional cooperation

(x) Meaningful engagement and civil society participation

(xi) Sustainable development

(xii) Asylum seekers, refugees, the stateless, internally displaced persons, labour and forced migrants

(xiii) Rights of migrant and informal sector workers

(xiv) Transitional justice mechanism to effectively address past violations of human rights

(xv) Use of energy, multiple uses of water, forest, mines/minerals and land

(xvi) Human rights-friendly legal mechanisms to end all forms of 12 violence

(xvii) South Asian Water Convention

(xviii) Banning the production, use and transfer of landmines, cluster munitions and improvised explosive devices

(xix) Developing a regional human rights charter, and effective and participatory human rights mechanism

(xx) Amend the 'SAARC Convention on Preventing and Combating Trafficking in Women and Children for Prostitution' to broaden mandate and scope

(xxi) Sexual and reproductive health rights (SRHR)

(xxii) End to militarisation

(xxiii) Dalits

(xxiv) Dignity of workers

(xxv) Indigenous people

(xxvi) Review of the Free Trade Agreements (FTAs) and Bilateral Investment Treaties (BITs)

(xxvii) Patriarchy in governance

(xxviii) Absence of labour as a SAARC area of cooperation

(xxix) Tax evasion

(xxx) Legal reform

(xxxi) Transformative change

(xxxii) Implementation of existing SAARC mechanisms: charters, declarations and conventions adopted by SAARC in the previous summits, and the full ratification and enforcement of all core international human rights instruments.

The list is long and, considering its performance, the SAARC inter governmental organisation and the People's SAARC would not share the same vision without a rethinking of the existing SAARC system.

Today, SAARC is all but a dormant institution, periodically coming to public attention with irregular SAARC summits that attract regional media attention for a short while.

REVIVING SAARC AS AN ORGANISATION OF RELEVANCE

To revive SAARC as an organisation relevant to the common people of South Asia, and to ensure that it provides a platform for the people to engage with, it needs to rethink the existing system and reorganise itself.

First, the protection and promotion of individual and collective freedoms and rights of the people of South Asia being intrinsic to the overall consolidation of democracy in the SAARC region, a regional human rights mechanism must be established. In itself, this is not a new idea in the SAARC region but one that is yet to gain the support of South Asian leaders who are the ultimate decision makers.

The People's SAARC, as discussed earlier, has called for a South Asian human rights charter and mechanism towards the promotion and protection of human rights and social justice in South Asia. Forum Asia, a wider Asian civil society organisation, has been working in recent years in consensus building across South Asian communities towards the establishment of such a regional human rights mechanism. A regional civil society—Working Group on a South Asia Human Rights Mechanism—exists as well.

Second, SAARC must revisit the Charter of 1985, taking into consideration globalisation and interconnectivity of the people, and the more or less borderless virtual world. The idea of the internal affairs of a nation being a domestic affair of little consequence to the region and outside and, therefore, internal affairs of a nation state being outside the scrutiny of other states is a misconception today, the realities of the 21st century being different. As such, SAARC too needs to give careful consideration to the removal of 'non-interference in the affairs of other States' as collective scrutiny and regulation in promoting democratic values and a democratic culture are today necessary to achieve the primary objectives of SAARC.

The success of regional organisations, most notably the EU, derives from the advancement of the region from war and conflict among member states to greater regional cooperation, as well as the development of an independent regional institutional mechanism as distinct from regional governments (Mehrotra, 1997). Examples are to be found in the European Parliament to which members are elected directly by citizens of European nations, and the European Court to which citizens can directly refer disputes.

South Asia, too, can start working towards developing independent institutional mechanisms to strengthen SAARC as a region. A major advantage in taking such a path, as in the setting up of an institutional, independent, South Asian Human Rights Mechanism, would be the opportunity for the South Asian region to oversee and regulate itself and develop collectively as a region where all peoples are equal.

◆

#This chapter was first published in 2015 in the *IIC Quarterly*, Vol. 41, Nos 3 and 4.

NOTES

1. The seven countries that founded SAARC are: Bangladesh, Bhutan, India, the Maldives, Nepal, Pakistan and Sri Lanka. Since then Afghanistan has been admitted as a full-fledged member and some other countries, including Iran and China, carry special observer status with SAARC.

2. SAARC Secretariat (1985) *SAARC Charter*. Article 1 http://saarc-sec.org/saarc-charter/5/

3. SAARC Secretariat (1985) *SAARC Charter*. Article 2 http://saarc-sec.org/saarc-charter/5/

4. SAARC Secretariat (2009) SAARC Charter of Democracy. http://saarc-sec.org/SAARC-Charter-of-Democracy/88/

REFERENCES

Maass, Citha D. 1999. 'South Asia: Drawn Between Cooperation and Conflict' in Eric Gonsalves and Nancy Jetley (eds.), *The Dynamics of South Asia: Regional Cooperation and SAARC*. New Delhi: Sage Publications.

Mehrotra, Lakhan Lal. 1997. *Towards a South Asian Community*. New Delhi: Indian Council for Cultural Relations.

◆◆

16
SOUTH ASIAN REGIONALISM
A People's Movement Perspective

RAKHI
SEHGAL#

People's SAARC has emerged as a common platform of progressive South Asian social movements and mass organisations that seek to work collectively for the democratisation of South Asian society, dignity of people and distributional justice.

SHARED SOCIO-CULTURAL HISTORY OF THE REGION

The people of South Asia not only share a contiguous geographical space, but also a social and cultural history that shapes our lifestyles, belief systems, cultural particularities, material practices and social relationships. Our natural environments are related, interdependent, and form elements of a common ecosystem. There is a similarity in our life practices which have been influenced by one another. On the other hand, the unique diversity of our region in all aspects has enriched the common heritage, and we celebrate a sustained history of mutual respect for one another.

However, there also exists tremendous suspicion, hostility, intolerance, disinformation, misinformation and prevention of interaction amongst the people in order to maintain the status quo. This acute sense of insecurity has led the South Asian nations towards increasing militarisation in the name of enhancing national security. Simultaneously, democratic debate and dissent on many vital issues is being curbed across South Asia by governments.

POTENTIALITIES OF SAARC AND SOUTH ASIAN REGIONALISM

It is widely acknowledged that SAARC lags behind the world trend of regionalisms such as ASEAN, European Union, OAS, Mercosur and others. In fact the world over, regionalism has emerged as a response and basis of engagement with processes of globalisation. South Asian people's movements believe that SAARC must strive to respond to people's needs and initiatives so that egalitarian social structures are built and strengthened.

Economic policies pursued by the ruling classes and parties of the region created conditions of exclusion and marginalisation, and denial of rights, justice and democratic freedom in different countries of the region. The logic and thrust of the policies and programmes of SAARC have also failed to address the issue of people's economic, social and cultural rights. Instead, it appears that for the most part, SAARC has been a forum at which our governments posture against one another or put in place agreements to serve the interests of the elite and corporate bodies.

The formation of SAARC in 1985 had been welcomed by people across the region, as it had roused hopes and aspirations amongst them for a better South Asia and the hope that SAARC would enhance people-to-people linkages, free flow of people across the borders of the region and mutual cooperation amongst the people to build strong, vibrant societies that would be democratic, ecologically balanced and socially just and sustainable. It was also hoped that SAARC would usher in a new era of prosperity and a regionalism that would be qualitatively more humane, egalitarian and secular (promoting religious harmony, respecting each other's religious and cultural beliefs). These hopes have been belied by the functioning of SAARC since its formation.

RECLAIMING THE REGION FOR DEEPENING DEMOCRACY, SOCIAL JUSTICE AND PEACE

Ordinary people are finding themselves more and more politically alienated, denied fundamental rights as well as access to instruments necessary for realising their rights. The State, which is conceived as a space for peaceful resolution of conflicts, remains fragile even as it is capturing more and more draconian powers of control aimed at curtailing people's movements and legitimate forms of organisation and resistance. More and more decisions affecting the everyday lives of people are being dictated by multinational corporations and global financial institutions to which there is no democratic access and from where there is no accountability.

There is no real move, and nor can we expect one, from the government and economic elites toward real integration that is based on cooperation, equity, fair trade, solidarity and complementarity. Hence, the impetus will have to come from civil society and people's movements. Contemporary experience around the world shows that in fact it is the people's movements that can deepen the process of democracy, contend ideologically and politically with all forms of regressive and chauvinistic regimes, viewpoints and ideologies, and build a secular framework for peaceful coexistence.

Reclaiming the region and developing sustained regional alternatives requires that we amalgamate politics and the economy that serves people. Reclaiming the region means recreating regional integration based on principles of human rights: people-centred and people-oriented. The challenge, then, for civil society and people's movements in the South Asian region is to come up with and assert an alternative vision of regional integration or new regionalism based on the needs and aspirations of the people of the region while also taking into consideration different levels of development. Effective regionalism must challenge systematic marginalisation of people, groups, communal divisions, degradation of the environment and impact of climate change. To do this, South Asian people's movements must forge solidarity across the borders to challenge the dominant neoliberal growth model that is at play currently and which has been violently restructuring the region's economic policies, the cultural life of the people, and directly or indirectly devaluing the values and institutions of democracy.

With this understanding, South Asian people's movements (women, youth, peasants, labour, socially marginalised groups) and civil society organisations have over the last decade organised themselves as People's SAARC with the hope of deepening people-to-people solidarity and crafting a collective and common vision of South Asia as well as engaging with South Asian governments in order to realise a people's vision of South Asia.

As host of the 18th SAARC Summit 2014, the Government of Nepal recognised the need to ensure participation of ordinary people in the SAARC processes and took the initiative to form a Citizen's Advisory Committee to give voice to the people of South Asia in the SAARC process. People's SAARC hopes this path-breaking precedent becomes a regular mechanism of SAARC engaging with civil society and people's movements of South Asia.

RENEWED EMPHASIS ON SAARC AND THE SOUTH ASIAN NEIGHBOURHOOD

People's movements also welcome the renewed focus on SAARC by Prime Minister Modi and by member countries and believe that 'Deeper Integration for Peace and Prosperity' (the theme of the 18th SAARC Summit) is possible only when this cooperation goes beyond the needs of regional elites and corporates, and allows and enables the people of South Asia to build their regional identity and shape democratic institutions for peace and prosperity.

Prime Minister Modi's emphasis that the South Asian neighbourhood comes first is welcome but is viewed with caution by its neighbours and South Asian people's movements, given the Indian state's tendency to prioritise what it sees as its 'national self-interest'. The test of India's emerging power status and leadership role will lie in how India's unilaterialism shapes up in its neighbourhood and if it is generous and pushes breakthroughs on several contentious issues bedevilling the region. In fact, if India is to be a leading South Asian country, then it has to help shape a democratic space of regionalism and emerge as a legitimate articulator of the region on a global level.

It is important to recognise that diversity and nation building processes in South Asia have led to a wide array of internal conflicts which have, over time, become militarised. Unevenness of democratisation in South Asia is linked to the unevenness of internal conflicts and the fact that the predominant framework for addressing conflicts has been the military framework instead of a democratic framework.

It is ironical that South Asia, which is home to the largest number of impoverished people and malnourished children, is also the most militarised region in the world today, and one of rising religious fundamentalisms creating instability, fear and fractures in the polity. Increased securitisation and militarisation of South Asian states and society in the name of combating 'terrorism' and national security threats and increasing arbitrary detention, torture, custodial rape and extra-judicial killings have reduced space for democratic dissent. While old challenges have not been addressed, new challenges have emerged in the form of climate change and environmental degradation, which are of transnational dimensions; extraction of natural resources; food, water and energy crises and resource grabbing by governments and corporates. These require collective regional responses. But the South Asian states continue to be caught up in and straightjacketed by competitive militarism in the neighbourhood to the detriment of building a robust and vibrant regionalism, as well as of enabling meaningful and substantive change in the lives of South Asian people.

Given its history, India cannot become a totally militarised state, and neither is it in India's interest to have other South Asian countries become militarised. In fact, the Indian state is unwilling and unable to deal with demonised neighbours or with armed dissent within the country. Ironically, while on the one hand, South Asian states are preoccupied with security, on the other hand, they are abdicating their responsibilities toward their citizens. Therefore, dominance of the military framework poses a grave threat to the ordinary people of South Asia.

It is the understanding of people's movements that if democracy in South Asia is not strengthened, it will be difficult to sustain democracy in India too. Moreover, without sustaining peace and democracy and building South Asia as a zone of peace, no South Asian government will be able to deliver on its promises of development, governance and inclusive growth.

EVOLUTION OF PEOPLE'S SAARC

The journey began with a small group in Bangkok in 1992 discussing the idea of initiating a people's process in South Asia to extend people-to-people solidarity for democracy and human rights. This was followed by a meeting in Kathmandu in February 1993 and another in May 1994 to discuss the ways to foster cooperation, solidarity and action at people's level in a fragmented South Asia. The 1994 meeting resulted in a declaration, *Toward People's SAARC: Statement of Concerns,* sharing ideas for strengthening regional cooperation and initiating wide regional and national dialogues towards the formation of People's SAARC.

The Regional Secretariat of People's SAARC is based in Kathmandu, and the India country process established the first People's SAARC Country Secretariat in New Delhi in 2013.

People's SAARC-India has initiated a process of articulating the issues from people's movements within the perspective of the SAARC framework and building a network of people's movements with the capacity and legitimacy to engage with the SAARC process and with our respective governments.

We have organised thematic programmes such as the 'South Asia Beyond Borders' series (discussions on Pakistan, Nepal, Bangladesh and Afghanistan); a joint symposium with South Asian Alliance for Poverty Eradication (SAAPE) on 'Demilitarisation, Democracy and Social Justice in India'; a roundtable on 'India's Look East Policy' and an international symposium on 'South Asian Water Commons' among other activities.

Working groups are evolving to deepen our substantive engagement on thematic issues such as South Asian Water Commons, Caste Discrimination and Social Exclusions, South Asian People on the Move: Labour, Migration Refugees, Right of Minorities in South Asia, Climate Change, Trade and Investment and Transitional Justice in South Asia.

Our focus this year is on the different dimensions and aspects of borders, especially borders as they impinge upon the daily lives of people—South Asian refugees; transboundary sharing of rivers; paucity of trading posts and fencing of borders, and its impact on petty trade that sustains the livelihoods of people living on borders; impact of political borders on lives of pastoralists and fisherfolk, to name a few. To give expression to the shared desire of South Asian people to transcend political borders that have divided communities and families and instead celebrate our shared social, cultural and historical heritage, we will shortly be organising a joint Border Peace Festival in Rajasthan (India) and Sindh (Pakistan) and a PSAARC Caravan across some parts of South Asia.

◆

#This chapter was first published in 2015 in the *IIC Quarterly*, Vol. 41, Nos 3 and 4.

17
SEWA'S SISTER-TO-SISTER INITIATIVE FOR PEACE AND WORK

REEMA
NANAVATY#

Home to a quarter of the world's population, and also to both the world's poorest and richest peoples, South Asia is one of the most densely populated regions in the world. Offering both hope and opportunities in the coming decades, it is prone to the recurring challenges of deadly disasters, economic downturn and internal conflicts, as well as a diversity of democracy demographic dividend, and the possibility of sustainable and climate-compatible development. Some countries, like Afghanistan and Sri Lanka, are the worst sufferers, with three consecutive decades of internal conflicts and recurring disasters. All of these have not only destroyed physical and human assets, but the fabric of society as well, and killed hope in humanity and peace. The future seems dark. Work is scarce. Peace distant. The worst off are women who are widowed, burdened with the task of nourishing their families or disabled husbands in a harsh socio-political environment with a lack of education, skills, employment, income and security. Rarely have women faced light and darkness, prosperity and poverty, hope and loss juxtaposed with each other in this region. And this conundrum is shared by women all over South Asia. When women meet at an interpersonal level, in meetings at policy events, or for work, they invite the sisters of SEWA (Self-Employed Women's Association) to come closer.

This need to come closer, to explore peace and find employment, attracted our attention at SEWA. But the question was: Should SEWA work outside India with other poor women, and on what basis? In the end, the call of one poor sister to another overcame the boundaries of time, policies, nationality, economy and society. SEWA has now been working in South Asia for almost nine years. Work began in Afghanistan in 2006, and in Sri Lanka in 2010, with war-affected widows and women who were in trauma, with no hope of survival. Violence was on the rise. Attacks were frequent. Work was being lost and the work space was shrinking. The future of their children was the only ray of hope and area of concern for these affected women. SEWA ignited their hope and self-confidence, and, from then on, the journey began, with women forming their own organisations in those countries, with trade and service delivery at the grass-roots level for developing the local economy, and peace and prosperity at the household level. The focus was on employment and the ability to use skills to access markets, to increase incomes and to build productive assets. Once income and assets were in somewhat solid shape, the march began—the access to water, the demand for sanitation, the use of road and transport, and sending children to schools and hospitals. A few more steps were taken by local sisters along with SEWA sisters to open bank accounts, use finance, and build and take local leadership positions in shops, bazaars and village organisations. This process was slow but steady. Women fell back on schedules, faced many reverses, but steadily moved ahead. In these war-torn countries, SEWA has organised over 3,000 war-affected women and promoted their trades with a consolidated turnover of USD 613,766.

SEWA's journey of hope and survival in Afghanistan began in 2006, where 1.5 million widows in Kabul alone were struggling with the survival of large families with day-to-day challenges owing to their illiteracy, social oppression and the absence of an income. SEWA, with its moral responsibility, initiated the work of skill building, first by setting up women's vocational training centres in Kabul. The only soothing touch for Afghan women at that point was the income by which they could support their children. SEWA developed a cadre of Afghan master trainers who inculcated Gandhian principles together with skills, set up vocational training centres in Kabul, and trained 4,000 war-affected Afghan women from Kabul and other provinces. These trained sisters formed and registered their own organisation, Baagay Khazana SABAH Association[1] in 2013, with 3,500 women participating actively. This was their own organisation, which worked at their pace and to their requirements. The Association helps their members in getting work and providing security of income by promoting their enterprises, by placement programmes, and by providing trade and facilitation support.

The Association has, to date, achieved an average annual turnover of USD 100,000 with an average income of USD 55 to 219 a month. Women use this income to feed their families, repair homes, send children to schools and visit doctors when needed. The income is invested in raw material, in storage facilities and in marketing. Trade and enterprise also open up avenues of work for unemployed youth, satisfying their aspirations, which helps prevent their participation in malign acts born of frustration. Youth, both male and female, want work. But where is employment to be found in these conflict-ridden economies? There can be no peace where there is no work.

This mainstreaming of war-affected women helped to start a programme with SEWA's SABAH for the further development of their trades and businesses. SEWA helped the Association to set up its own Trade Facilitation Centre in Kabul, and expand trade and businesses covering more war-affected women from four different provinces of Afghanistan. Women produced goods at home, at each other's homes as well as at their centre. At SEWA, the journey was not so smooth, but was successful enough to expand the mindset of male members, creating an understanding and acceptance of the right of women to work and earn. Men were amazed and often also agitated. Some were angry. But, in the end, when the children were fed and the home was repaired, most were happy to see women's work take them closer to peace. Happy families, satisfied youth, improved sources of income, developing Gandhian principles and acceptance for women in society were conditions that automatically gravitated towards peace and prosperity. However, all this was not easy. For example, Gandhian ideas were hard to apply, but truth had its appeal. Non-violence showed a way ahead from poverty, a march by grass-roots sisters which has now begun weaving peace in the social fabric, a slow but confident progress. Their slogan, '*Mohamaye Eaki Haste*' (We are all one) in the Dari language, was sounded again and again when these women from Kabul came to Ahmedabad to meet SEWA sisters and Elaben, SEWA's founder. Elaben pointed out how work can lead to possible peace, but there could be no peace where there is no work.

Sri Lanka's extended three-decade-long ethnic civil war damaged its social fabric, with serious consequences for both short-term survival and longer-term recovery. Children were also used as a tool in the war as child soldiers or forced into child marriage to prevent forceful involvement in the war. Over 90,000 people lost their lives and thousands of families are still grieving in the areas where SEWA works. A large number of people are still facing the challenges of physical and psychological casualties. SEWA began in 2010 by accepting the invitations of local poor women to work with them and understand their challenges. The social, political and cultural environment in Sri Lanka was different from that of Afghanistan, but the soul, heart and concerns of sisters are the same anywhere. Thus, with the same hope and concern for the starving children and war-affected women, SEWA began by developing bonding and work opportunities on similar lines of capacity building, along with the inculcation of Gandhian principles. A cadre of 40 Sri Lankan sisters was developed as master trainers and proceeded to set up two centres in the war-affected rural and urban areas of Batticaloa—the Trade Facilitation Centre and Community Learning Centre. During the course, 960 sisters were trained and have now formed the first-ever cooperative society in the history of Sri Lanka for war-affected women at the grass roots, which is registered at the provincial level—Women's Self-Employed Development Cooperative Society (WSDCS). The cooperative has achieved a turnover of USD 474,823 with an average monthly income of between USD 27 and 168. The cooperative has gained popularity and the attention of NGOs, companies and other women who have started entering into agreement for its services in Batticaloa and other parts of the country. This arrangement is also being extended to women of other ethnic communities. More women are being incorporated into this march, with the slogan, 'Nangal, Ellaru Mondray' (We are all one [in Tamil]).

The regional rural economy, which is predominantly agrarian, is rain fed. There is a water crisis for both domestic and agricultural use due to global warming. Again, women are the worst sufferers since they bear responsibility for their families and farm lands. SEWA's time-tested philosophy of women and work has allowed women to lead the greener livelihoods' initiative to combat global warming in seven countries of Asia. The importance of water in human life, and the challenges faced by women, has led SEWA to develop the concept of Blue Fund, with the twin objective of enabling women's access to water for every intended productive use with the help of microfinance. This creates the infrastructure, service and mechanism for water at the village level under women-led water chains, which also ensures livelihood security through the Blue Water concept. This women-led water supply chain has been developed in all SAARC countries, which creates awareness and develops the capacities of local communities for the productive usage, management and fair distribution of water.

The urban economy of South Asian countries is mostly dependent on home-based workers and service providers. Again, women are the largest invisible workforce which, working from home, runs the economy. In South Asia, women till farms, but men own them. Women water farms, but men own harvests. Women make doors and windows, but men market them. Women make bricks, but men make walls with them. With the objective of organising these women to help them overcome their trade challenges, SEWA has initiated a programme for economic empowerment by developing women-led value chains of the trades of home-based workers. South Asian cities are also factories. Every home of the poor woman is her factory, store, shop and also where she lives, where she makes over 1,000 items and stores over 3,000. The programme was started in India, and these women's organisations and Trade Facilitation Centres have been set up in Afghanistan, Sri Lanka, Nepal, Bangladesh, Bhutan, Pakistan and Sri Lanka. They have supported and strengthened the capacities and skills of women, and value chains of trade of 8,286 women workers, and achieved a turnover of USD 500,000.

It has been observed by SEWA that the plight of home-based workers is the same across countries and continents, and that it requires a multifaceted approach in overcoming the challenge. With this in view, SEWA has promoted an organisation called HomeNet South Asia, an international network of home-based workers' organisations, policy-makers and researchers, which is committed to working towards the recognition and visibility of home-based workers as full-fledged workers, with appropriate laws, policies, social security and economic rights. HomeNet is also actively assisting rural home-based workers, especially artisans such as embroiderers, organising and forming networks and marketing linkages. HomeNet promotes projects, programmes and workshops such as SABAH, which helps home-based workers to be recognised as workers in the economy, with the rights and benefits of mainstream markets.

SEWA's Gandhian philosophy and 42 years' experience has helped sisters believe that the key to a fair, peaceful and secured society is in the hands of women and their work. This approach has allowed SEWA to successfully roll out programmes across South Asia. SEWA has deployed a well-tested method—the integrated approach to sustainable livelihood generation by initiating the programme of understanding the local situation and the demands of local women. Essentially, this strategy follows four important directions:

(i)   Development of local human resources by building skills and capacities of local women at the grass roots.

(ii) Setting up the physical infrastructure, which can facilitate the economic activities of grass-roots sisters, to provide fair trade and distribution within their reach.

(iii) Setting up a grass-roots organisation for organised strength, visibility and capital, and networking for creating linkages, and to facilitate women to use their skills to generate an income.

(iv) Providing institutional managerial support to women to run their own organisation.

Through SEWA's work, over 12,000 grass-roots sisters across South Asia, who were deprived of opportunities for socio-economic growth, could develop enterprises and gainful employment. Most of these women have either joined small-scale businesses or organisations. This number is small, but what it indicates is important: given the chance, women in South Asia can find employment that builds peace—work that is gainful, sustainable, and not harmful to both the economy and ecology. It generates a peace that envelops families, communities and countries. Over 90 per cent of the trained women found positions where they could apply their newly learned skills.

Sixty per cent were able to earn a monthly income in the range of USD 34 to 90, compared to the average of USD 15. Over 50 micro-enterprises have been established. Women have invested towards seed capital for their business plans and started production, and developed backward–forward linkages, running entire supply chains by themselves.

All this has helped to foster a sense of ownership and accountability. The local organisation acts as a non-governmental, non-political, democratic, non-ethnic and secular set up that is committed to providing work, i.e., employment opportunities that will provide women and their families with a stable income, afford them a secure livelihood, water, food and, ultimately, peace. In the hands of women, work turns into peace.

◆

#This chapter was first published in 2015 in the *IIC Quarterly,* Vol. 41, Nos 3 and 4.

NOTE

1. SABAH is the acronym for South Asian Business Association of Home-based Workers. Prompted by SEWA and HomeNet South Asia, it organises the home-based workers in the neighbouring countries and builds their supply chain, thereby connecting them to the market.

◆◆

18

TRAFFICKING AND VULNERABILITIES OF CHILDREN AND WOMEN
An Analysis

ANURADHA
KOIRALA#

The South Asian Association for Regional Cooperation (SAARC) is dedicated to improving the welfare of the people of South Asia through economic growth, social progress and the cultural development of the region. It endeavours to achieve the six regional objectives stated in its charter through the principles of sovereign equality, territorial integrity, national independence, non-use of force, non-interference in the internal affairs of other States, and peaceful settlement of all disputes. Two significant consequences that derive from observing these principles are that decisions at all levels are taken on the basis of unanimity, and contentious issues are excluded from formal deliberations.

Children and women in South Asia are very vulnerable and prone to violence (human trafficking, sexual abuse, domestic violence), as well as natural disasters. UNICEF's *World's Children* (2010) states that the number of children under 18 in South Asia was 614 million, nearly 28 per cent of the world's total child population and greater than that of Europe, the Americas, Oceania and half of Africa combined. Every analysis and projection indicates that children in South Asia will be more vulnerable than ever due to natural calamities brought about by the impacts of climate change and rapid urbanisation that the region is experiencing on an unprecedented scale.

Climate change will impact food security, nutritional standards and human health, negatively affecting children to a greater extent than any other age segment of the population. The migration of poor rural households to urban areas in search of employment will expose children to the poverty and squalor of urban slums and increase their vulnerability to exploitation of many forms, including trafficking.

Protecting children during disasters from violence, exploitation and abuse is an integral component of protecting their rights to survival, growth and development. Their particular vulnerability to illness, malnutrition and abuse, their uniquely dependent social status and the fragility of their physical and mental development require special attention in the design and implementation of any disaster response, recovery and preparedness programme.

South Asian countries have demonstrated consistent concern and commitment for the protection and development of children's rights, being signatories to the Convention of the Rights of the Child, 1989, and its two optional protocols of 2000. Further, they adopted the World Declaration on the Survival, Protection and Development of Children, 1990, and endorsed the eight-fold Millennium Development Goals, 2000, six of which related directly to children. Heads of states and governments of South Asian countries signed the SAARC Convention on Regional Arrangements on the Promotion of Child Welfare in South Asia in 2002, and further adopted the SAARC Social Charter in 2004, which places strong emphasis on the promotion of rights and well-being of the child.

Human trafficking, especially that of children and women in South Asia (India, Bangladesh and Nepal), is a consequence of, and impediment to, socio-economic development, threatens national, regional and international security and, most importantly, the security of individuals. It has been estimated that more than 200,000 girls and women are trafficked annually for commercial sexual exploitation in South Asia. The focus on trafficking, either as an issue of illegal migration or prostitution, still dominates the discourse of trafficking in these countries, which prioritises state security over human security and does not adequately address its root causes as well as the insecurity of trafficked individuals. Vulnerability factors, such as structural inequality, culturally sanctioned practices, poverty or economic insecurity, organ trade, bonded labour, gender violence—all of which are further exacerbated by corruption— have remained unrecognised in academic and policy areas. Such underlying causes must be given due emphasis, and in particular corruption, which fuels human trafficking and threatens the human security of the trafficked in South Asian countries. The socio-economic structure is weakened by organised criminal activities, leading to the spread of corruption and infectious disease such as HIV/AIDS, and producing violence and greed that harms both states and their citizens.

Historically, the movement of people within the countries of the region has been common and, while on the move, people may become more vulnerable to exploitation in several forms. Trafficking for commercial sexual exploitation is considered the most virulent form in South Asia. As countries in this region experience rapid changes in economic, political, demographic and labour trends as an outcome of globalisation, the increasing demand for cheap labour coupled with burgeoning populations encourage migration, whether legal or illegal. The movement of young girls and women from Bangladesh and Nepal into Indian brothels, the Middle East and other destinations is common. At times of hardship, this starts out as illegal migration and ends up as trafficking. Such migration takes place with the backdrop of its origin and destination in the sending and receiving countries. The origin of this migration is associated with structural inequality, poverty, illiteracy and lack of opportunities for livelihood, whereas the destination is linked to the need for cheap labour.

In South Asia, the debate on human trafficking has been mostly dominated by two approaches: prostitution/sex work and migration. The first approach is debated by activists and practitioners as to whether prostitution should be banned or considered a legitimate trade. The second approach focuses on the supply/demand nexus of trafficking and stresses on promoting safe migration by separating trafficking from illegal migration. Anti-trafficking intervention by governments, NGOs, International Non-Government Organisations (INGOs) and other donor agencies is basically centred on these two approaches. It is important to consider that trafficking has been rarely referred to as an issue of individual security, both in academic research and policy intervention. The SAARC Charter on Human Trafficking also exists contemporarily.

THE EMERGENCE OF HUMAN TRAFFICKING

Although there is recent growing concern, human trafficking is not a new phenomenon. The origin of modern-day human trafficking dates back to the late 19th century. The movement against the transatlantic slave trade during that period provided the framework to abolish the 'white slave trade' which symbolically represented the notion of 'female sexual slavery' as the result of trafficking in white women for prostitution. Following the movement, the first international legal instrument, the International Agreement for the Suppression of White Slave Traffic, formed during 1904–10, acknowledged trafficking in white women for prostitution in Europe. But changes in racial notions and inadequate law enforcement later caused it to be replaced with another convention called Trafficking in Women and Children in 1921. Later, the International Convention for the Suppression of the Traffic in Women of Full Age was adopted in 1933 by the League of Nations, focusing on the distinction between adult women and female children.

These early anti-trafficking conventions were eventually consolidated into the 1949 Convention, known as the Suppression of the Traffic in Persons and of the Exploitation of the Prostitution of Others, which essentially referred to trafficking as a problem associated with prostitution. Thus, having made a beginning in the early decades, a series of international instruments against trafficking was adopted throughout the 20th century. Finally, the early years of the 21st century witnessed the first major, widely and internationally accepted, Convention Against Trafficking in Palermo, Italy. In 2000, as an outcome of previous international legal efforts, the UN Trafficking Protocol on Suppression of Trafficking in Women and Children was adopted. According to Article 3 of the Protocol,

> Trafficking in persons shall mean the recruitment, transportation, transfer, harboring or receipt of persons, by means of the threat or use of force or other forms of coercion, of abduction, of fraud, of deception, of the abuse of power or of a position of vulnerability or of the giving or receiving of payments or benefits to achieve the consent of a person having control over another person, for the purpose of exploitation. Exploitation shall include, at a minimum, the exploitation of the prostitution of others or other form[s] of sexual exploitation, forced labor or services, slavery or practices similar to slavery, servitude or the removal of organs (United Nations Office of Drugs and Crime, UNODC, 2004).

Human trafficking has always been a subject of huge debate, both in theory and practice. This debate has grown with its focus on the relationship between the problem of trafficking and other relevant issues such as prostitution, migration, organised crime and human rights. Trafficking is often equated with prostitution, a view that holds that its only purpose is prostitution and that all trafficked persons are sexually exploited. Those who take this position believe that prostitution should be abolished in order to stop trafficking (radical feminist/abolitionist view). Opposing this view is the other group (liberal feminist/sex worker) that acknowledges prostitution as sex work, arguing that migrant sex workers should not be categorised as trafficked persons, or that all sex work is not necessarily the result of trafficking. This view is rooted in the demand for the legalisation of prostitution. On the one hand, the migration approach to trafficking explains the supply and demand chains of trafficking in the backdrop of the irregular movement of people across borders and focuses on a restrictive migration policy to reduce the problem in source countries. On the other hand, it considers trafficking as a problem of illegal migration that threatens the security of host countries. This view sees trafficking partially as an illegal migration problem that often leads to the prosecution of the trafficked rather than traffickers. These circumstances raise the issues of human rights abuse of trafficked persons in the destination countries. The notion of state security does not help to understand this crucial point. Neither does it help to address the root causes or vulnerability factors of trafficking.

In addition to the debate over whether trafficking is a problem of prostitution or of migration, the following questions must be emphasised if trafficking is to be successfully combated: Why does trafficking take place? What are its underlying causes? How does it cause human insecurity?

MAJOR INTERNATIONAL AND LEGAL INSTRUMENTS

Trafficking in human beings attracted rapidly growing attention in the latter half of the 1990s. Today, it is regarded as a developmental issue as well as an expression of the absence of gender equality. It has found a place on the developmental policy agenda and become the target of international developmental cooperation measures. Therefore, a growing number of governmental and non-governmental players have begun to tackle this problem, and a variety of actions are being taken in areas such as migration, organised crime and human rights. Despite the diversity of actions and points of departure, a common pattern emerges of a strategy characterised by three main components: (1) preventive measures, (2) strengthened legislation and more vigorous investigation and prosecution of offenders, and (3) protection and support for victims. Initially, players—mainly governments and intergovernmental bodies—focused on policies and more vigorous prosecution of offenders, while the job of providing support and help to victims was left to NGOs.

Normative provisions have been given greater prominence and further developed at an international level through the United Nations and regionally. There is now an international regulatory framework in place. However, the norms have not yet found expression in national legislation or government policies. The central document in force today is the UN Convention against Transnational Organised Crime and its Protocol to Prevent, Suppress and Punish Trafficking in Persons, Especially Women and Children. The Convention and its protocols were adopted and opened for signature in Palermo in December 2000.

A major contribution of the protocol is that it provides the first legally binding, comprehensive definition of trafficking in human beings to be agreed upon by the international community. The instrument contains provisions on a range of issues, including criminalisation, assistance to and protection for victims, the status of victims in the receiving states, repatriation of victims, preventive measures, actions to discourage the demand, exchange of information and training, and measures to strengthen the effectiveness of border controls.

It stipulates that state parties must adopt or strengthen legislative or other measures to discourage the demand that fosters all forms of exploitation of persons, especially women and children, which leads to trafficking. Nepal has not yet ratified this protocol, and civil society organisations have been lobbying for its installation.

The UN Convention on the Elimination of All Forms of Discrimination against Women (CEDAW), with its optional protocol on the right of individuals, or groups of individuals, to submit individual complaints to the Committee on the Elimination of Discrimination against Women, focuses on the human rights of women. The Convention—which dates from 1979 and has been ratified by three-quarters of the world's states—provides the basis for realising equality between women and men by ensuring women equal access to opportunities in political and public life. State parties agree to take all appropriate measures, including legislation and temporary special measures, so that women can enjoy all human rights and fundamental freedoms.

The 1989 UN Convention on the Rights of the Child (CRC) has now been ratified by almost all countries. The Convention applies to all persons under 18 years of age and covers children's civil, political, economic, social and cultural rights. It addresses the right of children to have their basic needs met, to be protected against discrimination and exploitation, the right to express their views and to have them respected. State parties—nations which have ratified the UN Convention on the Rights of the Child (CRC)—are all committed to protecting every child from all forms of sexual exploitation and to adopt such measures as are necessary to prevent the sale, or trafficking, of children. State parties are responsible for ensuring that national legislation is in accord with the articles of the Convention.

In May 2000, the UN General Assembly adopted a protocol optional to the CRC on the sale of children, child prostitution and child pornography, which extends the protection provided under the Convention. The protocol is now in force, and guidelines on reporting by state parties have been drawn up. State parties are required to prohibit and penalise the acts and activities set out in the optional protocol, which includes provisions on the extradition of persons charged with crimes under the convention, and on international cooperation aimed at preventing crimes.

SOCIO-ECONOMIC AND CULTURAL IMPACT OF HUMAN TRAFFICKING ON CHILDREN

Traffickers use psychological manipulation and coercive methods to control their victims and to make their escape virtually impossible by destroying their physical and psychological defences. Reported methods include physical, sexual and psychological violence; isolation; deployment in areas unknown to them; dependence on alcohol or drugs; controlled access to food and water; and monitoring through the use of weapons, cameras and dogs. Children who experience commercial sexual exploitation

(CSE) confront all the dangers associated with sexual abuse; they are also subjected to routine beatings and abuse by traffickers, employers, pimps, brothel owners and customers. It is the extent and persistence of the psychological and physical abuse, and the coercive, deceitful and exploitative relationship with traffickers that distinguishes trafficking from other maltreatment. Numerous accounts suggest that the emotional and physical trauma, and unrelenting abuse and fear present grave risks to physical, psychological, spiritual and social–emotional development. Case studies suggest that CSE 'damages physical and emotional well being of the victims because of the persistent physical, sexual and psychological abuse that accompanies it on a daily basis'. Children who have been exposed to complex trauma, such as prolonged physical abuse, sexual abuse, emotional abuse and neglect, violence and torture, are at increased risk for a number of symptoms and behavioural characteristics, including attachment, stigmatisation and alienation, emotional regulation, dissociative adaptations, cognitive functioning and self-image.

EDUCATIONAL DEPRIVATION

Children who are trafficked are robbed of the few educational opportunities available to them and, thus, a chance to improve their future economic situation. Related research has identified the adverse outcomes of educational deprivation among victims of neglect (psychological and emotional) and abuse (physical and sexual).

PHYSICAL HEALTH PROBLEMS

Victims experience inhuman living conditions, an inadequate diet, poor hygiene, beatings and abuse, neglect, and the denial of their basic human rights to health care and protection, resulting in lasting health problems. Victims of CSE are further threatened by unsafe sexual practices, heightened risks of frequent unwanted pregnancies and their attendant complications, unsafe abortions and sexually transmitted diseases such as HIV/AIDS.

EMOTIONAL WELL-BEING

The experiences associated with trafficking can lead to lasting psychological challenges such as physical and emotional trauma associated with removal from their families, homes and communities;

subsequent encounters involve substantial harm through physical, emotional and sexual abuse. Case studies have reported adverse emotional effects, including depression, hopelessness, guilt, shame, flashbacks, nightmares, the loss of confidence, lower self-esteem and anxiety. The negative messages that they routinely receive can influence their sense of worth, leading to feelings of self-blame. Empirical research on child maltreatment has identified numerous adverse consequences for victims. Psychological abuse associated with ongoing threats, isolation, and witnessing the abuse of others, negatively affects self-worth, personal goals, relationships with others, and seriously jeopardises emotional well-being. Emotional and physical neglect are associated with social and emotional withdrawal and behavioural problems.

STIGMATISATION AND DISCRIMINATION
Survivors face acute problems in reintegrating with their families as they are severely stigmatised. Once a girl is trafficked, she faces hate and blame, especially in the South Asian context.

SOME MITIGATING MEASURES
Analyses from South Asia provide practical examples and lessons for the implementation of key components of a comprehensive rights-based approach to child trafficking. This includes awareness-raising, community mobilisation, political and social commitment, networking and cooperation, victim assistance and sustainability.

AWARENESS-RAISING AND COMMUNITY MOBILISATION
Community traditions and practices can sometimes contribute to an environment in which children are vulnerable to abuse and exploitation. Community mobilisation and raising awareness of child rights, risk factors associated with child exploitation and neglect, and support services to ensure child protection have proved to be important tools that serve to empower communities to assert the rights of children and women, and prevent child exploitation and abuse, including trafficking.

GOVERNMENT INVOLVEMENT
Successful anti-trafficking initiatives require the active involvement of the government, at local and central levels, and the long-term

commitment of all stakeholders. The political commitment required to address and prevent child trafficking should focus on all its forms as well as on broader child protection issues in both countries of origin and destination, as well as in initiatives for cross-border cooperation.

NETWORKING AND COOPERATION

Strong networking and cooperation among actors from the community level right up to the central government has proved to be an important success factor in tackling child trafficking. Further collaboration is needed among the countries of the region to share information, exchange expertise, coordinate prevention, care and protection practices, promote repatriation and reintegration, all of which must be fully guided by the best interests of the child. Such initiatives need to safeguard the rights of the children they seek to protect.

VICTIM SUPPORT

Victim support and psycho-social counselling need additional capacity building, especially at the national level, given the lack of professionals in the region with skills sufficient to counsel traumatised children. It is also important to support the families of the children concerned to ensure that children are properly reintegrated into their communities. Family members and other relatives are sometimes associated with exploitation and abuse of children, including trafficking. However, it is essential to ensure that the best interests of the child are a central concern when taking action against traffickers, since prosecuting their parents or family members may cause children additional harm.

CARE, PROTECTION AND REINTEGRATION

Reintegration remains a challenge in the region, and few organisations monitor children who have been returned to their communities, or document the successes and failures of reintegration. Mental health and social factors may be more difficult to address than the economic challenges of reintegration. Activities for the care, protection and reintegration of rescued trafficked children need to be integrated into a holistic framework. The quality of these practices should be regulated through national minimum standards. They also need to be strengthened through training caregivers and capacity building for a wide spectrum of care and protection services. Attention should be paid to strengthening reintegration practices, including mechanisms to ensure children's safe reintegration, and the development of community-based, care-giving options. Repatriation may not always be in the best interests of the child; therefore, each case should be assessed individually. Capacity building of professionals in areas such as psychosocial support, quality control and development, and the implementation of minimum standards needs further work. More attention is needed to support children's mental health and to address social factors, including teaching life skills.

NON-DISCRIMINATION
Women and adolescent girls are typically the focus of, and are actively involved in, initiatives aimed at preventing discrimination. Involving boys and men is crucial to overcome gender discrimination, violence and abuse. Discrimination and social exclusion also need to be further addressed by strengthening the participation and empowerment of marginalised children and adults. It is important to address all diversity issues, including discrimination, on the grounds of national and ethnic origin, ability, social status, caste, gender and age. Sexual exploitation of boys is an area that needs further attention. Both adults and children should be provided with information on the sexual abuse of children of both genders.

POVERTY
Poverty remains a challenge throughout the region. Linking child protection to activities aimed at economic empowerment of children and families is important. Agencies that support livelihoods are needed to help develop sources of family income, thereby reducing the risk of exploitation and trafficking of children. However, it is important to recognise that not all poor children are being trafficked and to learn the factors that increase or decrease children's vulnerability.

BEST INTERESTS OF CHILDREN
For caregivers, police, judicial authorities and others, determining the child's best interests and taking decisions to implement them

is seldom a simple or clear process. Clearly defined mechanisms and procedures, including guidelines for decision making, case management and minimum standards, help contribute to reliable and effective procedures to determine and implement a child's best interests.

NATIONAL CHILD PROTECTION SYSTEMS

National child protection systems should be developed, guided by children's rights and mobilised at all levels. Such systems address the prevention of trafficking and the responses required to assist trafficked children. They include child-friendly, legal, medical and psychosocial services; community mobilisation for child protection; training of service providers; and data collection, analysis and dissemination. A systematic approach is necessary to recognise the linkages between violence, abuse, exploitation and trafficking, and to address the root causes of child protection issues.

POLITICAL SUPPORT

It is important to ensure political support for issues such as:

(i) Ratification and effective implementation of the most important international legal instruments by all countries, including through the harmonisation of national legislation, the adequate mobilisation and use of resources, and the implementation of effective programmes and interventions.

(ii) Drawing up and financing national plans of action on child trafficking, or considering child trafficking within other national planning processes.

(iii) Development of national strategies for collaboration between the government, non-governmental organisations, international partners and children.

As the Founder and Chairperson of Maiti, Nepal, I have found the modus operandi of trafficking in the past two decades to have become increasingly organised. In the past, India used to be the only trafficking destination for Nepali girls. More than 12,000 girls and women are being trafficked from Nepal for commercial exploitation. Further, I have found that trafficking in the course of migration to the Gulf and African nations is very challenging, as it is a state-permitted process that confers the fundamental right to migration. Today, organised crime syndicates are involved in the sale of minor girls with the aid of fake documents and distorted details. Most importantly, internal trafficking is equally an alarming area of concern. Entertainment sectors might well be considerably good revenue-generating areas for the government, but the sexual exploitation of minors is something which attracts the attention of human rights defenders like me. Since 1993, Maiti has been able to rescue 29,000 girls from sexual slavery. My fight to find sustainable solutions to these issues will continue in the days to come.

◆

#This chapter was first published in 2015 in the *IIC Quarterly*, Vol. 41, Nos 3 and 4.

19
SOUTH ASIAN LITERATURES
Beyond Borders, across Boundaries

NAMITA
GOKHALE

MALASHRI
LAL#

*The signifiers, whether they are images or characters or episodes, or even
so-called structures and archetypes, may be the same in different periods
and regions, but the signification goes on changing.*

A.K. Ramanujan

A distinct South Asian literary identity, drawn from
interconnecting languages, culture, food, music and oral
heritage is emerging in modern fiction, and in social media.
It cuts across the boundaries of religion and ideology, and stretches
the limits of static political maps. Be it the commonality of Urdu
through much of Pakistan, Punjab and Uttar Pradesh; or Bangla
along the shores of the Padma river; or Tamil, one of the classical
Indian languages, spreading through India and Sri Lanka, South
Asian literatures present an intricate web of interdependency.
Adding to the strands are the merging and blending dialects of
spoken languages. Whether it is Saraiki, Multani and Sindhi across
India, Pakistan and the Sindhi diaspora, or Maithili featuring as
the second language in Nepal and the official language of Bihar, or
the fact that Nepali is itself one of the 22 official Indian languages
with a numerically larger base in India than in Nepal, the linguistic
and literary topography of South Asian countries have a common
imprint of tradition and creative imagination.

This interlinked pattern in the region makes it different from
'Western' pedagogical models which inscribe hierarchies between the
oral and the scripted, the epical and the modern, English and 'other'
languages. Without being needlessly contentious, it is important to
understand that ancient lineages and shared identities in Asia's past

find reflection in contemporary geographies of South Asia which are constituted differently than in other parts of the world. Western categorisations fail to grant recognition to the prolific linguistic and literary play in South Asia.

It is perhaps worth remembering that the word 'India' harks back to the 'Indies', for in the imagination of Portuguese and Spanish seafarers India was conceived only in the plural. The name 'Indies' (to describe the region) is derived from the river Indus and was used to connote parts of Asia that came under Indian cultural influence. In history, the matter gets enormously complex with colonial mediations as shown by Sheldon Pollock in his edited volume, *Literary Cultures in History: Reconstructions from South Asia* (2003). Ancient languages transit into newer forms, as evolving cultural practices create ever-changing contexts, and power structures determine which language groups get priority. So, the literary imagination of South Asia gets interpreted through a variety of perspectives as the 'Indies' of old yields to a flux of new political identities. We see today a constant straining for self-definition in each country, even though the common threads of the past tug at the expediencies of the present.

SINGULAR PLURALITIES

It has been observed that whatever one may say of India, the opposite is equally true. Linguistic groups and literary traditions collide and yet coexist, with some tangled thread of connectivity described as 'many languages and one literature'. The whole is greater than the sum of its parts and the flowering of new writing and the affirmation of new voices across India's multilingual map is drawing the intrigued attention of the world.

While Salman Rushdie's *Midnight's Children* (1981) was a watershed which impacted how the world viewed South Asian writing, the author's magical prose also transformed the manner in which this writing examined itself. Although some critics categorised it as a valorisation of the 'post-colonial exotic', Pico Iyer's famous essay 'The Empire Strikes Back' described it as 'a call to free spirits everywhere to remake the world with imagination', opening up 'a new universe by changing the way we tell stories and see the world around us'. It is useful to note that though Rushdie is a votary of English writing, the voice of Saleem Sinai, Rushdie's main character, reclaimed the spoken sounds of the Bombay/Mumbai streets into English literary usage. The sinuous, stylistic flow also reflected the texture and grain of Urdu, which is an important part of Rushdie's literary inheritance. Rushdie's English writing thus carried a residue or subtext of Urdu, just as writers such as Amit Chaudhuri, Jhumpa Lahiri or Chitra Banerjee Divakaruni carry the lilt of Bangla, in a confluence of linguistic culture and usage.

We need not enter into a discussion on Indian writing in English, the scope, accomplishments and aspirations of which are copiously documented. We may look instead at the other languages that porously inhabit each other across the political borders of South Asia.

The Urdu tradition, in the footsteps of Saadat Hasan Manto and Faiz Ahmed Faiz, mirrored both a determined social commitment and a strong sense of comic subversion. Pre-Partition Urdu was a secular, agnostic language, one capable of both the most brutal irony and the highest romanticism. It was used by Munshi Premchand, Rajinder Singh Bedi, Krishna Chandar, Qurratulain Hyder, Ismat Chughtai and Ghulam Abbas, in the syncretic linguistic tradition of Urdu/Hindustani. Post-Partition Hindi, the new national language of India, was shorn of its Urdu and Hindustani traces and influences, and was immensely the poorer for this loss. During the 1950s, as Pakistan entered into cycles of politico-military dominance, restrictions on free expression led to a heightened use of symbol and metaphor, thereby avoiding direct conflict with repressive forces. Across the border, in India, Urdu stayed alive in Punjabi writing. Today, it is alive in Bollywood, it is flourishing in both prose and poetry, and in translation too. Shamsur Rahman Faruqi's recent work, *Kai Chand Te Sare Aasman,* is considered one of the greatest works of Urdu prose ever penned and appreciated equally in India, Pakistan and the global Urdu diaspora.

Fortunately, Pakistan today is witnessing a literary liberation, a brilliant blossoming of talent in its highly visible international English language writers. From Zulfikar Ghose, Bapsi Sidhwa and Sara Suleri, a new generation of names come quickly to mind— Kamila Shamsie, Mohsin Hamid, Aamer Hussein, Nadeem Aslam, Mohammed Hanif, Musharraf Ali Farooqi, Daniyal Mueenuddin, Bilal Tanveer and H.M. Naqvi, among several others. In the words of novelist Kamila Shamsie, 'Pakistani writing is like the new fast bowler on the scene.' There is vital interaction among Urdu writers across the border of Pakistan and India and a finer understanding of a nuanced past. The post-Partition aspects of rural Punjab, Pakistan, find sensitive portrayal in the work of Ali Akbar Natiq. From this side of the border, Joginder Paul's fictional works are widely read not only in India, but also in Pakistan.

Other national literatures common to both India and Pakistan, such as Sindhi, have retained a distinct voice despite being marginalised for various political reasons. Sindhi literary traditions date from the heroic ballads of the 17th century, including *Shah Jo Risalo*, a poetic compendium of lyrics by Shah Abdul Latif Bhittai. But politics and geography suffered a traumatic disconnect in 1947. In 1952, the Sindhi Abadi Sangat was structured as a literary forum. While Karachi remained its original locus of activity, the movement quickly spread to other cities in the region as the desire to preserve a linguistic identity emerged strongly. The Sahitya Akademi of India recognised Sindhi as one of its languages in 1955. Today, research and contemporary writing in the language is fairly profuse, especially in journals, though the sense of a fragmented history colours its emotional landscape.

Along with such retrievals of neglected languages, one may list Multani and Saraiki, both considered 'regional' in character and yet claiming a rich literary corpus. Multani is an ancient language still spoken in the southern areas of Punjab, Pakistan, and has historical links with Sindhi as well as Saraiki. Lately, linguistic revivals have pushed Saraiki into prominence, and this language, spoken in western Punjabi areas, now features at the Lahore Literary Festival, introducing the popular folk tales associated with Ghazi Khan along with modern fictional writers such as Ismail Ahmedani.

A comparable weave of plurality is visible in Nepal. Like other South Asian literatures, Nepal too has its enduring epic transmitted through versions of orality and now popularised as 'Muna Madan' by Laxmi Prasad Devkota. Retelling an 18th century ballad, it speaks of a merchant from Kathmandu who must leave his bride and proceed on a journey with unknown risks to Tibet. However, literary continuities in Nepal have been severely hindered by political upheavals. Writers have been vocal about this; therefore views of, and within, the country are refracted through both Nepali and English. Writer Manjushree Thapa observes:

In the 1990s and before, members of Kathmandu's cloistered literary establishment—almost entirely 'high caste men'[—]would write Kathmandu-based literature; and only a few regional writers who had won recognition from the establishment would write about their particular communities ... The rest of Nepal remained almost wholly unwritten. This insularity had become quite untenable by the time the war started [in 1996]; and yet it persisted until the war's end.

Thapa's own collection of political essays, *The Lives We Have Lost,* captures the disquieting turbulence in the history of Nepal from 1990 until 2009. In the post-revolution era, Nepali literature has grown into a vibrant corpus ready to contend with issues of politics, family, history and Nepal's relationship with the world. No more a landlocked country in its creative imagination, the global experience is reflected in new works such as *The Gurkha's Daughter* by Prajwal Parajuly and *Palpasa Café* by the bestselling author, Narayan Wagle.

Bhutan, too, carries the same double-edged relationship between English and the sonorous native tongue Dzongkha that was declared the official national language in the 1960s. Religious texts, Buddhist hagiographies and classical commentary are still written in Dzongkha, a language based on old Tibetan, and now compulsorily studied in schools. Knowledge traditions continue to emphasise the psychological sciences that cover Buddhist doctrines. An ancient epic of Gesar, common to Bhutan and its neighbours, appears in several versions, and storytelling has gathered a modern emphasis. The writing in English is a parallel tradition heard at 'Mountain Echoes', the annual literary festival held at Thimphu and Paro. Among the popular writers is Kunzang Choden, the first Bhutanese woman to write a novel in English, *The Circle of Karma* (2005), her other works being folktales, children's stories and a cookbook. Gathering rapid fame is Karma Phuntsho, author of a comprehensive narrative *History of Bhutan* (2013) in English, and philosophical discourses in Dzongkha. The coexistence of English and Dzongkha is harmonious.

Sri Lanka has followed a different template. An extraordinary array of international talent, such as Michael Ondaatje, Romesh Gunesekera and others have drawn literary inspiration from their homeland of Serendip. Shehan Karunatilaka's debut novel,

Chinaman, attracted praise for writing engagingly about cricket, a game for which passion runs high in South Asia. In Sri Lanka, there is a conflicted racial and linguistic struggle because the distances and differences between Pali, Sinhala and Tamil literature have yet to find coexistence on amicable ground. Tamil Eelam literature of resistance is strongly political and incantatory, voicing its disillusionment in poetry and song, fiction and prose. Cheran's collection of poems, *In a Time of Burning,* captures three decades of civil war with brutal frankness, and Naomi Munaweera decides to tell the story as fiction in *Island of a Thousand Mirrors.* Tamil, the language of protest in Sri Lanka, is also one of India's most prolific literary and classical languages, and one which is powerful in its use of transgressional and transformative strategies.

Both India and Bangladesh, and their respective diaspora communities, continue to engage in a tryst with the Bangla language, radical and mellifluous in the same breath. The Bangla firmament shines with legendary writers and poets such as Syed Shamsul Huq, Shamsur Rahman, Humayun Ahmed and Muhammed Zafar Iqbal, as well as many younger names. Global outreach is captured by writers, including Monica Ali, Tehmima Anam, Shazia Omar and Kaiser Haq—all in English. Under the influence of Rabindranath Tagore and Kazi Nazrul Islam, traditions of poetry and music remain strong in Bangladesh, of which the popularity of singer Rezwana Choudhury Bannya is substantial. Fiction by Selina Hossain is highly rated and being extensively translated. Nurul Momen, often called Natyaguru, is credited with the revival of theatre and the integration of avant garde styles. Historically, Bangladesh shares a troubled heritage with Pakistan as well as West Bengal. However, over the last decade, literary negotiations with a traumatic past have yielded a distinct Bangladeshi identity.

MANY LANGUAGES, ONE LITERATURE

And so we come to India, that paradox of paradoxes, where similar patterns of linguistic unity and diversity show up on a completely different scale.

In a country with 22 official national languages, 122 regional languages, 4 classical languages, 1,726 mother tongues and countless dialects, the diverse and polyphonic expression of literary identity in modern-day India is both daunting and inspiring. Although colonisation and the imposition of English stifled the vitality and outreach of many Indian languages, today, after decades of suppression, writers are compulsively returning to their own tongues with new creativity and inspiration.

The various *bhasha* (language) clusters in India are distinctive, yet traverse a common heritage and core identity. Grass-roots writers, in the many languages, have both a contemporary voice and an enduring connection with classical traditions—here it is essential to mention Hindi, Bangla, Tamil, Malayalam, Kannada, Marathi, Odiya, Assamiya, Punjabi, Gujarati, Bhojpuri and Urdu traditions. Novels, short fiction, poetry and experimental writing are flourishing in each of these, along with a robust practice of literary criticism. English is an Indian language, of course, and also the first language of many writers from the North-east, including Mamang Dai, Temsula Ao, Robin S. Ngangom, Janice Pariat and others who cover a gamut of genres. However, indigenous writing from the North-east is increasingly making an appearance through young voices who wish to excavate forgotten tribal practices.

The novel is not a homegrown literary form, but has adapted instinctively to South Asian practices. The first Indian novel, *Indulekha*, was written by Chandu Menon in Malayalam in 1889. Novelists such as Srilal Shukla, Uday Prakash and Alka Saraogi in Hindi; Mahasweta Devi and Sunil Gangopadhyay in Bangla; Ambai, Sivasankari, Salma, Bama, Charu Nivedita, Sivakami and Ashokamitran in Tamil; U.R. Ananthamurthy in Kannada and M.T. Vasudevan Nair in Malayalam are just some of the great and beloved names of modern Indian literature.

India's two most enduring epics, the Ramayana and the Mahabharata, inform both the folk (*desi*) and classical (*margi*) traditions. A pan South Asian cultural and aesthetic vocabulary relates to these epics, leading to the many Ramayanas that bring delightful adaptions to the social contexts of the narratives. As the famed Kannada writer, U.R. Ananthamurthy observed, 'There are two languages which are understood all over India—the Ramayana and the Mahabharata. One can easily refer to the characters from these epics and [these] make sense to anyone.'

Mythology remains a constant on Indian bestseller lists. The passionate exploration and reinterpretation of epics within different languages and genres is often surprising to Western academia which tends to categorise myth as a static area of study. The gods are alive in India and much of the rest of the region: Mythology is not merely a theoretical subject, but a topic of vital and immediate relevance to the act of living meaningfully. The interplay between the ancient heroic stories and contemporary situations has resulted in an outpouring of essays, plays, films and novels, including the hugely popular novel, *The Palace of Illusions* (2008), by US-based Chitra Banerjee Diwakaruni; the Ramayana series (2003–6) by Ashok Banker; the record-breaking *The Immortals of Meluha* (2010) by Amish Tripathi; *Chanakya's Chant* (2010) by Ashwin Sanghi and *In Search of Sita: Revisiting Mythology* (2009), which is co-edited by both of us. The entire South Asian region revels in its peculiar versions of the Ramayana, binding it in a narrative fabric where the main strands are recognisable but the hues, infinite. Our work on Sita imagines her in the Ashoka Vatika in Sri Lanka; other tales see Hanuman as Rama's acolyte with a bagful of antics. Ravana himself is variously interpreted as a villain or a sage. Recent books by Devdutt Pattanaik, Samhita Arni and Arshia Sattar present Sita in myriad ways by building upon the possibilities of the essential tale. The Mahabharata likewise gives infinite range in imagining where the Pandavas spent their years of exile, and especially the period of 'agyatvasa'. Languages and geographies melt into vocalising a timeless cultural trope: the good versus the evil.

Retelling epics rejuvenates oral traditions. Many of India's Adivasi and other marginalised societies, for long mistakenly described as 'illiterate', are repositories of oral literatures that have been transmitted through generations. Across India, fragile and endangered cultures have held on to a continuity of intangible heritage—through folk song, woven narratives, timeless ballads and local epics. These are often transposed into the mainstream imagination, but in that process, many face the dilemma of being forgotten, of being distorted in translation, or of losing their fluidity and being embalmed through academic archiving. For example, Ghafaruddin Mewati is a balladeer of an unbroken secular tradition dating from the 18th century when the Muslim composer Sadullah Khan appropriated the Hindu Mahabharata tradition for his own poetic ends. Today, Mewati's young grandson Shahrukh is the enthusiastic recipient of 14 generations of this mindfully nurtured heritage, but it is doubtful whether he, or others like him, will be able to sustain it.

Among the marginalised, Dalit writers have emerged as a distinct group protesting their rejection by mainstream Indian literature and now asserting their sensibility. They are, in a sense, conscience keepers of a democratic India. Kancha llaiah, one of the major ideologues of the caste struggle, wrote a moving editorial piece in the *Deccan Herald*: 'Literary festivals teach how to connect oneself to social mass culture if one is doing transformative writing. If it helps even a section of oppressors to identify with the viewpoint of the oppressed, writing becomes more meaningful.' In India, where many feel so passionately about the country's multiple literatures, it is crucial that common spaces must be available for society to share its problems—and anger is a very important part of the process. This is valuable, because it is a thinking anger, a talking anger, an anger that leads to creative energy, rather than a stone-pelting anger. For example, the late Om Prakash Valmiki's autobiography, *Joothan* (Leftovers), with its vivid portrayal of personal deprivations, cannot fail to arouse sensitivity about the travails of the outcaste.

Several marginalised and suppressed voices—those of Dalits, women, LGBT and others—are using their newly emergent micro-literatures to subvert oppressive hierarchies and prejudices. Women writers, in particular, are making a significant impact in the literary environment of India's many languages, even in the face of resentment from an established patriarchal setup. A few years ago, in 2011, V.S. Naipaul claimed that women write differently from men and he can deduce the writer's sex by reading 'a piece of writing and within a paragraph or two'. Women writers are 'unequal to me', Naipaul announced grandly, and proceeded to label all writing by women as 'feminine tosh'. Such prejudice was not new as, on another occasion in India, Naipaul had angered Nayantara Sehgal and Shashi Deshpande with his words: 'My life is short. I can't listen to banalities .... And this thing about colonialism, this thing about gender oppression, the very word "oppression" wearies me.' Women writers today are vociferous in protesting against inequities that are legacies of a social schema no longer acceptable in a global modernity. Neither Dalits nor women, nor writers of the North-east, are ready to blend into an undifferentiated homogeneity. Their voices against oppression are mediated by matrices of caste, class, language, ethnicity and such variables leading to questions about inherited beliefs.

In the South Asian context, fiction today provides a surrogate space for writers of an alternative sexuality, allowing them to honestly wrestle with their identities in a still largely patriarchal, homophobic society. Such 'gendered' writing is not easy. Feminist publisher Urvashi Butalia narrates how:

> For the last decade or more, I've been working with Mona Ahmed, a hijra, on writing her life. Mona lives in a large compound called Mehendiyan—named after the mehendi trees that once dotted its gardens—close to the walls of the old city of Delhi. Here, local lore is still rife with the stories of a legendary hijra couple, Sona and Chaman, whose lives were split, like those of millions of others, at Partition.

Eventually, this will become a fascinating tale of invisible lives but, meanwhile, says Butalia, one may recall:

> India and Pakistan are among the few countries in the world where eunuchs still exist. Deprived of their traditional roles as caretakers of harems, their main occupations are offering of blessings in return for money or *badhai* on auspicious occasions such as weddings, the birth of children, etc., or begging, or sex work.

In a relatively new genre, literary narratives such as A. Revathi's *The Truth About Me: A Hijra Life Story* (2010), and *Our Lives, Our Words: Telling Aravani Lifestories* (2012), show the transgendered body as an arena of political and individual assertion.

CULTURE AND CONNECTIVITY

South Asian literature, in its many voices, languages and avatars, retains an underlying warp and woof of cultural connectivity. India is, and always has been, a *bahubhashit* (multilingual) society. The Vedas, the earliest remembered expression of our literary culture, urge invoking the gods in many languages.

Over the years, an unprecedented interest in South Asian literature and its increasing articulation have fuelled a need for vigorous interpretation of the contradictory, often conflicting, realities of India and the region. Engaged levels of debate on literature and society in these regions, which are fractured by political identities and joined by linguistic legacies, are to be encouraged. International communities are rediscovering their roots in South Asian languages such as Urdu, Nepali, Bangla and Tamil. India has had a peculiar hierarchy in languages. On the surface it appears plural, polyphonic, but between those many languages, there has always been a clear, dominant one. The aesthetic distinction between 'desi' and 'margi', the folk and classical styles, has transmuted but not disappeared. Historically, Sanskrit was at the helm, followed by local median languages, and then folk tongues and dialects. Somewhere along the line, in the process of colonisation, English effectively replaced Sanskrit as the elite and aspirational tongue. As India found its own voice, and national languages flourished in an environment supported by media and technology, the balance shifted back to the local bhasha languages, bringing today a constant transaction between English and its 'other'.

Like democracy, translation must seek equity. There should be no dominant bias between the two languages, and the cultural cues within the work need to be projected for effective literary translation. This is naturally not an easy process, requiring intensive dual-language skills and cultural knowledge. However, while it is generally easier to translate between cognate rather than non-cognate language clusters (Marathi to Gujarati being easier than Marathi to Mizo), the link language for translation in the Indian literatures still often tends to be English. This middleman role is a mixed blessing and, while opening up a larger readership, can sometimes result in a double-distortion and distancing in the translation process.

Indians, both in their homeland and abroad, have achieved an intimate ability to use English for portraying Indian contexts. Arundhati Roy, Vikram Seth, Amitav Ghosh, Kiran Desai, among others, are notable international writers with deep Indian roots while being open to global sources. On his novel, *An Equal Music*, Vikram Seth said that inspiration could come from anywhere:

> The impulse could be a character, like in this case, someone looking rather darkly at the Thames. Or it could be a shred of conversation, like 'You will marry who I choose.' Or it could be a wonderful literary work like *Eugene Onegin*.

However, the debate on the supremacy of English over other languages keeps surfacing. In the 1990s, Salman Rushdie had made a contentious comment on Indian literature, claiming that both fiction and non-fiction by writers working 'in English' was proving a more important body of work than that produced in the so-called 'vernacular languages'. Writers in the Indian bhasha languages are still hostile to him on this count. The recent spat between Rushdie and Bhalchandra Nemade brought matters to a boil once again as Nemade belittled English language writers, and Rushdie retaliated in equally harsh terms.

Such uneasy debate about Indian languages, including English, will persist. South Asia, in the literary space, is beginning to look at its own reflection, creating a mirror within its own frame, rather than viewing itself in the refracted approval of an imagined Western audience. The publishing industry is growing at an unprecedented rate, with a combined potential readership of nearly 1.67 billion people across South Asia. And somewhere between these many vibrant languages, interpreting and reinterpreting themselves, there exists a unity of criticism that comes through shared aesthetic and common critical methodologies born of commonalities in cultures.

'UPSTAIRS, DOWNSTAIRS, INSIDE-OUTSIDE'

While Indians live in many languages, they are rarely self-conscious of this plurality. We would like to conclude this discourse with a tribute to the 'curious perversity' of our complex literary culture and the conviction that this spontaneous and accepting multilingualism will persist, and flower to greater glory, in its unaccountable 'upstairs, downstairs, inside-outside' trajectory.

The Kannada writer U.R. Ananthamurthy has said,

> there are at least three languages in our lives: one is the home language, the other is the street language, the third is the upstairs language....I cannot live in only one language. I live in English, I live in Kannada, I live in Sanskrit, and so many translations.

To quote A.K. Ramanujan: 'By a curious perversity I read Tamil constantly in the Kannada area, Kannada in the Tamil area, studied and taught English in India, and India and Indian languages in the US.'

The connections and conjunctions of this 'upstairs, downstairs, inside-outside' arc mirrored in an array of over 70 literary festivals that have found voice and value across South Asia in the last decade. The inspirational Jaipur Literature Festival, now the largest free literature festival in the world, has created a platform and a model of multilingual literary appreciation across languages, and the class and community divides that come with them in this part of the world. A literary community is slowly but surely being forged, where a multilingual and vociferous social media also plays a crucial part. Literary festivals in Karachi and Lahore, Kathmandu and Thimphu, Galle and Yangon, Mumbai, Kolkata and Bengaluru, are spaces to think through continuity and change and the challenges of modernity as reflected in the narrative and cinematic arts. In an environment where writers and thinkers are butchered and hounded simply for the act of thinking and writing, these platforms are witness to the new roots and wings of literary experience across South Asia.

◆

#This chapter was first published in 2015 in the *IIC Quarterly*, Vol. 41, Nos 3 and 4.

20
SPEAKING THE UNSPEAKABLE OR THE LIMITS OF REPRESENTABILITY

FIRDOUS
AZIM[#]

Colonial literature is replete with hints of unspeakable acts, especially 'native' atrocities against women. The lustful Turk, the lascivious Arab, the savage African and the revengeful Indian are stereotypes spawned by this sphere of writing, and prurient descriptions of such acts have proliferated in colonial accounts. Joseph Conrad's *Heart of Darkness* seems to somehow shift the focus from the easy binary between the colonial Other and the European, as the European himself is shown to take part in the rites and customs that mark the savage Other. Kurtz, fabled as the most successful ivory agent, participates in the performance of unspeakable acts. This duality is kept intact through the contrast in the description of both his majestic African mistress and rather bland European fiancée. The fascination with the African woman further acts as a warning against an intimate involvement with the wilderness of Africa, as she is delineated in terms that hint at a sexual plenitude unavailable in the homeland. Kurtz's mourning fiancée is an example of what is missing in the European homeland. The nature of these acts is perhaps made clearer in Francis Ford Coppola's film *Apocalypse Now* (1979), with its vivid portrayal of cannibalism, uncontrolled sexuality and a total breakdown, both of physical and mental faculties, as the grossly obese Kurtz figure gradually comes into view. 'The horror, the horror', are Kurtz's famous last words. This horror is not of unspeakable acts witnessed, but of unspeakable acts participated in and brought to view.

Nineteenth-century European literature conflated the colonial encounter with the sexual, placing the colonised in the position of passive and oppressed femininity. Meanwhile, the dangers which the colonising conquering male was confronted with were shown to lie in the blurring of these positions. The strong us-and-them division, thus, becomes blurred in Conrad's fiction, conflating male and female positions, or the difference between the strong and the weak, the conqueror and the conquered. The violence and violations, and the ambivalent positioning in 19th-century English fiction are explored from the conqueror/coloniser or male point of view. It then becomes interesting to look at the nature of the delineations by changing the narrative to a woman's one, and the delineation of 'unspeakable acts' not from the male, but the female point of view. Kurtz's vulnerability, or the horrors that he experiences, emerges from the uncertainties of the victor's position. How are such vulnerabilities experienced by the body on which unspeakable acts are committed, and how does sexuality, sexual desire and social–political positioning find expression in such a context?

These are the questions that are brought forward in Shaheen Akhtar's *Talaash* (2005). This chapter is an attempt to understand how a female narrative voice can be deployed to talk about rape, war and violence. Set during the liberation struggle of Bangladesh, the novel takes us through the student movement of 1969, the war of 1971, and to the early years of independent Bangladesh. The heroine, Mariam, or Mary as she is known, is a young girl who is lost in the displacement that occurs during the war, winds up in an army camp, is rescued in December by freedom fighters, and then struggles to find a place for herself in the newly independent nation. Love affairs, marriage and friendship—she is betrayed at every step and tossed about in her journey through life, never to find a footing anywhere. The breakdown of subjectivity parallels the breakdown of national promises and dreams, and the novel becomes a parable of the nation.

The framing of *Talaash*'s narrative brings about the comparison with *Heart of Darkness*. The novel is ostensibly told by Mukti, who is a researcher born on 26 March 1971—the night of independence. Like Rushdie's children, Mukti is a midnight's child, and her name—freedom—is emblematic of the nation. She is part of a research team which is tracing the lives of *birangonas*,[1] 34 years after independence.

However, the narrative voice fluctuates, and Mukti acts more as a commentator than a narrator. Mukti is trying to frame a definite history, 'she trails the footprints of the murdered' (Dutta, 2011: 36). However, when it comes to the birangonas, this trailing is impossible, and Mukti's voice is foregrounded at times to express wonder, sorrow or bewilderment. The novel uses different genres of representation, juxtaposing the historical events with stories and plays, using drama as a way to portray dramatic historical events. The third-person omniscient narrator takes over as Mary embarks on a picaresque journey through the Bangladeshi landscape and its history. At each stage, she is vulnerable, sexually and emotionally. The book, and Mary's story, begins with her love affair with Abed, a student leader who insists on her participation in the movement, ignoring her pregnancy. On that fateful night when the Pakistani army cracks down on the city of Dhaka, she has a miscarriage. Ironically, the researcher Mukti was born on that same night. The picaresque story is narrated in a stream-of-consciousness style, symbolically representing Mary's vulnerabilities. The journey from her Dhaka home to her village has to traverse Sundarir Khal— Sundari's Swamp—that appears as a wetland, where generations of women went missing. Mariam and her brother Montu have to cross this place on their journeys back to their village, and the fear of getting lost besets both brother and sister. Their fears are amply realised when one loses his life in the war, and the sister loses any position within the community and country.

Before going on to the central portion of the narrative, which is set during the war, it is important to consider the nature of Mary's loss and, through her, the loss suffered by all birangonas. The national narrative has framed this as the loss of honour of our mothers and sisters. Feminists have been protesting this phrasing, insisting that rape is not equivalent to a loss of honour, but is a crime and violation of the woman's body. But a feminist articulation evades us every time we try to talk about the women not as victims, but as survivors. Was there a sacrifice involved, or were the women passive victims? Where is the heroism in these women's lives? From this perspective, *Talaash* is a wonderful exploration of what it means to have been continually raped, put at the sexual service of the enemy, and the ways in which this experience is indelibly printed on the body and mind of the survivor.

The question of honour is thoroughly examined. Mary is no virgin, having lost her 'honour' to Abed, whose attitude and treatment of her is as callous and selfish as her rapists-to-be. The miscarriage is described in terms of the blood that oozes out of her and becomes one with Sundari's Marsh. Hence, sex and blood, and the hapless victimised woman, are already associated. When Mary flees, she is protected by Rameez Sheikh, a man who had been convicted of the murder of his wife, and castigated by 'good' middle-class Bengalis who find shelter in the ironically named Swargadham, or heavenly abode. Handing her over to the Pakistani army could have been done by her protector: but, then again, was it? Identities that the national narrative has divided into clear binaries of the collaborator or *razakar*, and the freedom fighter or *muktijoddha*, are made ambiguous, as the people fleeing are hapless, bewildered and uncertain of their destinations.

The central portion of the novel is associated with the sojourn in the Pakistani camp. Juxtaposed with our knowledge of what happened in those camps is the uncertainty of Mary's recounting. Did she have a dupatta; or was she wearing a sari? Was there a fan in the room? asks Mukti. She is not sure of anything, but thinks that she did have a dupatta, and, yes, there was a fan, as there were in a schoolroom. Then why did she not hang herself? wonders Mukti. The uncertainty of the answers hints at the unspeakability of the violations performed, as Mary throws questions back at Mukti. 'Can one explain all this? Is there a language to describe this experience? What language shall I use?' (ibid.: 89). Mary's inability to give definite responses to the questions posed to her is part of the limits of representability, both artistic as well as of historical recounting. Despite this, it is not as if the women themselves were unaware that they would be asked to bear testimony, and even as prisoners in the camp had hoped that strands of hair or pieces of cloth would bear witness to their situation in the future. This inability to express is accompanied by an inability to comprehend. The researchers and social workers, both immediately after the war and 28 years later when Mukti's research project begins, are themselves shocked and rendered speechless.

The book contains references to Nilima Ibrahim's path-breaking recounting of her interviews with birangonas in *Ami Birangona Bolchi*. She had rushed to interview women who had chosen to go with the Pakistani army to prisoner of war camps in India, preferring to be with their rapists than remain in Bangladesh.

The explanations that they had offered to the completely puzzled Nilima Ibrahim, using words such as revenge, had left her more dumbstruck than ever. Mukti's research also brings her face to face with attitudes and emotions that are completely beyond her ken, and the mutual incomprehensibility is part of the reason such women could not be easily rehabilitated within the national discourse.

The incomprehensibility that is part of this story of violation, violence and torture is enhanced when it is interspersed with a scene of desire—with roses, perfumes and silk saris. Mary recounts a scene of love while painting a picture of a Major Ishtiaque proffering her sympathy and understanding. This scene is incongruous and belies belief, as indeed there is no evidence that snow-white sheets and wine and roses were a part of the arts of seduction used by the Pakistani army. This moment of fantasy—of a moment when the mind transgresses the bodily limitations to find a realm of plenitude and desire—is surprisingly marked by a scene of complete recognition. While Mary is beguiled, or beguiles herself, into thinking of this man as her lover, someone who will take her to the Shalimar gardens where she will find her place among the women in Lahore, where the act of rape will be replaced by one of love and fulfilment, a chance glance at a photograph brings her back to reality. A photograph of a woman slips out. She is apparently the major's wife, and lines of a letter hoping that he is being faithful to her and requesting him not to fall into the snares of long-tressed Bengali women also become visible to the deluded Mary. Staring at this photograph, Mary seems to merge into that other woman in the georgette dupatta. The two women function as mirror images, as Mary is jolted back to the realisation that Major Ishtiaque can never love her, that he is her enemy, and all the ghazals and the roses bear no significance for her. The binaries—Pakistani/Bengali, friend/enemy, lover/rapist—establish themselves in a moment of recognition, as the woman in the photograph and Mary blend into each other, even while they are completely separated into irreconcilable positions.

The search, thus, becomes a narrative of a woman's search for social and sexual position, even in the midst of untold violence and violations. Made to slip in their own blood and excreta, stripped of all clothing, somehow desire springs in the mind and the position becomes that of a lover and not a rape victim. The division between the collaborator and the patriot—the willing mistress of the Pakistani major and the violated birangona or war heroine—that the national discourse tries to establish, is blurred. This ambiguity of position becomes even more telling after independence, as Mary slips and slides between conflicting roles—wife or prostitute—when every sexual act feels like rape, and husband/rapist and sexual customer blur into each other.

Talaash can be read as a focused attempt to foreground the voice(s) of the raped women of 1971. In the course of the narration, the book becomes a parable of the nation itself, and of the limitations of the efforts of national history-writing, which has had to struggle with the question of war-time violence against women. Historical writing on the issue of war rape has remained incomplete and unsatisfactory, with major attempts by Nayanika Mookherjee (2003) and Yasmin Saikia (2012) to address this issue. Research in Bangladesh has concentrated on first-person narratives or accounts of the women's lives after independence.[2] With the recent declaration by the Government of Bangladesh that birangonas be recognised as muktijoddhas or freedom fighters, the issue has come afresh to public limelight. However, the honouring of birangonas as muktijoddhas can also be seen as a further elision, an example of our collective inability to confront the nature of suffering and violations. Personal experiences of these women will still elude historical accounts, and the unspeakability of their sufferings keep the women unrepresented.

POSTSCRIPT

In the Light of What We Know, Zia Haider Rahman's debut novel of 2014, tells a very different story. Hidden within this narrative of 21st-century global politics and finance is a picture of a birangona. Tossed very casually into the story is an allusion to the hero's—Zafar's—parentage. The nameless narrator, while trying to understand Zafar's sense of alienation, delves into his childhood, and as part of the explanation brings in the question of his parents:

'more than the few facts I have at my disposal which don't even tell me how I came to know that his father, his true father, was a Pakistani soldier who raped his mother, and that this mother, his true mother, was the younger sister of the man who raised him as his own son' (Rahman, 2014: 137).

The source of information is vague, belying 'the facts', thus bringing to notice the repetition of the word 'true'. Truth and facts are juxtaposed, not to bolster each other, but to show how even vague facts can elicit 'real' truths.

The picture of the woman herself—'the true mother'—was given fuller treatment earlier in the novel. Ten-year-old Zafar had been sent back to his village home and lived with a woman for two years, who, although not introduced as his mother, is presented as a symbol of motherhood. She is described in terms of a painting, never given voice, but made to become an emblem of silent suffering and maternal love. To quote:

> I saw, then, a form on the verandah of the main house, sitting on the step. I could make out a dash of long black hair, iridescent in the darkness, and the drape of a white sari over the bent form. The woman's head was nestled in her crossed arms, which braced her hunched-up knees (ibid.: 88).

The 'remarkable geometric precision' of this description freezes the birangona into an image of eternal suffering. To her child, she is the mythical mother figure, a repository of love and affection. But the tale gives us no further information, which makes this rendering powerfully artistic—silent, despite the garrulity which marks the narration.

This narrative is also involved in another 'tracing'—that of the breakdown of its central character, Zafar. Zafar winds in and out of his story, apparently seeking an ultimate truth which, he feels, might lie in the sphere of mathematics. But his love of mathematics leads him to an arena of uncertainty, exemplified in the mathematician Godel's uncertainty principle, which shows how the truth eludes even the purest form of philosophical enquiry. Even more elusive then for Zafar is the spoken word, through which a novel, or a life, is narrated. As he says to his friend:

> No one can tell their own story ... They're the most untrue stories of all, the stories we write ourselves, by our own hand and in the first person, where our own dishonesty is hidden from us. Everyone has a region of privacy, things they keep from the world, but that region is only a protective layer behind which are the things they themselves cannot see, a layer shielding them from themselves (ibid.: 312).

What is this that lies hidden, the truth that cannot be spoken? The novel ends with a scene of unspeakable horror, another scene of rape, as Zafar encounters Emily, his ever-elusive girlfriend, in a hotel room. Described as 'violence-becoming' (italics in the original), the act is hinted at, rather than described. Zafar goes on to say:

> I have said enough. I wanted to tell you something, I thought I would be explicit, make it clear what I did, leave no room to hide, but now I know I can't. I came this far, down the long river, visiting spurs and detouring to tributaries along the way, but here at the brink of the cliff, where the river meets the sea, I don't know how to speak the unspeakable (ibid.: 547–48).

The narration reaches its own limit, and is faced with the unspeakable horror of unrepresentable facts.

We have also come full circle. Trying to examine the ways that violated bodies can be made to speak the horrors to which they have been subjected, we come back to the limitations of representability, to unspeakable horrors. The offspring of a rape, is Zafar doomed to perform such an act himself? Is there no space for redemption? This was a question that Saikia's research had posed, but in Zia Haider Rahman's work, the trope of rape seems to echo the unspeakable acts with which we had begun. The rape of the white woman by the man of colour, the warnings and fears that beset the colonial encounter is played out once more. All students of English literature are made to question the actual occurrence of the events in the caves in E.M. Forster's *A Passage to India*. Was Adela really attacked, or, was she merely hallucinating? What is this 'region of privacy' that is hidden even from the protagonist? The journeys to the heart of darkness are endless and are repeated time without number.

◆

#This chapter was first published in 2015 in the *IIC Quarterly*, Vol. 41, Nos 3 and 4.

NOTES

1. Birangona, or war heroine, is a title that was awarded to survivors of war rapes in 1971 by the then Prime Minister Sheikh Mujibur Rahman. Meant to honour the women, the efficacy of this title still remains questionable, as very few women came forward to take this title, or felt that Bangladesh has honoured them in any way.

2. The paucity of research on the topic is indeed telling. Sarmila Bose (2011), in her controversial book, accuses Bangladeshi historians of not adequately researching the war of independence. This is an accusation that definitely is true in the matter of birangonas. Yasmin Saikia's (2012) is an interesting recounting, which tries to bring in the remorse and guilt suffered by Pakistani perpetrators, and can be seen as a plea for reconciliation and forgiveness.

REFERENCES

Akhtar, Shaheen. 2005. *Talaash.* Dhaka: Mowla Brothers. Translated into the English by Ella Dutta. 2011. *The Search.* New Delhi: Zubaan. All references to the text are from the English translation.

Bose, Sarmila. 2011. *Dead Reckoning: Memories of the 1971 War.* London: C. Hurst and Co.

Conrad, Joseph. 1899. *Heart of Darkness.* UK: Blackwood's Magazine.

Forster, E. M. 1924. *A Passage to India.* UK: Edward Arnold.

Ibrahim, Nilima. 1994. *Ami Birangona Bolchi (The Voices of War Heroines).* Dhaka: Jagrata Prakashani.

Mookherjee, Nayanika. 2003. 'Ethical Issues Concerning Representations of Narratives of Sexual Violence in 1971.' www.dristipat.org/1971

Rahman, Zia Haider. 2014. *In the Light of What We Know.* India: Picador.

Saikia, Yasmin. 2012. *Women, War and the Making of Bangladesh: Remembering 1971.* Durham, N.C., USA: Duke University Press.

◆◆

21
A BROKEN SHARD
Sri Lankan Writings in English

ASHOK
FERREY[#]

Thirty years is a long time, as we in Sri Lanka know: we who have suffered through a war that lasted almost that long. Thirty years is even longer than the span of a generation, that curious length of time it takes for the human race to slough off one skin and grow another. Thirty years is the perfect distance from which to look back at that old version of yourself, whether you look back in anger, sorrow or joy. So what do we see when we look back at SAARC over this divide?

First of all, a word of warning to the reader: It is difficult for any one of us to weigh and appraise the whole picture on our own. Each of us holds just one tiny fragment of the truth, a broken shard which, if placed carelessly and out of context, will only serve to distort, not clarify, the picture. I cannot speak of the changes 30 years have wrought on the economics or the development, the science, the technology, or even—God help us all!—the politics of SAARC. My own piece of shattered glass happens to be the Arts, particularly as they relate to English language writing in Sri Lanka, and this is the bit I will attempt to hold up to scrutiny in this essay, catch what light from it you will. It is up to you the reader to place it where it belongs, in that vast mosaic of the general scheme of things. But be advised: what I write about does not relate to the current state of either Sinhala or Tamil writing; however much I would wish it, my knowledge simply does not extend to those spheres.

I returned to this country only a year or two after SAARC was initiated, at a time when writing was the last thing on my mind. Curiously, writing seemed to be the last thing on the country's mind, too. But all that was about to change with the advent of the 1990s.

There were, to my mind, a couple of seminal events that were part of this change, either as cause or effect. The year 1991 saw the publication of Yasmine Gooneratne's *A Change of Skies*, a look at Sri Lankans in a foreign land through foreign eyes. The writer was actually a Sri Lankan-born Australian academic who could comment on our society with a clarity and affection that only an ocean separating her from us could give. It opened our eyes to ourselves. It told us truths about ourselves we had always known but never publicly acknowledged.

This was followed in 1993 by the publication of Carl Muller's *The Jam Fruit Tree*. This last book, particularly, caused huge waves in the small, rather stagnant pond that was then the sorry state of English writing in Sri Lanka. It was a warts-and-all look at the Burgher community—the mixed race community (the mixture of colonial and local)—that was such a vibrant part of our society. Native Sri Lankans had always looked upon Burghers as white— they ate 'white' food after all and they spoke English, albeit with a particular Burgher accent; they had a happy-go-lucky devil-may-care attitude to life, which might have had not a little to do with their fondness for liquor. No, they were definitely white when looked at through our rather prejudiced coloured eyes. The colonial whites, meanwhile, looked upon them with ineffable superiority and condescension as being decidedly native; if not dangerously so, like the 'real' natives. This put the Burghers in a unique position, where the colonial masters looked to them for the day-to-day running of the island. The Burghers, to a large extent, ran the railways, the post, the schools: they were the keepers of the system. They worked hard, they played hard. And it was Carl Muller who nailed them, with his witty and percipient writing, his bawdy descriptions of Burgher life in the raw. The book caused outrage when it first appeared. The Burghers, who had been clinging precariously after independence to the last tattered shreds of respectability in an ever-increasing sea of nativeness, rose to a man in revolt. Carl Muller was reviled and vilified. And everyone read the book; and everyone loved it, though very few admitted to the fact.

These two books in particular looked at Sri Lankans with fresh eyes, showing us versions of ourselves we had tried so hard to keep under wraps all these years, assuming nobody would guess. Suddenly, it was open season on Sri Lankan society, where anything could be written about and discussed, however embarrassing. The subject matter of the Sri Lankan novel had suddenly exploded, to include just about anything. A third event set the seal on this sudden boiling over of the sea. Michael Ondaatje, the Sri Lankan-born Canadian author, had just won the Booker Prize for his *English Patient*. He used a portion of his winnings to set up a Sri Lankan literature award, naming it the Gratiaen Prize after his mother, Doris Gratiaen. Carl Muller promptly won that very first year for *The Jam Fruit Tree*, and Sri Lankan English literature was on its way. Suddenly, everyone in Sri Lanka was a writer. Elderly aunties who had hitherto painted genteel watercolours of sunsets and stilt fishermen decided that yes, they too had really been writers all along, much misunderstood of course. There were Asian Development Bank (ADB) economists and purveyors of bottled water who were discovered to be writers. There was even a former builder turned personal trainer (me).

But what has all this got to do with SAARC, I hear you ask. Surely the Arts are the one branch of human endeavour that by definition flies solo, without the help of outside influences? Why would it need, or be influenced by, an amorphous organisation that is above and beyond its ken? Surely art is an organic sort of plant that flourishes despite—rather than because of—the society around it? This is absolutely correct. But I would forward two reasons why a strong cultural framework like SAARC is necessary for growth. The first is that magic word, *patronage*. All art needs the money that patronage brings, to survive: it is the oxygen that gives the plant life. But at the same time, money is a word that all artists affect to despise (though secretly adore). Without it, all the good ideas of art shrivel up and die. Patronage was the single biggest reason for the Italian Renaissance coming into being. So what about the individual governments of each of these countries? Do they not have a duty to promote the Arts, and are they not better placed to provide the patronage art needs? The sad trouble with governments is that when they provide the money, they expect the artist to dance to their tune, particularly in South Asia; although it is galling for any government anywhere in the world to give money to an artist and sit back and watch that same artist bite the very hand that fed him. And we artists have very sharp teeth.

How is the patronage of SAARC any different? By its very *disinterestedness*, I would venture to answer. Because SAARC is essentially above and beyond mere government, it can take a disinterested view of the arts of any country, promoting them without any agenda, hidden or otherwise. Yes, I do understand that in actual practice, any artist selected for SAARC patronage is all too often chosen through tiresome bureaucratic government procedure, but there is more chance of this changing than any possibility of a government changing. There is less chance too of SAARC attempting to dictate to the artist, because SAARC does not (or should not) have any ideological agenda. SAARC is like the rather elderly (the 30-year-old, remember?), rich benefactor, who gives you the keys to his library and tells you, Go on, write that novel, you know you have always wanted to. Perhaps in practice this does not happen yet. But we artists can live in hope!

There is another reason why an organisation like SAARC is particularly important to a relatively small country like Sri Lanka. One of the reasons for English writing to take so long to get going here is the relatively small readership in the country. This is a problem that India never had. So it is no surprise that Indian English writers are a good 20 years ahead of the rest of us. They have always had a rich ongoing cultural exchange with their compatriots in the diaspora, and a ready readership in that diaspora hungry to read anything they produced. This foreign readership ensured that the 'local produce' was kept up to the mark, and that there was a ready market for it. Most importantly, in those early days, acceptance of this local literature by a foreign readership ensured a sort of 'validation' of the product. If it was good enough for them, it was certainly good enough for us. But English literature in India has come of age, and validation is no longer seen as necessary. Indian writers have gone on to win major international prizes for their work; there is no longer that sniffy, rather patronising attitude towards the language they use—on the contrary it has become almost a language in its own right, with its own vocabulary, its own phrases, its own pronunciation.

What about Sri Lankan English? Sadly, we are nowhere near that stage, for the simple reason that we do not yet have a diaspora of critical mass (and even if we did, there were better things for it to worry about up to now, like that small matter of a 30-year war); but we are getting there. Till then, it is a long hard slog for us 'native' writers. Why is it, asked the worthy editor of a local newspaper recently, that the only Sri Lankan writers of any note (Ondaatje, Selvadurai, Gunesekera, de Kretser) live abroad? Perhaps he could not see the answer staring him in the face: that they only became writers of any note *precisely* because they went abroad. Selvadurai, for instance, would have been hounded out of town if his *Funny Boy* (which happens to be Sri Lanka's first gay novel) had been published here. The novel would have been stifled at birth. But because it has been thoroughly 'validated' abroad, it is now acceptable local currency, and indeed much fêted and admired.

In spite of those early heady days of Carl Muller, there is still, too, a sort of apartheid at work in relation to the subject matter of Sri Lankan writing: what is permissible from the pen of an expat writer is seen as absolutely not kosher from a home-grown one. Whether this is a sort of self-censorship by local writers (especially when it comes to touchy subjects such as politics and religion) is not entirely clear. What is plain is that Sri Lankans will put up with much more from a 'corrupted' expat Sri Lankan (and hugely enjoy the corruption as a sort of guilty pleasure!) than we will from a local, who 'should know better' and who we feel should aspire to higher standards. Perhaps exposure to other SAARC writers will broaden our perspectives and lower these rather false standards that we have set ourselves.

One of the reasons why that poor editor is so disgusted with the state of local literature is its extremely variable quality. Here in Sri Lanka, editors, proofreaders and discerning publishers are extremely thin on the ground—to say nothing of a truly sophisticated readership. There is no infrastructure in place for writing to become healthy and grow to international standards, no possibility of valuable feedback from experts. It is amazing what can happen to a raw manuscript in the hands of a good editor. Till then, any young aspiring writer is all alone, shooting in the dark. He has to struggle along with the very poor standards of journalism all around him, the very poor standards of spoken English to which he is exposed and very little access to books he might want to read. The British Council library—the only decent library on the island for English fiction—has been steadily cutting back on its lending section, preferring to concentrate on language classes which are naturally more lucrative. It might be argued that books can be ordered on the internet, but this is a costly business for any

Sri Lankan. Writing is very much an organic thing: what you hear and absorb is what you in turn will produce in your work, whether you like it or not. Our English-speaking society as a whole needs to up its game; till that happens, our standards will remain low.

So how can SAARC help? In terms of population, SAARC is definitely one of the biggest groups of nations in the world. Here you have a ready-made diasporic critical mass, if only it could be persuaded to set up a dialogue with those languishing local authors in individual countries. By doing so, it would—inadvertently or not—help set a gold standard for local South Asian literature. Because its combined English readership is extremely large, it automatically has a pool of editors, proofreaders and publishers that could help those countries with smaller readerships. If these works are read, critiqued and reviewed by this common wider audience, you will have the benchmark so necessary to pull these books up to the mark; this international readership will also provide the 'validation' so essential for local authors to be accepted within their own societies. Does this in fact happen at the moment? Probably not; at least not to the extent required. But any growth of long-lasting value is slow, so there is hope.

If one thinks of the relatively new phenomenon of literary festivals, there is suddenly this growing pool of South Asian writers on which these festivals are beginning to draw, and this process is beginning to set the standards for regional literature. A new hunger has been created for regional writing, as opposed to the more traditional appetites for Western literature. These South Asian festivals have been hugely helpful in pushing the cause of local literature forward, and it would be relatively easy for SAARC to become involved, either through the existing mechanism of these festivals, or simply by providing sponsorship. This is without discounting SAARC's own festivals, of course.

So what, then, is the current state of play with regard to Sri Lankan literature in English? Sadly, not everything in the garden is rosy. The proto-renaissance of the early 1990s seems to have died down, somewhat. Entries for the Gratiaen Prize seem to get steadily lower in quality as the years go by. Is this due to the drop in the general standard of English, or is there a more deep-rooted malaise at work here? Is it just that young Sri Lankans are simply not interested in reading and writing? Or are they being encouraged by their peers to concentrate on more financially lucrative pastimes—the traditional ones of doctor, lawyer or engineer? For whatever reason, that palpable charge of enthusiasm that existed in the 1990s and in the first decade of the 21st century is very much a thing of the past. There is, too, a very real problem of suitable judges for these prizes. Local judges seem to be simply not up to the job. All too often they take the easy way out, by succumbing to cronyism and influence. The upper echelon of Sri Lankan society is very small; it is very easy to get through to the people that matter—'everyone is somebody's somebody', as they say around here. Here, too, SAARC might be invaluable: in providing a gene pool of outside judges who would have no local agenda, and would therefore be able to give unbiased judgments.

The Galle Literary Festival (the original plans for which were hatched at my dining table eight years ago) has sadly died a natural death. It was an astounding success while it lasted, and did more for local English writing than almost anything else. We are all still waiting for it to rise again, phoenix-like, from its ashes. It has been three long years since its demise, though, and nobody is holding their breath.

So there we are. Speaking purely from my rather narrow perspective—that of English writing in Sri Lanka—there is now a large hole in the ozone layer; a vacuum waiting to be filled. Patronage, critical mass, validation, international standards—all issues waiting to be addressed. Is there anyone out there? SAARC, where are you?

◆

#This chapter was first published in 2015 in the *IIC Quarterly,* Vol. 41, Nos 3 and 4.

22

HUMAN RIGHTS BEYOND THE STATE
Generating Spaces for Rights in Society

AFSAN
CHOWDHURY
ZERRIN AFZA
NABALESWAR
DEWAN#

The Universal Declaration of Human Rights (UDHR) was articulated and formalised in the context of World War II. Essentially, it reflected the principles of the Allied Powers and the Four Freedoms upheld by them: (1) Freedom of Speech,[1] (2) Freedom of Worship, (3) Freedom from Want and (4) Freedom from Fear. Although it was 'international' in nature, it failed to take into account some specific violations, particularly racist and ethnic ones, which prevailed within the 'national' societies of the signatory countries.

The UDHR was meant to uphold the 'ideology' of Western values and paradigms that affirmed that the state was the primary custodian and, thereby, protector of rights, an understanding of the relationships that arose as a by-product of the conflict between the leading Western powers. However, it did not particularly consider other rights-related situations that crop up in societies, or outside the state agency-dominated space, since that was not the situation in the West. It did not also deal with violations that occur in the name of defending the freedoms in various situations of cold and hot conflicts (Kovler, 2011: 7).

The UDHR also ignored the uneven development of various states in the 'Universe', and how that development influenced the Human Rights (HR) status, its application and understanding by various UN member states and their citizens. The focal point of the UDHR 'ideology' is that the state, and the concurrent narrative of promoting a strong state, is responsible for protecting HR while acting as the distributor of social services. The HR discourse is, therefore, largely based upon the behaviour of strong, developed states. The UDHR is preconditional upon the state in existence at the end of World War II. It is not a continuing narrative reflecting new realities in the state, as well as society (Englehart, 2009: 163–80).

Those who control state power control the HR status. States differ from each other, but rights are universal and the same indicators are used to measure both strong and weak states, making comparisons difficult. Meanwhile, rights at the social level have been relatively ignored, including the role of society, both as the preserver and violator of rights. This chapter looks at rights beyond the state and the situation of rights in weak states. It also explores societies in weak states and if they reduce, or can expand, the rights space through the functioning of informal institutions.

◆◆◆

EXPERIENCING THE STATE IN WEAK STATES

Bengal, in general, and Bangladesh in particular, has been a marginal zone within imperial India from the period when human settlement began. The land was known as 'Ashura' under the Aryans and visitors required cleansing rituals after returning from this geographical zone (Rafi, 2006: 13). As people living in a delta, they developed their culture around notions of survival without external support from an imperial monarchy of which it was, at best, a nominal part. It was ignored by the great Aryan takeover of indigenous societies in the early stages, as it was far away from the Indo-Aryan centres, but came to their notice when the settled agricultural revolution of the neolith period provided them with an economic incentive (Schendel, 2009: 67).

The Aryan expansion and the migration of Aryan warlords to the area began after the 7th century BC onwards, and the ruling class comprised Aryan Brahmin–Kshatriyas before the Turko-Afghan takeover in the 13th century (Rafi, 2006: 11–13). However, the area was not 'Aryanised', and, although a series of powerful chieftains ruled the area, traditional forms of social systems prevailed, rooted in an ethnic and socially mixed society. The Bengali language is a mix of several tongues as well, including the Sanskrit-based 'Magadhi Prakrit', and these Bengali people—an ethnically mixed linguistic group—lived as junior members of an area politically dominated by Aryans (ibid.: 14).

Subsequently, significant social change took place by virtue of the agricultural revolution of the Mughals under Akbar, which saw Mughal administration/state reach the villages. The purpose was to increase royal income from agriculture in a newly morphed topography with great promise. It was not the formal state machinery that acted as the intervention agent, but those identified as 'charismatics', or Muslim holy men, who doubled as agricultural entrepreneurs. Thus, religion or social ideas and customs travelled, rather than the state machinery. Tax collection was the purpose, not social change. However, distance, illiteracy and traditional customs played a part in formulating religious systems in the area as well. Bengal evolved its own brand of syncretistic Islam, often called 'popular Islam', which was also a mix much like its ethnic identity. Its rain- and flood-dependent agriculture flourished, from which the state emerged. This was an informal state and social zones often remained outside state interest and perhaps, control, partly because nobody had much interest in them (Eaton, 2003: 1204–1760).

It was during rural Bengal's third agricultural revolution—also its most negative—that state influence was enhanced. Under the Permanent Settlement of 1793, introduced by the British, Bengal's agriculture was brought under colonial state control as a project for the development of capitalism in agriculture by the state. State intermediaries—zamindars or landlords—acted as agents of the state, and many social and customary rights enjoyed by peasants were taken away in favour of the zamindar. Subsequently, this taxation system pauperised the peasantry and led to several large resistance movements by the rural poor. Agro-capitalism in Bengal was unsuccessful as the expected investment by the landlords did not take place. Hence, the sector, as a whole, declined. Thus, modern institutions, which could serve citizens through services, never developed significantly in the increasingly urban-run state. Instead, the peasants experienced the state dominantly in the form of the tax collector, rather than the service provider. Absentee landlordism resulted in the rise of intermediaries who became default state representatives and so the system, as a whole, never strengthened its service delivery role (Schendel, 2009: 58–60).

◆◆◆

Between Pakistan's independence in 1947 and Bangladesh's in 1971, the state was locked in a nationalist struggle involving the established Pakistani elite and the emerging middle-class elite of East Pakistan. Pakistan was focused on the development of the 'security state' against an Indian invasion, but left East Pakistan/Bengal out of this arrangement, partially because it was not part of the Pakistani state's internal perception of itself. Consequently, West Pakistan became 'Pakistan', although income from lucrative agro-products of Bengal funded a significant part of the Pakistani state.

Conflict between Pakistan and East Pakistan reached a peak in 1966 when it transpired that East Pakistan was outside any protection plan devised by Pakistan against external military threat. Almost coincidentally, the nationalist Manifesto—six points of the leading party, Awami League (AL)—was published, and the final phase of the state arrangement was ushered. Being ignored in the state's development had always been a grouse, and it peaked in the 1969 mass upsurge and later in the 1970 election, when the Bengali nationalist AL won almost all the seats (Chowdhury, 2007: 229–328).

From 3–26 March, the formal 'Pakistan' state in East Pakistan almost ceased to exist when the Pakistani army refused to hand over power to the elected party. At the local level, the informal state replaced whatever formal mechanisms existed. On 26 March, the Pakistani military took charge and the state's condition continued in a state of collapse till independence in December 1971. Following the military crackdown, the barely present Pakistani state ceased to exist and from it emerged a series of small Bangladeshi pocket states. They were bound together by their resistance, not law or dicta. Although the Pakistani state was able to establish military control by end-April 1971, the state, in a functional sense, had died. It was the lack of the state structure, down to the lower levels, that forced Pakistan to rely on paid patriots of the village-based, local government and their lackeys. Being pro-Pakistani became an economic activity. The resistance activities were run by the elite in the rural areas and backed by the exiled government which was located in India. Thus, the state was at best, in limbo. It was this state that was handed over to Bangladesh after it became independent in December 1971, both as a contemporary and historical legacy (Chowdhury, 2007: 229–328; Schendel, 2009: 161–70).

The limitations of this state were clear from the outset. The administration was not in any shape or position to impose a functional government. Between 1972 and 1975, there was increased violence at all levels. Not only were state leaders targeted, but the rise of radical Left parties, the politicisation of the military, extra-judicial killings, failed elections, famine, etc., produced a chaotic method of state-making. This dismal situation began to peak in 1974, when Emergency was imposed and, by 1975, the state had drifted into one-party rule. By the end of 1975, Sheikh Mujibur Rahman, the founding leader of the democratic nationalist movement and most of his family members were killed by a rogue branch of the state military, several coup d'etat had taken place, major leaders of the AL were killed in jail, a Leftist–military uprising was put down and, finally, the country slipped under martial law (Schendel, 2009: 181–82).

The state was not in a healthy situation, and if HR is contingent upon state protection, then it was in a dismal state too. This was the challenging foundational era faced by Bangladesh.

◆◆◆

The constitution was passed on 4 November 1972 with four major state principles: democracy, socialism, secularism and nationalism. It was influenced by the Indian version, but it was not a concrete or complete statement of national will. Its historical relationship with social ideas and collective aspirations was somewhat vague, given the enormous basic changes brought to it by an independence war. Contradictions began to emerge with each of the principles soon after its birth (Hossain, 1997: 113).

Nationalism became a divisive element. First, it conflicted with the non-Bengali Adivasi population on the denial of their identity when Bengalis spoke about a single identity for all Bangladeshis. Subsequently, Chittagong Hill Tracts Chakmas and other communities opted for armed militancy from 1976 to 1986 (Chakma, 2014: 111–38).

Socialism was a far cry for the state and, with little economic discipline, it became everyone's business to uphold and no one's business to implement. Both corruption and the lack of economic benefits in general created negative feelings about this principle.

Socialism often became synonymous with state-owned enterprises and the attendant practice of asset-stripping (Hossain, 1997: 125).

Secularism and democracy were the two most troubling principles, because constitutional secularism was perceived differently from its intentions. While secularism was explicitly explained in the constitution under Part II Article 12, public perception among many was that secularism meant 'lack of religion'.[2] It appears that people did not want the state to be present in the religious space which was considered more social than legal. State success was, therefore, contingent upon social and economic success, which would justify its inclusion. Finally, democracy took a big hit when Sheikh Mujibur Rahman amended the constitution and established one-party rule, making all the elements of the state-guiding democratic instrument problematic (Rafi, 2008: 166; Islam, 1984: 556–73).

A history of the constitution does not make for comfortable reading as 16 major amendments have been made till date, many of which were either to legitimise the illegitimacy of military rule, reduce the power of the judiciary, or introduce new systems of electoral or state management. The result has been the weakness of the state system and the rise of alternative institutions to provide services to citizens. With parliament never functional, a judiciary not able to keep up with demands and its access beyond the capacity of most people and an executive, which is generally not considered accountable for services delivery, the indicators for a reduced state are visible. The issue is also about the alternatives emerging in view of this reduction.

◆◆◆

SOCIETY AND APPLIED RIGHTS

Societies are traditional survival mechanisms, but a society's position in the 'weak state' scenario is unusual. Many societies have supported the politics which, ultimately, spawned the state within which they are located, but the point is about the relationship between the two. States are expected to reflect the beliefs of society, but in weak states the inability, or refusal to do so, may cause rights violations. Societies in isolation from mechanisms to guard rights will violate them as well. State documents, or the constitution, will contain the highest level of collective aspirations, but they may flow down to society inadequately, since the informing mechanism between the two is weak. This lack of communication is a major issue of rights realisation.

The position of minorities at the social level is a two-tiered one.

(i) If the law and order regime is frail, as it is in a weak state, 'powerful criminal' elements, taking advantage of the situation in society, damage minority rights.

(ii) Social values can be dominated by group interests, historical conflicts, inadequate access of resources, a collective sense of threat to social values, etc., which leads to exclusionary and anti-diversity practices. The state can act as the protector of diversity rights, but in a weak state that protection is eroded, state–society partnership is affected and rights fail (Rafi, 2008: 162–67).

In Bangladesh's case, the state attempted to ensure minority rights through the introduction of 'secularism' in the constitution, as stated in Part II, Article 12. However, this endeavour was unsuccessful since the state could not provide protection to minorities due to the weak construction of the concept and its application, as well as the conflict between the application and perception of the societal notion of what secularism represented in the constitution of 1972 (Hossain, 1997: 125)

The state could not provide secular security through the formal arrangements of the constitution. It was thought that the will of the state could override the conflicts between communities and power exertion by the elite at various levels through legal means. However, not only is there little evidence that the situation improved during the 'secular' era, but the later change in the constitution, under which Bangladesh moved from secularism to proclaiming Islam as the state religion,[3] created the space for political conflicts over the issue which did not make the minorities less vulnerable. As a result, the inter-community relationship has become a political issue overriding other positions. The state also did not, or could not, exert enough pressure on anti-diversity forces in society, where it has been historically located, thereby enhancing minority vulnerability (Hossain, 1997: 138; Rafi, 2008: 15–38).

SECULARISM[4]

Secularism, as defined in the constitution, is as follows:

The principle of secularism shall be realised by the elimination of:

   (i)   Communalism in all its forms;
   (ii) the granting by the state of political status in favour of any religion;
   (iii) the abuse of religion for political purposes;
   (iv) any discrimination against, or persecution of, persons practising a particular religion.

The *secularism* principle was adjusted in the constitution in 1977 by adding bismillah-ar-rahman-ar-rahim (In the name of Allah, the Beneficent and the Merciful) before Article 12. This was incorporated in the *Fifth Amendment Act*. The *Eighth Amendment Act,* which was passed on 7 June 1988, further amended Article 2 of the constitution by declaring Islam as the state religion.[5] But none of these amendments explicitly withdrew any rights prescribed in the constitution for the minorities.

The existence of the state at the grass-roots level is limited, as it invariably is in any weak state. Rural societies operate under a power-sharing system, whereby the state allows the rural elite relative freedom to control grass-roots government institutions. These are centres of power but do not provide services to all, while traditional institutions continue to survive even as their resources are increasingly reduced.

One example illustrating the new discourse lies in the field of poverty reduction and social development. The Specially Targeted Ultra Poor (STUP)[6] programme of BRAC[7]—the world's largest non-state social services delivery agent—was significant, as it showed that the extreme poor, who are outside the state's lens, can be lifted out of poverty through a civil society alliance of the village elite, private sector development and the poor themselves. Although there was no state policy to remove extreme poverty, BRAC developed a 'Policy of Action', which led to the reduction of extreme poverty.

The number of extreme poor is 27.6 million, which constitutes 17.6 per cent of the total population. By December 2014, a total of 1.7 million households (7.05 million of a total of 27.6 million people) had been covered. The 20.55 million people that remain will be covered by 2016.[8] It was also possible for the state at the periphery to participate in such a project through service provisions which were not part of its formal service delivery policy. Thus, the state, in some sense, was appropriated into societal initiatives and was able to influence national policies on extreme poverty alleviation. Accordingly, citizens' access to rights could take place without the state as the principal narrator.

Generally, the low level of application of governance policies indicates that the state is not the only construct in operation and society continues to hold values and apply them, both negative and positive, which may support or run contrary to state-held views. It has made the need to have a stronger, more deliberately organised, society essential to sustain the rights of the people even when the constitution is not at work.

APPLIED RIGHTS AND SOCIETY

Rights exist in several spaces—state, societal and, finally, personal. Human rights largely concern the rights-based relationship between the state and citizens. But apart from the violation of individual rights by the state, there are societal violations of rights and, finally, the rights-related relationship between state and society.

While individual rights are spelt out in the constitution as a formal act of declaration, no such documents can exist for society. Nor are significant measurements available for society's relationship with rights. Thus, the focus on the description and protection of rights is dominantly state-based, largely excluding social situations which, in weak state situations, demand greater attention as they are more active in this area. Rights are perceived to exist or originate dominantly from social space formalised in state documents, but there is no formal recording of most violations emerging from this social space, nor are there any mechanisms where formal complaints can be made and thus recorded. The question is not whether state or society is guilty of violation, but that both may violate the same right in different spaces. Hence, a discussion of the constitution, and rights ensuing thereof, is limited in a weak-state situation. But in a social situation too, there is no adequate diagnosis of rights violation. This applies in the case of what is understood as secularism/inter-communality, etc. Since the analysis of rights is state-based, there is little study about its location, protection, interaction and, finally, its relationship to other rights' spaces.

While the state's attitude to minorities is detectable in law and policies, social attitudes towards them have developed in customs and practices. The state may be abstract in its understanding of secularism, but the manner in which it views the social level is determined also by people's sense of loss and gains and not just attitude. The perception of rights and violations is conditioned by the threats and opportunities of inter-communal relationships and positions. For example, the security strategy in the Chittagong Hill Tracts, where long-standing hostility exists between Adivasi and settler communities, the conflict is in reality between Adivasis and the state rather than between two communities, one outsider and the other indigenous there. Elsewhere, the state may either have limited contact with social groups, or is not in conflict with society, with the dominating conflicts being socially internal.[9]

Communalism is also an exclusion issue, one that is related to social development. It exists in various spaces, including in efforts to bridge state and society through the organised management of the problem so that initiatives can create social capital (Rafi, 2008: 39–55).

◆◆◆

CAN ANTI-COMMUNALISM BE A DEVELOPMENTAL ISSUE IN A WEAK STATE?

Understanding communalism as a developmental issue is useful where development links state and societal agencies. In Bangladesh's case, where the developmental sector is fairly successful, state gains of ethnic and religious diversity are low, with all minorities experiencing major discrimination.

To address anti-communalism/diversity as a developmental issue, methods of standard developmental analysis were applied to identify problems and their sources. The reason behind this approach was to locate it outside the constructed idealistic state/constitutional space to judge if it could exist in the less formal social space, where different communities live together but often in hostile situations. This could help to locate rights from the purely state space and policy to developmental and behavioural space as well.[10]

The problem of defining the state–society relationship may also be due to the non-availability of indicators to measure rights status in social constructs. Indicators for the state are available, and the relationship between constitutional documents and state practices is described and recorded in judicial discourses. While the constitution is a final product, supposedly of public will, there are opportunities to distort this and a flawed political system may affect its role significantly when the state is in transition. For example, Bangladesh's constitution shifted from the secular to a state with Islam as the state religion, though with safeguards in place for minorities, and is recorded in the amendments. But social situations have a longer time frame, changes take place over time and record-keeping mechanisms are limited. Society's relationship with the state on rights issues is also not immediately visible. Exploring ways to conceptualise social rights and violations, whether state-inspired or not, are needed. The social space not only generates rights and violations, but can also support the individual in rights preservation and, by extension, help the state.

Understanding why, and how, societies communicate with the state is important. For example, why does land-grabbing of minorities' land take place when the state forbids it? Much, therefore, may depend on the identity of the perpetrators, who act as members of society, but use the state to gain advantages or represent it formally or otherwise. Could there be tacit approval, then? In that case, unless one can identify the specific intent of the criminal, it may be seen as a communal act. But in a power-based relationship, the powerful take advantage of the powerless, irrespective of identity. In a sense, this crime is a secular act, but if it affects an entire vulnerable community, it becomes a communal problem for that community. It is inspired by greed and not communalism. However, while the overall impact is a criminal communal act, is the identity of the perpetrator a communal one or that of a powerful individual? The encouraging, and discouraging, factors behind communalism need to be understood in the context of social and community values, and action.

The BRAC Diversity Pilot Intervention Project's objective is a collective encouragement of inclusion at a social level.[11] This addresses not just majority–minority relations, but discrimination within both groups as well. The project goes beyond the constitutional rights discourse and enters societal perceptions and conversations. The following case study of the project illustrates the challenges:

CASE STUDY

Harilal Robidas is a resident of Baniachong in the district of Habiganj, located in the Sylhet division. He is, by caste, a cobbler. His neighbours, with whom he has positive relations, are all Muslims. He has not faced discrimination at their hands, he says. But he faces problems with people from within his own community. Robidas observes:

> I give donations at the time of Puja but I am not allowed inside the temple. I have to worship and receive Prasad standing outside the temple. In the market, I am not given tea in cups and even the barber doesn't touch my hair. I have never [been] invited to any community event. I sometimes think of complaining to the police station about my treatment. But then I think, what's the point? God has created me as a person of lower caste so it's no fault of human beings. I wish I could go away to another place where I would not be known as a lower caste but I love this village. Maybe one day things will get better.[12]

Several points are raised in this case study:

(i) Exclusion is not community-specific, nor caused by demographic power. It appears to have universal tendencies. Discrimination by Hindus exists along with complete exclusion by Muslims.

(ii) Most acts of exclusion and discrimination are informed by multiple sources—historical as well as community belief. Robidas' economic status primarily informs us of the level of his vulnerability.

(iii) The state's value-structured constitution is a weak presence and does not/cannot ensure equal, or near equal, rights and does not seem to influence social values.

(iv) Although the state is weak, people still consider it to be as the final provider of relief and rights.

(v) There is no significant social mechanism to provide relief within the community level, and no institution is planned for by anyone.

The Diversity Project focuses on the exploration of the means of assistance in producing social rights, and mechanisms to ensure their practice. It attempts to encourage the creation of resilient rights spaces within informal social space and develop methods to initiate a dialogue for rights between all the parties involved by building diversity units at the grass roots through analysis and action. In addition, the project aspires to a developmental and social space, besides the state and the constitution.

◆

#This chapter was first published in 2015 in the *IIC Quarterly*, Vol. 41, Nos 3 and 4.

NOTES

1. United Nations Universal Declaration of Human Rights, 1948.

2. The Constitution of the People's Republic of Bangladesh, Part II, Article 12, p. 4.

3. The Constitution of the People's Republic of Bangladesh adopted on 4 November 1972, p. 4—Secularism; p. 105, 5th Amendment; pp. 109–10, 8th Amendment; pp. 157, 159–60, 15th Amendment.

4. The Constitution of the People's Republic of Bangladesh adopted on 4 November 1972, Part II, Article 12, p. 4—Secularism.

5. Ibid.

6. Challenging the Frontiers of Poverty Reduction (CFPR)—Targeting Ultra Poor (TUP) Programme, BRAC. 2004. Phase-wise coverage progress report, 2014.

7. BRAC, an international development organisation based in Bangladesh, is the largest non-governmental organisation in the world measured by the number of employees and the number of people it has helped as of November 2012. BRAC was known as the Bangladesh Rehabilitation Assistance Committee and then as the Bangladesh Rural Advancement Committee. Currently, BRAC does not represent an acronym.

8. Challenging the Frontiers of Poverty Reduction (CFPR)—Targeting Ultra Poor (TUP) Programme, BRAC. 2014. Phase-wise coverage progress report, 2014.

9. Diversity Project Document, Advocacy for Social Change, BRAC. 2015. Process Flowchart and Causal Layered Analysis (CLA).

10. Ibid.

11. Diversity Project Document, Advocacy for Social Change, BRAC. 2015.

12. The case study was collected from Baniachong, Habiganj district, as part of the Baseline Survey on Social Discrimination under the Diversity Project in Sylhet division, conducted by BRAC's advocacy programme.

REFERENCES

Chakma, Ananda Bikash. 2014. 'Peace Building in the Chittagong Hill Tracts (CHT): An Institutional Approach', *Journal of the Asiatic Society of Bangladesh* (Hum.), Vol. 59 (1). http://www.asiaticsociety.org.bd/journal/HJ2014%281%29_6_Ananda.pdf

Chowdhury, Afsan. 2007. *Bangladesh 1971: History of Bangladesh War of 1971*, Vol. 1. Dhaka: Mowla Brothers.

Eaton, Richard, M. 2003. *The Rise of Islam and the Bengal Frontier.* Berkeley: University of California Press, c 1993 http://ark.cdlib.org/ark:13030/ft067n99v9/

Englehart, Neil. A. 2009. 'State Capacity, State Failure and Human Rights', *Journal of Peace*, Volume 46, No. 2.

Hossain, Syed Anwar. 1997. 'Islamic Fundamentalism in Bangladesh: Internal Variables and External Inputs', in *Religion, Nationalism and Politics in Bangladesh.* Chapter 2. New Delhi: South Asian Publishers.

Islam, Syed Serajul.1984. 'The State in Bangladesh under Zia (1975–81)', *Asian Survey*, Vol. 24 (5). doi:10.1525/as.1984.24.5.01p0162r, JSTOR 2644413

Kovler, Anatoly. 2011. '*Human Rights in a Contemporary Society and European Values: Critique of Europeanism.* CEURUS EU–Russia Paper No. 1. Tartu: Tartu University Press.

Maiese, Michelle. 2004. 'Beyond Intractability: Human Rights Protection'. (http://www.beyondintractability.org/essay/human-rights-protect)

Mazumder, Sadrul Hasan and Faustina Pereira. 2013. BRAC Property Rights Initiative. BRAC–USA, BRAC Human Rights and Legal Aid Service Progress Report, July–December. New York and Dhaka.

Rafi, Mohammad. 2006. *Small Ethnic Groups of Bangladesh: A Mapping Exercise.* Dhaka: Panjerri Publication.

———. 2008. *Can We Get Along? An Account of Communal Relationship in Bangladesh.* First Edition. Dhaka: Panjerri Publication.

Schendel, Van Willem. 2009. *A History of Bangladesh*. London, UK: Cambridge University Press.

23

DIVERSITY MANAGEMENT IN SAARC COUNTRIES

FAIZAN
MUSTAFA#

Diversity management, through minority protection, is the true hallmark of a *civilisation*. Mahatma Gandhi was of the view that the claim of a country to civilisation depends on the treatment extended to its minorities. Lord Acton added another facet: 'The most certain test by which we judge whether a country is really free is the amount of security enjoyed by minorities.'

Minorities are essential groups within larger societies whose members share a distinctive collective identity of their own. There are many possible bases for distinctive identity, such as religious beliefs, ethnicity, language, common historical experiences, place of residence, etc. All South Asian states are plural societies and are mosaics of distinct peoples, whose identities and aspirations may, or may not, be accepted by those who hold state power. Its rich diversities make it an interesting region to examine for diversity management. The failure to evolve a satisfactory solution to minorities' rights led to the partition of Pakistan and the subsequent creation of two countries: Pakistan and Bangladesh. Religious, linguistic, ethnic and cultural diversities in themselves are not causes of war or conflict; it is the refusal to accept diversity that causes strife, war and partitions. For minority communities, minority rights represent limits to what the majority, which in democratic polity largely controls the state, may impose. Freedom of religion, the right to speech, equality and non-discrimination on the basis of religion, language or race, the right to use their own language and script, and to preserve their distinctive cultures, are all limitations against unjust or unfair preferences of the majoritarian state. Minorities everywhere face discrimination of varying kinds and forms.

Jawaharlal Nehru, in the *Young India* issue of 15 May 1930, rightly observed:

> The history of India and of many of the countries of Europe has demonstrated that there can be no stable equilibrium in any country so long as an attempt is made to crush a minority or force it to conform to the ways of the majority. There is no surer method of rousing the resentment of the minority and keeping it apart from the rest of the nation than to make it feel that it has not got the freedom to stick to its own ways.... *It matters little whether logic is on its side or whether its own particular brand of culture is worthwhile or not. The mere fact of losing it makes it dear.* Therefore we in India must make it clear to all that our policy is based on granting this freedom to the minorities and that under no circumstance will any coercion or repression of them be tolerated ... we can also lay down as our deliberate policy that there shall be no unfair treatment of any minority. Indeed we should go further and state that it *will be the business of the state to give favoured treatment to minority and backward communities* [emphasis added].

In South Asia, until recently, Hindu-majority Nepal was a Hindu state, and there are demands to drop secularism from its new constitution. Muslim-majority Pakistan, Bangladesh, Afghanistan and the Maldives are Islamic states. Although Buddhist-majority Sri Lanka stops short of declaring Buddhism as the state religion, it does place it foremost. Bhutan, in its 2008 constitution, declared Buddhism as the spiritual heritage of Bhutan. However, Hindu-majority India is a secular state. SAARC has all kinds of minorities, but some SAARC constitutions recognise only religious minorities. Minorities are grossly under-represented in all SAARC countries in all spheres, especially in the institutions of the state. With the exception of India, the majoritarian character of the states is clearly visible and minorities continue to face situations of varying degrees of discrimination, exclusion and neglect. An attempt will be made here to examine the constitutional provisions of SAARC nations to assess the state of diversity management. Since India is a truly secular country, with the best minority protection provisions, Indian law on minority rights will be first discussed and, subsequently, the laws of other SAARC countries will be compared with the Indian position.

Religious minorities alone constitute 19 per cent of India's total population. The rights of minorities were debated at length in the Indian Constituent Assembly, as framers wanted to ensure full and meaningful protection to minorities. Accordingly, special safeguards were guaranteed to minorities and were incorporated in the chapter on fundamental rights, with a view to instill in them a sense of confidence and security. The minorities were satisfied with the pledge of Sardar Patel that 'our mission is to satisfy every interest and safeguard the interests of all the minorities to their satisfaction'. It is within this context that the provisions of freedom of religion (Articles 25 to 28) and the rights of minorities (Articles 29 and 30) were incorporated in the constitution. Justice H.R. Khanna rightly observed:

> these provisions enshrined a befitting pledge to the minorities in the constitution of the country whose greatest son had laid down his life for the protection of the minorities. As long as the constitution stands as it is today, no tampering with those rights can be countenanced. Any attempt to do so would be not only an act of breach of faith, it would be constitutionally impermissible... .[1]

The attribution of such enormous importance to minority rights immediately after Partition is indeed appreciable. Justice Venkatarama Ayyar explicitly remarked in the *Kerala Education Bill*:

> It is well known that during the Middle Ages, the accepted notion was that Sovereigns were entitled to impose their own religion on their subjects, and those who did not conform to it could be dealt with as traitors. It was this notion that was responsible during the 16th and 17th centuries for numerous wars between nations and for civil wars in the continent of Europe, and it was only latterly that it came to be recognized that freedom of religion is not incompatible with good citizenship and loyalty to the State, and that all progressive societies should respect the religious beliefs of their minorities. It is this concept that is embodied in Articles 25, 26, 29 and 30 of the constitution.[2]

Constitutional law experts recognise the Indian Constitution as an exceptionally far-sighted, progressive and modern document.

The underlying argument for minority rights—that individualistic universal rights are not of much use in a heterogenous country such as India—presaged the discussions on multiculturalism, difference and the rights of minorities that mark contemporary political theory by about 66 years.

Article 29(1) lays down that, 'Any section of the citizens residing in the territory of India or any part thereof having a distinct language script or culture of its own shall have the right to conserve the same.' This provision signifies two vital dimensions. First, it concedes that different groups do have different cultures and all people may not have only one culture; these linguistic and religious cultures are valuable for their members; that members of minority cultures can face disadvantages in a majoritarian society and that, therefore, these members need to be given explicit rights to conserve their own culture. Second, the right to culture is an individualistic right, i.e., individuals have been given the right to preserve their distinctive culture. Subsequently, Article 30 guarantees that all religious and linguistic minorities shall have the right to establish and administer educational institutions of 'their choice'. Article 350-A provides for adequate facilities for instruction in the primary stage of education in the mother tongue, and Article 350-B for the appointment of special officers for linguistic minorities.

It is shocking to note that a single-judge bench of the Allahabad High Court held that Muslims are not a minority. The judgment was subsequently stayed. Interestingly, although the term 'minority' has been used at four places in the constitution, no definition of the term 'minority' exists in the constitution and that, probably, was the reason for the Allahabad High Court's anxiety. But the High Court was clearly bound by the apex court's decisions in which the Supreme Court had consistently held that any group, which is less than 50 per cent in a state, is a minority. The Indian Supreme Court has given the widest possible interpretation to the minority rights provisions of the constitution, and there is no doubt that the world over, Article 30 is a unique provision as it permits minorities to set up educational institutions of their choice, including universities. The religion-based personal laws of minorities, such as the customary laws of Nagas, have also been constitutionally protected.

Unlike several other SAARC constitutions, there is no religious qualification attached to holding the highest constitutional positions. There is a National Minorities Commission and National Minorities Educational Institutions Commission to deal with the problems of minorities. In spite of these provisions, communal riots, attacks on churches, reconversion in the name of so-called *gharvapsi* (reconversion to Hinduism) and hate speeches are frequent occurrences, particularly after the Bharatiya Janata Party's (BJP) coming to power in 2014. The saffronisation of textbooks has also made a return. The extreme right does proclaim that India is a Hindu *rashtra*. Only Hindus can avail of the benefit of reservation as Scheduled Castes. Muslims are the worst-off among all minorities and have not really benefitted from the high economic growth of the country. Their socio-economic condition reflects poorly as compared to other religious minorities and they face multifaceted challenges in terms of identity, equity and security.

◆◆◆

Although Mohammad Ali Jinnah wanted Pakistan to be a secular state, fundamentalists soon took over and Pakistan became a theocracy. Islam has been declared as the state religion by Article 2, with the *Quran* and *Sunna* being proclaimed as the supreme law of the land. Only a Muslim can occupy the position of president and, practically speaking, only a Muslim can become the prime minister. Both in Pakistan and Bangladesh, even non-Muslim judges have to take the oath in the name of Allah before entering upon their offices. Pakistan merely recognises religious minorities, not linguistic, ethnic and racial minorities. As in India, the term 'minority' occurs at various places in the constitution, but no definition has been given. Ethnic minorities in Pakistan include Sindhis (14.1 per cent), Pathans (15.42 per cent), Mohajirs (7.57 per cent) and Baluchis (3.57 per cent). Urdu is the national language, even though it is the first language of only 10 per cent of the population. Religious minorities include Christians (1.59 per cent), Ahmaddiyas (0.22 per cent), Hindus (1.6 per cent), Shi'as, Isma'ilis, Bohras and Parsis. Unlike the Indian Constitution, Pakistan's Constitution segregates citizens on the basis of religion while according a privileged status to Muslims. Pakistan's Constitution does not recognise the right to convert. Ironically, while conversion to Islam is welcome, no Muslim can even think of converting to another religion as it involves the risk of losing one's life.

In 1974, Ahmaddiyas were declared non-Muslims by the National Assembly. They are barred by law from calling themselves Muslim, and using Islamic terminology such as *masjid* or *azaan* (call to prayer) entails criminal proceedings and imprisonment. From July 2003 onwards, Ahmaddiyas proceeding for Haj are required to officially denounce in writing the founder of their faith as a 'cunning person and an impostor'. While the Indian judiciary expanded minority rights through liberal interpretation, Pakistan's judiciary, on the other hand, has completely failed to protect its minorities in general, and Ahmaddiyas in particular.

Till 2002, there was a system of separate electorates under which Muslims elected law-makers on an exclusive list of Muslim electorates, and non-Muslim denominations voted only for their co-religionists under a separate voters' list. Seats have been reserved in favour of religious minorities in all legislative bodies, except the Senate. These seats are, however, filled with candidates appearing on political parties' lists in proportion to seats won by these parties in various legislatures. In reality, separate electorates had undermined the morale and political clout of minorities.

Minorities' concerns arise from several other sources, such as draconian blasphemy and *Hudood* (capital offences) provisions. Major changes were made by General Zia ul Haq as part of his Islamisation process. Under the blasphemy provision, a person found to be critical of the Prophet Mohammad (Peace Be Upon Him: PBUH), or his companions, could face imprisonment. Later amendments made the imposition of the death sentence mandatory for anyone defiling the name of the Prophet Mohammed (PBUH). These discriminatory provisions opened the floodgates of persecution of minorities, particularly Christians, attracting enormous international criticism and rebuke as the *Quran* does not prescribe any punishment for blasphemy.

Similarly, the arbitrary imposition of the *Hudood* ordinances on non-Muslims is grossly discriminatory and unjustified. In accordance with the law of evidence requirements, while Muslims can testify against non-Muslims, non-Muslims are not permitted to give evidence against a Muslim accused. Moreover, when a Muslim kills a non-Muslim, he can get away with payment of compensation to the victim's family, but this benefit is not available to a non-Muslim who happens to kill a Muslim, i.e., a non-Muslim is not permitted to pay blood money and, accordingly, he must face either the death penalty or imprisonment. There is further discrimination, as compensation for killing a non-Muslim is less than that for killing a Muslim. Thus, the life of a non-Muslim is less valuable compared to that of a Muslim.

◆◆◆

The creation of Bangladesh proved the two-nation theory wrong in South Asia. Bangladesh was partitioned from Pakistan in 1971 and was premised on democratic and secular principles. The original constitution, adopted in 1972, proudly proclaimed 'nationalism', 'democracy' and 'secularism' as fundamental principles. But within no time, Bangladeshi politics found itself within the twists and turns of majoritarianism. Unlike the Indian Constitution, Bangladesh's Constitution does not contain any special provision on minority rights. It is based on the premise that universal individualistic rights are enough for everyone, including minorities. Similarly, the declaration of Bangla as the only language clearly impinges on the rights of ethnic and linguistic minorities.

Bangladesh, too, represents a multi-ethnic, multi-religious and multilingual pluralistic society. Its people have a variety of beliefs. Several languages are spoken in different parts of the country. Approximately 10 per cent of the population comprises religious minorities, i.e., Hindus, Christians and Buddhists. While Buddhists are the third largest group (0.46 per cent), Christians make up the fourth largest group with only 0.26 per cent of the population. Next, there are also several small factions within the Muslim population: the Biharis, the Ahmaddiyas, Isma'ilis, Shi'as, Memons, etc., who are in the minority and need protection. Although secularism was one of the fundamental principles of the original Constitution of Bangladesh in 1972, it was, unfortunately, deleted from the constitution in 1977 by the Fifth Amendment by General Zia-ur Rahman. Islam was declared the state religion in 1988. Thus, both in Pakistan and Bangladesh, military rulers caused maximum damage to the secular fabric and initiated the process of Islamisation, which dealt the death knell to minority rights. However, in 2010, the Supreme Court of Bangladesh declared the Fifth Amendment unconstitutional and restored *secularism* as one of the basic features of the constitution. The Indian Supreme Court has also held secularism as part and parcel of the basic structure of the Indian Constitution. However, unlike Pakistan, Bangladesh's Constitution does not provide for separate electoral rolls on the basis of religion.

Chittagong Hill Tracts (CHT) covers 10 per cent of the total area of Bangladesh. It is the homeland of some 13 different tribes of which the Chakmas are one of the largest and account for more than 50 per cent of the CTH population. The religious persecution of indigenous peoples is common in CHT, with repeated incidents of destruction of Buddhist temples, aimed at taking possession of temple land, the routine harassment of Buddhist monks, the destruction of Buddha statues, etc.

Similarly, religious minorities outside CHT have also been displaced as a result of discrimination and regular incidents of communal violence. The Hindu community, in particular, lost much of its land due to the nationalist Vested Property Act of 1974. This Act was repealed in 2001, but there has since been no return or restitution of land to minorities. The Act has not been subjected to judicial review. According to one estimate, the total land taken over under the Vested Property Act, mainly from Hindus, is approximately 10.5 million acres. It affected 1.2 million households and 6 million Hindus. The missing Hindu population that has migrated en masse due to this land deprivation is estimated to be 6 million. Hindus were forced to flee from Bangladesh to India after the acquisition of their land by the government. It is common sense that when people lose their lands, they lose their livelihood. It also adversely affects their health, social security, education and freedom of religion.

◆◆◆

The island of Sri Lanka is an ethnically, linguistically and religiously diverse South Asian state. The Sinhalese make up 74.9 per cent of the population. The Sri Lankan Tamils live predominantly in the north-east of the island, forming the largest minority group at 11.2 per cent of the population. The Moors, who were descended from Arab traders that settled in Sri Lanka, are the third largest ethnic group at 9.2 per cent of the population. There are also Indian

Tamils who form a distinct ethnic group which comprises 4.2 per cent of the population. The British brought them to Sri Lanka in the 19th century as tea and rubber plantation workers, and they remain concentrated in the 'tea country' of south-central Sri Lanka. Most Sinhalese are Buddhists and most Tamils are Hindus. Most Moors are Muslims. In the context of the internal armed conflict, violence against civilians based on ethnicity and/or religion occurred routinely. Both parties to the conflict failed to take steps to prevent or stop incidents of communal violence involving Buddhists, Hindus, Muslims and Christians. Both the government and the LTTE targeted places of worship of various religious communities. Ever since independence, the socio-economic and cultural rights of Tamils were systematically and deliberately violated by state policies: through the disenfranchisement of the Indian Tamils; through state-sponsored colonisation of the north-east by Sinhalese settlers, frequently accompanied by forceful eviction of Tamils; through a discriminatory language, education and recruitment policy which pursued but one aim—the Sinhalisation of the state. As a result, today, more than 90 per cent of civil servants and 99 per cent of the security forces are Sinhalese, and there is an almost total exclusion of minorities in state institutions.

In an atmosphere of war triumphalism, coupled with ultra-nationalism after the LTTE wipeout, the dominant political voice is one of a resurgent 'political Buddhism', which wants to convert the multiethnic and multicultural country into a Sinhalese Buddhist nation.

Buddhism has been given a prominent place, and it is the state's duty to protect and foster the Buddha *sasana* (a term used by Buddhists to refer to their religion). But freedom of religion and conscience, including the freedom to have or adopt a religion of one's choice, has been guaranteed to all persons. The official language of Sri Lanka is Sinhalese, with a rider that Tamil shall also be an official language. Yet violations of language rights are the rule, not the exception. To check these violations, the Official Languages Commission Act was passed in 1991, which established the Official Languages Commission. Anyone who 'wilfully neglects to transact business, receive or make such Communication in Tamil' shall be punished. The Sri Lankan Constitution of 1978 has explicit provisions to safeguard the interests of its minorities, which were intended to dispel their fears. Chapters on Language Rights and Fundamental Rights also protect minority rights. The scheme of proportional representation in parliamentary and local government elections is another good provision, ensuring adequate minority representation in the legislature as against the first-past-the-post system that prevailed prior to 1978.

To support the drive towards national unity and reconciliation, the Lessons Learnt and Reconciliation Commission (LLRC) was set up in May 2010. But the LLRCs did not investigate human rights violations committed during the last stage of operations. With minorities voting against him, Mahendra Rajapaksha recently lost the presidential election.

◆◆◆

Hindus comprise 80.6 per cent of the total population of Nepal, other religions comprise 19.4 per cent and there are 59 indigenous nationalities, with 125 languages and dialects. Nepal's religious minorities comprise 2.96 million Buddhists (20 per cent) and 1.12 million Muslims (4.2 per cent). In addition, there are linguistic minorities, which include Gurung, Magar, Tamang, Rai, Limbu, Thakali, Sherpa, Tharu and Raute. Nepal has yet to ratify international instruments for 'minorities' and 'indigenous nationalities'. Article 4 of the Nepalese Constitution of 1990 declared Nepal a Hindu state. Nepali was declared the national language. However, the right to instruction in the mother tongue was given only at the primary level.

In 2007, after over 240 years of Hindu monarchy, Nepal became a secular state. The interim constitution, which was approved under UN's supervision, prohibits proselytising but allows all citizens to express their faith. The political and economic instability of recent years—linked to the power struggles between secular parties—has strengthened pro-monarchist Hindu movements, which are attempting to curb the rise in conversions since the end of the monarchy's reign.

Although the Constituent Assembly, mandated to draft a constitution, has not been able to complete its task due to an absence of consensus, the government has made repeated assurances that the new constitution would be secular, democratic, federal and committed to social inclusion. Interestingly, the Constituent Assembly has a substantial minority presence. Proportional representation and provisions for affirmative action, if included in the new constitution, would go a long way in giving meaningful protection to minorities.

◆◆◆

Minority rights face a threat from the 'one nation, one people' doctrine in Bhutan. While the 2008 constitution ensures smooth transition from absolute monarchy to constitutional monarchy, the constitution does give Buddhism a prominent place. Dzongkha is the national language of Bhutan. The *Chhoe-sid-nyi* (dual system of religion and politics) was established by the constitution itself, and, accordingly, Bhutan is unified in the person of the King who, as a Buddhist, is the upholder of the *Chhoe-sid* (religion and politics; temporal and secular). Buddhism has been declared as the spiritual heritage of Bhutan and Buddhist Drukpa Lineage is the state religion. A massive majority of Bhutan practises Drukpa Kagyu, or Nyingmapa Buddhism, both of which are disciplines of Mahayana Buddhism. The Nepali-speaking minority population practices Hinduism, Christianity and Buddhism. There are several cases of societal abuse or discrimination based on religious affiliation, belief, or practice, including the teasing of, and sometimes refusal of admission to, non-Buddhist children in schools, and verbal abuse against non-Buddhists in villages and interior areas. There are authentic reports of societal pressures on non-Buddhists to uphold the 'Buddhist spiritual heritage'.

◆◆◆

The Maldives comprise a chain of 1,190 small coral islands, lying about 675 kilometres south-west of Sri Lanka. Achieving full independence from British rule in 1965, it became a republic in 1968 and is the smallest economy in South Asia. The majority of its people are Sunni Muslims, although there is a small community of Shi'a, descendants of Indian traders. While not given official recognition, the Maldives also has small populations of Hindus and Buddhists. Its government took the positive initiative of establishing the Maldivian Human Rights Commission (MHRC) in 2003.

Islam is the state religion. The constitution, ratified in 2008, prohibits citizens from practising other religions and precludes non-Muslims from voting or holding public office. It is painful to note that even in the 21st century, religious freedoms of non-Muslims continue to be substantially curtailed. Also abhorrent is that non-Muslim foreigners are permitted to practise their religious beliefs only in *private*. Non-Muslims have not even been provided with places of worship. Moreover, there is a ban on the import of religious statues and icons. On the contrary, in India, freedom of religion is available to all foreigners in full measure, as Article 25 of the Indian Constitution guarantees freedom of religion to 'all persons' and not just Indian citizens.

◆◆◆

The Islamic Republic of Afghanistan, too, has different religious and ethnic minority groups, making Afghanistan a plural society. Minorities have suffered most in the past three decades of war and conflict. Ethnic minority groups, such as Hazara and Uzbeks, constitute approximately 15 per cent and 10 per cent of the population, respectively. Then, there are also smaller groups such as Baluch, Turkmen and Noristani, which constitute less than 3 per cent of the total Afghan population. About 20 per cent of the Afghan population follows Shi'a Islam, mainly the Hazara ethnic group, as against a massive majority of 80 per cent, which follows Sunni Islam. In addition, a very small population of Sikhs—estimated to be less than 50,000—lives in Afghanistan, mostly in urban areas. There are as many as 14 recognised ethnic groups. Ethnic identity remains a sensitive issue in Afghanistan.

Article 22 of the Afghan Constitution provides that all Afghans, men and women, should enjoy the same rights. Although conditions for minorities have shown a significant improvement after 2001, conditions of religious freedom continue to be highly unsatisfactory for dissenting Sunni Muslims, as well as for Shi'a Muslims, Hindus, Sikhs and Christians. In spite of respect for freedom of worship being enshrined in the Afghan Constitution, religious minorities continue to face violence and discrimination. As in Pakistan, the Maldives and Bangladesh, Islam is the state religion. Article 2 lays down that 'followers of other religions are free to exercise their faith and perform their religious rites within the limits of the provisions of the law'. Such 'limits and provisions' is to be construed as sanctioning discrimination. Moreover, 'no law can be contrary to the beliefs and provisions of the sacred religion of Islam'. The state has a duty to improve the conditions and upkeep of mosques and religious schools and centres, but a similar obligation does not exist with regard to Hindu and Sikh temples, and churches. Article 54 calls for the elimination of all traditions conflicting with Islamic principles. Additionally, Article 149 states that 'the provisions of adherence to the fundamentals of the sacred religion of Islam and the regime of the Islamic Republic cannot be amended'. As in Pakistan and the Maldives, the Head of State can only be a Muslim. The oath of allegiance to God and Islam has clear marginalising effects. It is strange that in spite of United States' and European powers' 15-year-long engagement with Afghanistan, the liberal human rights and minority rights' jurisprudence of the West is not reflected in the Afghan Constitution.

◆◆◆

It is a fallacy, or rather a heresy, to regard the rights of minorities as special privileges or mere concessions to them. These guarantees are essential in a democratic and pluralistic polity because, as Franklin Roosevelt correctly pointed out, 'no democracy can long survive which does not accept as fundamental to its very existence the recognition of the rights of minorities'. It would be in the interests of South Asian states to give full protection to minority rights, as without these rights, peace, progress, real development, and even their survival, would be at stake. These states should learn from the Indian management of diversity, which favours the 'salad bowl' theory and rejects the American concept of the 'melting pot'.

◆

\#This chapter was first published in 2015 in the *IIC Quarterly,* Vol. 41, Nos 3 and 4.

NOTES

1. The Ahmadabad St. Xavier's Society v. State of Gujrat (AIR1974SC1389).
2. AIR1958SC956.

◆◆

ABOUT THE EDITORS AND CONTRIBUTORS

EDITORS

RAJIV KUMAR is Senior Fellow, Centre for Policy Research, New Delhi, and Chancellor, Gokhale Institute of Economics and Politics (GIPE), Pune. He is an International Board Member of the King Abdullah Petroleum Studies and Research Centre, Riyadh, and the Government of India Nominee on Board of Governors of the Economic Research Institute for ASEAN and East Asia, Jakarta. He is a government nominee on the Central Board of the State Bank of India. He is also on the Board of Directors of the Indian Institute of Foreign Trade and the Institute of Human Development, New Delhi.

OMITA GOYAL is presently Chief Editor of the *IIC Quarterly*, Journal of the India International Centre. She started her career in the voluntary sector with the Indian Social Institute, New Delhi. Shortly thereafter, she moved into academic publishing where she has spent over 27 years. She worked at SAGE Publications India Pvt. Ltd for 20 years, leaving as General Manager. She took time off to work as a freelance editor for SAGE and other institutions, such as the World Bank, UNICEF, UNDP, Voluntary Health Association of India, Centre for Women's Development Studies, WHO, Institute of Social Studies, The Hague and TERI. In 2005, she was invited by Taylor and Francis to start a social science programme under their social science and humanities imprint, Routledge, as Publishing Director.

CONTRIBUTORS

ZERRIN AFZA holds an MA in Peace and Conflict Studies from Dhaka University and an MA in Environment & International Development from University of East Anglia, Norwich, UK. She is a member of the Diversity and Inclusion Cluster, BRAC, Dhaka.

FIRDOUS AZIM is Professor of English at BRAC University, and a member of Naripokkho, a women's group in Bangladesh. Her recent publications include an edited special issue for *Feminist Review,* entitled *South Asian Feminisms: Negotiating New Terrains* (2009) and a special issue for the *Inter-Asia Cultural Studies* journal, entitled *Complex Terrains: Islam, Culture and Women in Asia* (2011).

AMITA BATRA is Professor of Economics, Centre for South Asian Studies, School of International Studies (SIS), Jawaharlal Nehru University (JNU), New Delhi. She has worked extensively in the area of regional trade and economic integration. Her most recent book on the subject is entitled *Regional Economic Integration in South Asia: Trapped in Conflict.*

SANJAY K. BHARDWAJ is Associate Professor at Centre for South Asian Studies, SIS, JNU, New Delhi. His areas of specialisation include: Bangladesh (Identity, Politics, Security, Economic and Foreign Policy Issues in particular) and South Asian countries, in general. He has authored over three dozen articles and research papers on contemporary sociopolitical and economic issues of South Asia.

AFSAN CHOWDHURY is Senior Advisor, BRAC Diversity and Inclusion Cluster, and a professor at BRAC University. He is the author and co-author of a dozen books on history, human rights and literature.

NABALESWAR DEWAN is a member of the Diversity and Inclusion Cluster, BRAC. He has an MA in social science from the University of Queensland, Australia, and an MBA from Dhaka University.

KANAK MANI DIXIT is Founding Editor of *Himal Southasian* and Publisher of *Himal Khabarpatrika*. A journalist since 1971, Dixit has worked in the United Nations Secretariat between 1982 and 1990.

He is currently engaged in civil rights activism in Nepal in relation to peace, democracy and human rights, and in political commentary in *Himal Khabarpatrika*, *The Nepali Times* and *The Kathmandu Post*.

ASHOK FERREY read Pure Mathematics at Oxford University and is currently a guest lecturer at the Colombo School of Architecture. He is host of *The Ashoka Ferrey Show* on national television. His books— *Colpetty People, The Good Little Ceylonese Girl, The Professional*—were all nominated for The Gratiaen Prize, and *Serendipity* for the State Literary Award.

NAMITA GOKHALE is a writer, publisher and festival director. She has written twelve books, including several works of fiction. A founder and co-director of the famed Jaipur Literature Festival and of 'Mountain Echoes', the annual Bhutan Festival, Gokhale is committed to showcasing literature from across Indian languages. She currently curates 'Kitabnama: Books and Beyond', a multilingual book show on the national channel, *Doordarshan*.

ERIC GONSALVES served in the Indian Foreign Service in various capacities, including Ambassador to Japan and the European Union and as Secretary, External Affairs. After retirement, he was Director, IIC; Director, Asian Relations Commemorative Conference; Member, International Observer Group, Sri Lanka Elections; and President, Institute of Peace and Conflict Studies, among others. Gonsalves is currently Member, Governing Body, CPR, Delhi, and Convenor, Indian Delegation, BCIM Forum.

AKMAL HUSSAIN is currently Distinguished Professor of Economics, Forman Christian College University, Lahore, Pakistan, and Co-chair, South Asia Centre for Policy Studies. He has advised governments in Pakistan on economic policy from 1989 to 2001, and 2010 to 2011. He has helped build organisations aimed at poverty alleviation and development at the village, district, national and regional levels. Hussain has authored/co-authored 38 other internationally published books on development.

SAMAN KELEGAMA is Executive Director of the Institute of Policy Studies, Sri Lanka, and Fellow of the National Academy of Sciences, Sri Lanka. He was the President of the Sri Lanka Economic Association. He has published a number of books on Sri Lankan and South Asian economic issues in both local and international journals. Kelegama serves on the Boards of a number of government and private sector organisations.

RAJESH KHARAT is currently Associate Professor at the Centre for South Asian Studies, JNU. Previously, he has worked as Lecturer and Reader in Politics, University of Mumbai. He has published three books, over two dozen articles in various international and national journals, and edited volumes on contemporary issues in South Asia and, in particular, on the Himalayan region.

ANURADHA KOIRALA is Founder and Chairperson of Maiti, Nepal, which has been combating Human Trafficking since 1993. She has liberated 29,000 girls and women from sexual exploitation and rehabilitated them successfully in society. Koirala is the recipient of various national and international awards and felicitations, including CNN Hero, 2010.

MALASHRI LAL is Dean of Colleges and Professor of English at the University of Delhi. Her academic specialisation is in Women and Gender Studies about which she has eleven books. Among Lal's acclaimed co-edited volumes are *In Search of Sita: Revisiting Mythology* (2009), *Chamba-Achamba: Women's Oral Narratives* (2012) and *Tagore and the Feminine: A Journey through Translations* (2015).

HAROUN MIR is an independent political analyst based in Kabul and the Chief Executive Officer at the Business Integrity Network Afghanistan (BINA).

FAIZAN MUSTAFA is presently Vice-Chancellor of Nalsar University of Law. Earlier, he was the Founder Vice-Chancellor of National Law University, Orissa. His areas of interest include Copyright Law, HIV Law, Human Rights, Right to Information, Strict Liability Law and Religious Conversion Law. Mustafa was awarded in 2014 with the best SAARC Law Teacher Award.

REEMA NANAVATY has worked with SEWA since 1984 and currently oversees 3,200 self-help groups, 2,000 producer collectives, 110 cooperatives and 15 federations. Some of her initiatives are: rehabilitation programmes in Afghanistan and Sri Lanka; Trade Facilitation Centre model in SAARC countries; and RUDI, where women farmers and labour trade their agro-produce with each other and ensure livelihood security. Nanavaty was awared the Padmashri in 2013.

SASANKA PERERA is Professor in Sociology and Dean at the Faculty of Social Sciences at South Asian University, New Delhi. Beyond a long-term interest in the politics of education, his other research interests include ethnicity, nationalism, politics of violence, visual culture in South Asia and urban space. He is a poet, photographer and also edits *Society and Culture in South Asia*.

RASUL BAKHSH RAIS is Professor of Political Science at Lahore University of Management Sciences (LUMS). He is the author of *Recovering the Frontier State: War, Ethnicity and State in Afghanistan* and *War Without Winners: Afghanistan's Uncertain Transition after the Cold War*, among others. His current research interests are: Modernism, State and Challenge of Radical Islam in Pakistan, war and state in Afghanistan, and fall of the Bahawalpur State.

NIHAL RODRIGO retired from Sri Lanka's Foreign Service having served as Foreign Secretary; Secretary General, SAARC; Advisor to the president of Sri Lanka; and Ambassador to China, North Korea and UN Missions in New York, Geneva and Vienna, respectively. Rodrigo is currently Guest Lecturer, International Affairs, at Sri Lanka Defence College, South Asian Universities and think-tanks; and Board Member, Regional Centre for Strategic Studies, and Kadirgamar Institute, Colombo.

SHYAM SARAN has been India's Ambassador to Myanmar, Indonesia and Nepal, and High Commissioner to Mauritius in a career in the Indian Foreign Service (IFS) spanning 34 years. He was India's Foreign Secretary from 2004 to 2006. Upon retirement, he was appointed Prime Minister's Special Envoy for Indo-US civil nuclear issues and later as Special Envoy and Chief Negotiator on Climate Change. Saran is a recipient of the Padma Bhushan.

BEENA SARWAR is a writer, documentary filmmaker and artist, a journalist and activist in human rights and peace issues for over two decades. She is the Editor of *Aman ki Asha*, a peace initiative between India and Pakistan and is on the editorial board of *Himal Southasian*. Sarwar blogs at www.beenasarwar.com and tweets at @beenasarwar.

RAKHI SEHGAL is a scholar of international relations and a trade union activist organising in the auto industry in Gurgaon. She is a member of the National Executive Council of the New Trade Union Initiative (a national federation of independent trade unions), and since 2013 she has been a coordinator of the People's SAARC–India Secretariat.

SANGEETA THAPLIYAL is Professor at the Centre for Inner Asian Studies, SIS, JNU, New Delhi. She works on India's strategic interests in the Himalayas and Trans-Himalayas, India's relations with Central Asia, South Asian Security and Water Security in South Asia.

AISHATH VELEZINEE was the Chief Editor of *Adduvas Weekly* (2005–2007), served on the Maldives Judicial Service Commission (2009–2011) and as Deputy Home Minister (2011–2012). Velezinee has published extensively on the role of the judiciary in the Maldives' transfer of power and is currently a PhD researcher at the International Institute of Social Studies, Erasmus University, The Hague.

HABIB WARDAK is Programme Officer at Business Integrity Network, Afghanistan, and a graduate of the Department of Defence and Strategic Studies, University of Pune, India.

◆